# Détente and Papal-Communist Relations, 1962-1978

# Westview Replica Editions

This book is a Westview Replica Edition. The concept of Replica Editions is a response to the crisis in academic and informational publishing. Library budgets for books have been severely curtailed; economic pressures on the university presses and the few private publishing companies primarily interested in scholarly manuscripts have severely limited the capacity of the industry to properly serve the academic and research communities. Many manuscripts dealing with important subjects, often representing the highest level of scholarship, are today not economically viable publishing projects. Or, if they are accepted for publication, they are often subject to lead times ranging from one to three years. Scholars are understandably frustrated when they realize that their first-class research cannot be published within a reasonable time frame, if at all.

Westview Replica Editions are our practical solution to the problem. The concept is simple. We accept a manuscript in camera-ready form and move it immediately into the production process. The responsibility for textual and copy editing lies with the author or sponsoring organization. If necessary we will advise the author on proper preparation of footnotes and bibliography. We prefer that the manuscript be typed according to our specifications, though it may be acceptable as typed for a dissertation or prepared in some other clearly organized and readable way. The end result is a book produced by lithography and bound in hard covers. Initial edition sizes range from 400 to 600 copies, and a number of recent Replicas are already in second printings. We include among Westview Replica Editions only works of outstanding scholarly quality or of great informational value, and we will continue to exercise our usual editorial standards and quality control.

# Détente and Papal-Communist Relations, 1962-1978

Dennis J. Dunn

The Catholic Church and the various communist governments of Europe have been vitally involved in the process of détente, moving from the silence of the Cold War to the stage of dialogue despite the persistence of religious persecution in the communist world. In this detailed study of recent developments, Professor Dunn discusses the motivating factors in papal-communist relations and chronicles the major events in détente policy in the Soviet Union and those countries of Eastern Europe--Poland, Hungary, Czechoslovakia, and Yugoslavia--where the Catholic Church is at least nominally the religion of 30% or more of the population.

Dennis J. Dunn is associate professor of history and director of the Institute for the Study of Religion and Communism at Southwest Texas State University.

# Détente and Papal-Communist Relations, 1962-1978

## Dennis J. Dunn

Westview Press/Boulder, Colorado

*A Westview Replica Edition*

*Keston Book #14*

Published in 1979 in the United States of America by
    Westview Press, Inc.
    5500 Central Avenue
    Boulder, Colorado  80301
    Frederick A. Praeger, Publisher


Library of Congress Catalog Card Number:  78-21436
ISBN:  0-89158-197-9


Printed and bound in the United States of America

For my mother and father

# Contents

0263122

# Preface

Détente, the term commonly used to describe the psychological aspects of the armed truce which has existed between the Soviet Union and the United States and its Allies since the 1960s, remains an important feature of the contemporary world. The "relaxation of tension in international relations" -- to give the word its Russian rendering--has not yet yielded any epoch-making results, but is pursued by the non-Communist and Communist governments for their reasons which are not always the same. For the former, answerable as they are to democratic peoples with no love for war, détente implies a hopeful, progressive endeavor to replace polemics with the mutual tolerance and intercourse of normal, social life, with permanent peace as the objective. By the latter, it is sometimes viewed as a means, more efficacious than the sabre-rattling of the 1940s and 1950s (which produced the North Atlantic Alliance, the rearmament of Germany, and the costly skirmish of Korea), of promoting "the development of the world Socialist system." Presented originally by the West in the 1960s as proposals to reduce the danger arising from the confrontation of armed forces in Central Europe and the competition of the Super-Powers in strategic nuclear armaments, détente was taken up by Khrushchev as a useful way of furthering the "policy of peaceful coexistence" which had been defined in 1961 as "the chief aim of its foreign policy activity" by the Communist Party of the Soviet Union and has been ever since a basic element in its program. "Peaceful coexistence affords more favorable opportunities," the program asserts, "for the struggle of the working class in the capitalist countries and facilitates the struggle of the colonial and dependent countries for their liberation." This policy, while avoiding conflicts with capitalist powers which could lead to the

dreaded thermonuclear war, which would be fatal to
the prospects of the Revolution, leaves the USSR free
to pursue a double purpose: maintenance of the
nuclear stalemate with the U.S.A. and development of
diplomatic and economic relations in Europe, on the
one hand; extension of Communist power by "wars of
liberation" overseas on the other. Vietnam, Angola,
and Mozambique are examples of the latter, encouragement of Bonn's Ostpolitik, the Four Powers Agreement
of 1971 on Berlin, and the Nuclear Test Ban Treaty
of the former. The Helsinki Conference on European
Security and Cooperation, in which the U.S.A., Canada,
the Holy See, and all the European States (except
Albania) were persuaded to take part, was the most
ambitious attempt to exploit the pacific interests of
the heirs of the Christian Civilization in the interests of the Soviets' Peaceful Coexistence Policy and
to stabilize its western glacis. But the Iron Curtain remains.
    Such in outline is the story of détente. It is
important to bear in mind the dichotomy of motives in
pursuit of the official "relaxation of tension" between the Communist and non-Communist world when we
come to consider how relations between the Catholic
Church and the Communist governments of Europe have
been affected by it and the dialogue into which, in
pursuit of their distincitive purposes, they have
been drawn. Persecution of religion in the Communist
world continues along side of the discussions. This
work attempts to shed light on that apparent anomaly.
In the process, it seeks to elucidate Communist and
Papal motivation in such rapprochement as there has
been, and to chronicle the major episodes of it in
the Soviet Union, Yugoslavia, Poland, Hungary, Czechoslovakia, East Germany, Bulgaria, and Romania. Albania is also treated as the exception to rapprochement in Europe. The Communist-Catholic dialogue concerns the other Communist states as well, and has its
repercussions on the Church throughout the world; but
the major diplomatic developments nave been in the
above eight countries. The study of those developments is preceded by a chapter providing the historical perspective and background necessary to understand
the Catholic-Communist negotiations.
    It is a bold, possibly reckless, historian who,
writing in 1978, would attempt to write a book about
Catholic-Communist relations in the 1960s and 1970s.
There are no primary sources of an official nature
yet available and there probably will not be for some
time.

Nevertheless, studies of developements which shape history cannot be put off until all the proper documents are declassified. Catholic-Communist relations of the 1960s and 1970s, and, more specifically, the policy of rapprochement are such events: they involve the interaction of influences that make up the social texture and political concepts of modern civilization. The importance of these occurrences for Western culture, for the peoples of East and West Europe, for the United States, for the Third World, and the rest of mankind seems to justify the peril inherent in the nature of the book.

The London School of Economics and Political Science, and its distinguished Director, Professor Ralf Dahrendorf, saw the beginning of my research when I was there as a Visiting Fellow in 1975-76. The Ford Foundation, through Keston College, gave some financial assistance in the early and middle stages of my research. The Librarians of the Royal Institute of International Affairs, the London School of Economics and Political Science, Keston College, and Southwest Texas State University generously opened their holdings and provided me with necessary books, journals, and newspapers.

This book owes a primary debt of gratitude to Bohdan R. Bociurkiw (Carleton University, Ottawa), Michael Bourdeaux (Keston College, London), Sir John Lawrence (Keston College), Mr. John Eppstein (Keston College), Lucian Blit (London School of Economics and Political Science), Leonard Schapiro (London School of Economics and Political Science), and Walter Sawatsky (Mennonite Central Committee Scholar, West Germany). The above persons read all or parts of the manuscript and commented on it intelligently and incisively. Nancy McGown did the superb job of typing the final manuscript. I alone, of course, am responsible for the thesis, format, and any errors which might be in the work. I extend my gratitude, finally, to my wife, Margaret, for her insights, support, and patience.

D.J.D.

San Marcos, Texas
September 1978

# 1. Catholic-Soviet Relations Before 1962

Entire peoples find themselves in danger
of falling back into a barbarism worse than
that which oppressed the greater part of
the world at the coming of the Redeemer.
This all too imminent danger, Venerable
Brethren, as you have already surmised, is
bolshevistic and atheistic communism, which
aims at upsetting the social order and at
undermining the very foundations of
Christian civilization. . . .
    Pius XI, <u>Divini Redemptoris</u>, March 28, 1939

While the declared purpose of the Conference
which concluded at Helsinki on August 1, 1975 and
was followed up at Belgrade in 1977 was to promote
security and peaceful cooperation in Europe and to
fulfill the purposes of the Soviet government's
"peaceful coexistence policy," that government used
it to obtain international acquiescence in the territorial <u>status quo</u>, which it interpreted as legal
sanction for its annexations and the integrity of its
"Socialist Commonwealth" in Eastern Europe.  From the
end of World War II to the early 1960s, the Vatican
had resisted all Soviet efforts to gain legitimacy
for its annexation of the Baltic States, Bukovina,
Bessarabia, Eastern Poland, and part of Pomerania.
    At the same time, and indeed until the German-
Polish agreement of 1970, the Holy See refused to
adjust diocesan frontiers to the boundary changes in
post-war Europe until they were confirmed by peace
treaties.  Since the reign of Pope John XXIII, however, it has acquiesced in the existing <u>status quo</u> in
Eastern Europe, so the territorial question was no
deterrent to the presence at Helsinki of the peripa-
tetic Archbishop Agostino Casaroli, Secretary of the
Council for Public Affairs in the Papal Secretariat

1

of State. Does this mean that the Vatican has changed
its opposition to international Communism and vice
versa? What, in fact, has happened in Catholic-
Soviet relations since the 1950s when the Papacy and
the Soviet-led Communist world were implacable foes?
These questions introduce a development in Catholic-
Communist affairs which we have ventured to call
détente because of its visibility in the political
climate between the Soviet bloc and the West. This
book studies this development as it evolved in the
Soviet Union, Poland, Hungary, Czechoslovakia, Yugoslavia, East Germany, Romania, Bulgaria, and Albania.

To appreciate the novelty and significance of
Communist-Papal rapprochement, it is necessary to
review the Church's relations with the Communist
states before the 1960s. For the sake of organization, this chapter analyzes the Church's position in
regard to the Soviet Union. Its relationship with
the other regimes during those years is covered as
introductory material in successive chapters.

In a word, Soviet-Catholic associations before
the 1960s were antagonistic. The reasons can be
conveniently, if somewhat arbitrarily, organized
under three headings: the historical legacy, ideology, and the repressive nature of a totalitarian
regime.[1]

## THE LEGACY OF THE PAST: CATHOLIC-RUSSIAN RELATIONS TO 1917

The historical legacy which the Bolsheviks inherited from the tsars in regard to the Catholic
Church did not predetermine the relationship between
the Catholic Church and subsequent Communist governments and parties in the former Russian Empire and
in other countries, but it did influence that relationship. It is useful, therefore, to examine the
historical position of the Church under the pre-1918
Russian governments.

In general, Russian-Catholic relations before
1917 were unfriendly and often openly hostile.
Tsarist Russia was a theocratic state which inherited
the distinctive character and prejudices of the Orthodox Church, identified with the East Roman Empire of
Byzantium and, since the Schism from the West which
had become absolute by the end of the twelfth century,
refused to accept the authority of the Pope in the
older Rome.[2] Thus Russia, before the Revolution, was
the heir to a centuries-old opposition to the Latin
or Western Church, which had become the matrix of
civilization in southern, central, and western Europe.

It was in 988 A.D. that the Eastern Slav state of
Kiev--Kievan Rus--, founded by the Vikings, embraced
Christianity; and it was from Constantinople (Byzantium), not Rome, that the Faith came.  When Kievan
Rus broke up into a number of principalities, the most
westerly of them, except the great Republic of Novgorod, came under the rule of the powerful Catholic Kingdom of Poland.[3] But when the Golden Horde of the Mon-
gols, which subdued most of the other Russian princes,
itself began to lose its grip in the fourteenth century, it was the Orthodox principality of Moscow
which eventually emerged as the strongest, defeated
the Tartars, and proceeded to unite the Russian lands.
Reviving the tradition of Kievan Rus, and bringing
Novgorod under his sway with the heroic memory of
Alexander Nevsky's victory over the Catholic Teutonic
Knights, Ivan III made Moscow the national and religious capital of Russia.

Thus it is to those years that dates the continued ecclesiastical and political rivalry between the
Orthodox Russians and powerful Latin Catholic states
which lay to the west and south of them, Lithuania,
Poland, and Austria, whence had come the campaign to
evangelize the Western Slavs, many of whom were torn
between loyalty to Rome and loyalty to Byzantine
Christianity.  It was in order to bring them into, or
keep them in communion with the Roman Church that the
Holy See authorized in 1596 the formation of an
Uniate Church for the Ukrainians and Ruthenians under
its own hierarchy, retaining the liturgy and canon
law of the Orthodox Church--including the marriage of
parochial clergy.[4]  (It was and is the largest of the
various Uniate Churches (Armenian, Melikite, etc.)
formed about that time.)

But before the middle of the fifteenth century,
the Prince of Muscovy was not the head or leader of
Orthodox Christianity.  It was the Ecumenical Patriarch of Constantinople, subject to the East Roman Emperor who, though never having the power of jurisdiction of the Roman Pontiff of the West, was the first
among equals of the bishops and the forces of communion.  The capture of Constantinople by the Ottoman
Turks in 1453 made the Patriarch a Turkish subject--
as he still is.  This deprived him both of some of his
imperial aura and of his spiritual independence; and
before long the Patriarch and his court at the Phanar
were being used as an instrument of the Sultan's administration.  Russia then emerged as the strongest
Orthodox power and we find the Prince of Moscovy
taking the title of Tsar or Caesar,[5] and his
chief bishop the title of Patriarch.[6]  Soon Moscow

3

was proclaimed the Third Rome and the inheritor of the
whole tradition of World Government which the name
implied.  So we read in the charter of installation
of the Patriarch of Moscow in 1598:

> Because the old Rome has collapsed
> on account of the heresy of Apollinarius
> and the Second Rome, Constantinople is
> now in possession of the Godless Turk,
> thy kingdom, Oh pius Tsar!, is the Third
> Rome.  It surpasses with its devotion
> every other, and every other, and all
> other kingdoms are now merged in thy
> kingdom.[7]

This short summary is exerpted to show two important
ingredients of the Russian national character which
cannot be without influence even upon the present
Communist leaders of the country: one is the ingrained
hostility to Catholicism; the other a kind of mes-
sianic mission of world hegemony which unites itself
to the ambitions of the World Revolution.  So, Orthodoxy for the Great Russians waxed into a national
creed and, thus, not only aided the development of
Russian nationalism but ripened into an ideology of
Muscovite expansionism.  In the seventeenth century,
Muscovy reconquered most of the more easterly parts
of the Polish Empire, including the right bank of the
Ukraine.  Here western influences were strong.
    The partitions of Poland in the eighteenth cen-
tury and the Congress of Vienna in 1815 increased the
power of Moscow at the expense of the Austrian Empire.
The Russian tsar emerged from these events with the
greater part of Poland, including Lithuania, as a
kingdom under his jurisdiction, and thereby not only
secured his western flank, but also added to his
religious minorities a strong Catholic Church.
    From then until 1917, Moscow controlled sizeable
Catholic populations.  In general, its policies up
to the 1905 revolution were repressive, particularly
towards the Ukrainian-Belorussian Uniate Church which
was forcibly joined with the Russian Orthodox Church,
save for the Cholm diocese in Poland, in 1839.[8]  This
diocese was suppressed in 1875, but the Uniate Church
survived and flourished in that part of the Western
Ukraine (Sub-Carpathian Ruthenia) which was under
Austro-Hungarian rule.  The Constitution introduced
under Nicholas II by the Imperial Manifesto of October
1905 was more favorable to the Latin Catholics (the
Ukrainian-Belorussian Uniate Church continued to be

illegal) than previous tsarist policy had been, and so was the short-lived Provisional Government of 1917. In fact, in 1917, Metropolitan Andrei Sheptyts'kyi established a Russian Uniate Church under Exarch Leonid Fedorov.[9] This was not a premonition of what was to come but more a lull before the battle.

The Bolskeviks, in their attitudes toward the Catholic Church, revealed distinct continuities with its tsarist oppressors. In ill-treating the Catholic Church, the Communists in fact revealed such earlier justifications for dragonades against Catholicism as dynasticism, the claims of Moscow to be the Third Rome, and nationalism. Indeed, in many encounters, they actually adopted in detail the models of persecution which the tsars had devised. For example, in 1946, when the Kremlin forced the Ukrainian Uniate Church of Galicia to join the Russian Orthodox Church, it utilized virtually the same technique as Nicholas I had used to dispose of the Uniates in 1839.[10] It would be untrue, however, to attribute the inspiration of the Bolskevik's anti-Catholic position solely to the tsarist past. The basic attitude of the Communists towards Catholicism, while drawing upon the tsarist legacy, was structured by Marxism-Leninism.

IDEOLOGY

It is difficult to reconcile Communism and Catholicism philosophically. Each is an universal creed based upon principles irreconcilable with one another; and it is on doctrinal, not political ground that Marxism-Leninism has always been denounced by the Popes. Consequently, a reconciliation between the two in the part of the world with which we are concerned would only be possible on the assumption that Communism, as practiced in the Soviet Union and Eastern Europe, had changed the philosophical underpinnings of Marxism-Leninism. Or, of course, that Catholicism had altered its philosophical foundations. In that case, Catholicism would no longer be Catholicism and Communism no longer Communism. This is not to say that changes in emphasis within a religious or political system cannot happen without an alteration of character, but it is to argue that a transformation of principles does alter character. Otherwise, language has no meaning. The case has been made by a number of writers that Catholicism has not changed but that Communism has and that, as a political philosophy, it now respects human rights and liberties as evolved in the West and upheld by the Catholic Church. If that is the case, of course, Communism is no longer Communism, but a type of social democracy like that prevailing in Western Europe. Advocates of this theory point to the 1976 international Conference of Communist Parties in East Berlin where Soviet control of foreign Communist Parties was openly challenged. They also point out the promises of the Italian Communist Party (PCI) and the French Communist Party (PCF) to respect freedom. Possibly they are right in accepting the Communist protestations as sincere, but the fact remains that there is no Communist Party in power which respects the multi-party system of government and no Communist Party, in or out of power, has abandoned the policy of nationalization of the economy. All the European Communists, including the Italian and French, also continue to support the zigzags of Soviet foreign policy.[11] In addition, since the East Berlin Conference of Communist Parties, Moscow has balked at any deviation from the Soviet model by foreign Communists and has emphasized its dominant position in the World Communist Movement.[12] Personal freedom cannot be obtained by a mere act of will, but rather it is dependent vitally, among other things, upon the "ability of citizens to dispose of the material wealth that they create."[13] Furthermore, how is it that a party, like the PCF, "that only yesterday was 100 percent anti-democratic has overnight become 100 percent pro-democratic?"[14] In a preliminary report dated June 1977, the U.S. Commission on Security and Cooperation in Europe, a by-product of the Helsinki Conference of 1975, reported that the Soviet Union and East European countries have not eased East-West contact and that "the pattern of conduct by the Communist signatories remains basically unchanged."[15] Until such time as concrete proof as opposed to promises appear, it is prudent to assume that Communism has not fundamentally changed. Proceeding also on the assumption that Catholicism has not varied its basic premises, one is led to the conclusion that compatibility between Communism and Catholicism cannot logically exist at the philosophical level.

Historical Communism drew its inspiration from Marx, Engels, and Lenin, and was firmly grounded in historical materialism.[16] It is a quasi-religion which asserts a world view without a spiritual dimension. It claims that all reality is, in the first instance, material and, secondly, is determined by economic laws pushing mankind dialectically and inexorably forward through various economic and corresponding social stages toward Communism. Man has value, not as a free personality but as one element of the collectivity; he must be subordinated to the Communist Party and its political struggle to fashion an economically "classless society." Immanent in such a concept are the axioms that man is defined by his class position, that economics control history and determine social organization, and that political activity is extremely important in the realization of the Communist world view. Society, from the Communist perspective, is not only changeable but perfectable.

Catholicism, in common with other forms of Christianity and Judaism, places a great deal of emphasis upon the unique dignity and free will of every man and his dependence upon divine help to overcome his human imperfections. It stipulates that there are a spiritual order and a material order and that the former is above the latter. Man's life on earth, according to Catholic theology, is a crucially important preparation for life with God after death. Man's activities, his ideas and behavior, accordingly, should conform to that view. He must strive to live a good life, as indicated by Divine Revelation in the Bible and in the teachings and tradition of the Church. He cannot relinquish responsibility for his actions before God by submitting himself to the directions of a state, government, or political party. Endowed by God with life and a free will, man and reality are not directed nor fashioned by the laws of dialectical materialism.

In the Communist view, religion in capitalist society has two major characteristics. It is first the fantasy of man alienated from himself, other men, and reality by capitalism's division of his labor. End the division of labor, according to the Marxists, and one destroys "the opium of the people."[17] Secondly, religion is a principal tool of exploitation wielded by the bourgeoise against the proletariat. It is, as Engels declared, "the exclusive possession of the ruling classes, and these apply it as a means of government, to keep the lower classes within bounds."[18] Once the working class takes control of the means of production in an advanced industrial society, however, this support also, as Engels states, will vanish "and with it will also vanish the religious reflection itself, for the simple reason that then there will be nothing left to reflect."[19]

7

The Catholic Church, of course, denies that its existence depends upon such moorings. It considers itself to be a sacramental and apostolic Church founded by Jesus Christ for the purpose of helping man obtain salvation. It rejects completely the Marxist-Leninist notion that religion is a fantasy, a creation of man to soothe his alienation and that it is simply a mechanism manipulated by the ruling class to exploit the workers. Religion, in the Catholic mind, defines man and makes his existence meaningful.

The world views, then, of Communism and Catholicism clash on basic interpretations of reality, man, and history. Without one or the other altering fundamental positions, philosophical reconciliation is difficult to imagine.

Although Communism and Catholicism are ideologically opposed, it would not necessarily follow that Communists should attack the Catholic Church. Marx, in fact, once he had proclaimed religion to be the "opium of the people," had little to say about the policies which Communists should practice in dealing with religion. The omission is not fortuitous, any more than is his laconic advice on foreign policy or economic planning for socialists. According to Marx and Engels, the Communist revolution which will succeed capitalism will advance only in fully developed industrial countries and as a consequence of an internal breakdown of the economic and political system. When economic circumstances are pregnant in a particular society, the socialist revolution will be born naturally and axiomatically. It will not, according to Marx, be affected by international factors, such as imperialism, or by internal conditions (other than economics), such as a violent campaign against believers. Persecution of religion, from the point of view of orthodox Marxism, will not hurry the forces of history but may rather hinder them. In fact, the Communist Manifesto held that religion was becoming less and less significant in European societies.[20] As the economy and civilization evolve, religion, in the Marxist view, will have a diminishing influence on the future. Its exploitive tendencies will be weakened as the clash between capitalists and workers quickens and the proletariat is capable of identifying and eschewing religion as a weapon of bourgeois exploitation. In a highly advanced industrial society, the working class will be capable of dispensing with all the tools of capitalist manipulation, including the institution of religion.

8

As to the religious policy of a Communist state, again Marx and Engels say virtually nothing.[21] But they hardly need to because in a Communist state religion will have disappeared since the capitalist jugular vein from which religion drew sustenance would have been severed. Revolutions, of course, Marx admits, can take place in under-developed countries, but Communism will not grow unless and until the economic conditions are ripe and no quantity of political or religious activism will change that equation.

Lenin, however, in a major modification of Marx's nonpersecutory stand vis-à-vis religion, argues implicitly for an activist approach against religion as well as against the established order. His exhortations on religion--few though they may be[22]--mirror Marx's attitudes, but they do change Marxism's interpretation of religion. Lenin wanted to take power in Russia and, if he were to follow a literal interpretation of Marxism, he would have to forego his desire and await economic conditions to fructify in Russia. He opted, instead, for a political advance to socialism, as reflected in What Is To Be Done and Imperialism: The Last Stage of Capitalism. His activist stand, as implied, was affected considerably by the environment of late nineteenth and early twentieth century Russia. In a perspicacious study, Bohdan R. Bociurkiw stressed that Lenin's criticism of religion was precipitated, in the main, by his view of contemporary Russian Orthodoxy's weaknesses and its pivotal role in the tsarist system of government.[23] Lenin, in fact, adopted the antireligious positions of many of Russia's nineteenth century radical writers, including Belinsky, Herzen, Pisarev, Bakunin, and Chernyshevsky.[24] He believed an onset against organized religion was a direct attack against an exploitive social system, and thus, in contrast to Marx, a realistic modus operandi for the revolution.

Such, in general, was Lenin's basic view on religion. He favored direct persecution, but with an overriding proviso. Power, for the sake of fashioning the Communist state, was the priority for Lenin, and if an assault on religion was an obstacle to the achievement of power, it would be foregone.

That is, no tactic was allowed to obstruct a Communist coup d'état. In a passage which became of major importance in developing Communist antireligious policy, Lenin wrote:

> A Marxist must be materialist, i.e., an
> enemy of religion.  But he must be a
> <u>dialectical</u> materialist, i.e., one who
> organizes the struggle against religion
> not on abstract, purely theoretical
> grounds, . . . but concretely, on the
> basis of the <u>currently</u> proceeding class
> struggle, a struggle which is educating
> the masses more and better than anything
> else.  A Marxist ought to be able to
> judge the concrete situation as a whole;
> he must always be able to determine the
> boundary between anarchism and opportunism
> (this boundary is relative, mobile, and
> everchanging, but it exists); he must not
> fall either into the abstract, verbal, and,
> in fact, empty 'revolutionism' of the anar-
> chists, or into the philistinism and oppor-
> tunism of a petty-bourgeoise or liberal
> <u>intelligent</u>, who is afraid of the struggle
> against religion, forgets about this task
> of his, reconciles himself with faith in
> God, and is guided not by the interests of
> the class struggle but by petty, meager
> little calculations: not to insult, not
> to alienate or frighten away, [in line with]
> a wise rule: 'live and let live' etc.[25]

Once victory was secured, of course, then the Communists could act to defend their government by trying
to create a Communist society and that could involve
the suppression of religion.

Before October 1917, that is, before the Bolsheviks brought down the Provisional Government, Lenin
had to subordinate his antireligious principles to
expediency.  The reason was simply that the Bolsheviks, to win power, needed the backing or neutrality
of parties or groups which either considered religion
inviolate or thought it to be of no concern to social
democracy.  Among the latter would be most non-Bol-
shevik socialists.  In the former category would be
the peasantry, the working class, and the minority
nationalists of the Russian Empire.  The Bolsheviks
could not afford to write off any of these groups
by advocating a public persecution of religion.

Lenin, thus, would countenance religious persecution, but only if such a policy did not hamper his
attempt to gain power with which, once attained, he
could do what he wished.  His legacy to the Soviet

state, then, was ambivalent; while standing for a war against religion as opposed to waiting for it to bury itself, Lenin's admonitions could support any policy, including religious toleration, which served to strengthen political power.

SOVIET-CATHOLIC RELATIONS SINCE 1917

In November 1917, when the Communists took power in Russia, the basic ingredients for the creation of a totalitarian government were present: an ideology which worshipped power and a disciplined elite who were determined to implement that ideology. Additionally, the historical conditions of Russia greatly influenced the development of totalitarianism. Steeped in the traditions of autocracy and paternalism and torn apart by the World War, the Civil War (1918-1921), the Russo-Polish War (1920-1921), debilitating domestic disorders, and famine, Russia was an easy prey to a ruthless, determined, organized centralizing authority. The Communists wasted little time in beginning the process of building a veritable <u>Leviathan</u> of a state.

In terms of Catholic-Soviet relations, the issues were clear-cut. The atheism of the new Communist Government, added to the tradition of bad relations with Rome, pitted Church and State against one another from the beginning. But the loss of Poland, including Western Ukraine, Belorussia, and Lithuania left Soviet Russia from 1920 to 1945 without any substantial Roman Catholic population. (Between 1939 and June 1941, the Soviet Union held, for varying lengths of time, the Baltic States, Western Ukraine, and Western Belorussia.)[26] The small Catholic minority tried to adjust itself to the atheistic and hostile Communist authorities, but ultimately the Church could not reconcile itself to a government which strove with violence and terror to obliterate religion.[27] Initially, of course, the campaign was directed mainly against the Russian Orthodox Church, the State Church of Tsarist days to which the bulk of the Russian people belonged.

Once in power, the Bolsheviks did not hesitate "to prime" Russia for its socialist revolution in anticipation of Western Europe's socialist explosion. Lenin commenced, for example, a series of economic policies called "War Communism" and, in the religious sector, introduced anti-God legislation. By 1921, with the peasantry on the verge of rebelling against the economic policies and when it became apparent that the socialist revolution would not be racing across

11

Europe, Lenin made a tactical retreat, replacing
"War Communism" with the New Economic Policy or N.E.P.
From his point of view, this was purely and solely an
expedient retreat and would be maintained only until
his government was strong enough to industrialize and
collectivize the land forcibly, to transform the
peasantry into a proletariat, and the economy into a
socialist system.  Only when Russia had been converted
into a socialist state could the place of the Bolshevik Party be guaranteed and only then could the classless society develop.

   Although the Communists had been compelled to
make a tactical retreat on economic issues, they did
not feel forced to offer any concessions to the Orthodox Church in Russia.  Though there was much distress
among humble people at interference with their hab-
itual devotions, there was no major outburst against
the Bolsheviks' persecution of the Orthodox Church.
This was partly because it had been damaged in the
eyes of the peasantry through the hierarchy's identification with the Tsar and the ruling class of the
old regime and through Bolshevik propaganda which
spuriously depicted the Orthodox Church as refusing
to turn over its wealth to help feed starving peasants in the famine of 1921-22.[28]  Also, the Bolshevik anti-God campaign was selective and, thus, avoided a general reaction.  In fact, concessions to
religious sects and to Islam continued well into
the 1920s.[29]

   Catholicism, because it was relatively insigni-
ficant in the then boundaries of the Soviet Union
following the independence of Poland and Lithuania,
did not become a major target of the Bolshevik persecution until 1923.  The delay was no doubt due to
the impotence of the Church, the engrossment of the
Bolsheviks with Orthodoxy and other more pressing
economic and political problems, the fact that the
Papacy was helping with famine relief in 1921-22,
and the reluctance to antagonize a church strong in
the West, where the Soviet government, in its isolation, was hoping to win economic and diplomatic
concessions.  But the Soviet government's antipathy
toward Catholicism never abated.  Specifically, five
factors appear to explain the Soviet government's
inveterate hostility toward Rome.  First, because of
the ideological presuppositions of Marxism-Leninism,
the Communists believed Catholicism (and other religions) to be a fraud, and a "false teaching" which
were destined to be supplanted by Communist truth.
Secondly, the Catholic Church was an independent

12

institution which the Party could not manage ideologically and which, additionally, advocated a view
of reality which was incompatible with the Communist
theory of the world, thus, delaying the political
socialization of part of the Soviet people. The Catholic Church within the USSR was overwhelmingly a religion of national minorities having affinities with
the West--Poles, Germans, Lithuanians, some Belorussians, and some Latvians--, and its principles
appeared to hinder the absorption of these peoples into the Soviet system. The fact that many Catholics
were to be found near the sensitive borderlands of the
Soviet Union made them potential hazards to security.
Thirdly, the Communists, as pointed out above, could
not completely stifle their hereditary suspicion and
phobia of the Catholic Church. Fourthly, the young
Soviet government was convinced that the Church was
against its policies and that it supported anti-
Communist elements during the 1917 Revolution, the
the Civil War, and the Polish-Russian War--convictions
which branded the Catholic Church as a tool of the
foreign and domestic enemies of the Bolshevik system.
Finally, the Catholic Church, from the Communist
point of view, was an external, universal religion,
manipulated by an outside, supreme authority, the
Pope. It was not merely stronger, initially, than
Communist internationalism, but could impede and up-
set the Communist conversion of the world and some
of the goals of Soviet policy.[30] For these reasons
seemingly, the Soviet government launched in the
middle of the 1920s a brutal onset against the Catholic Church. The Kremlin was ready by then to attack
the Church because the famine was over, some Western
states showed no hesitation about working with the
USSR despite its policy of religious persecution
(for example, in 1922, Germany signed the Rapallo
Treaty with Moscow), and, finally, the Communists
were no doubt anxious to root out what they considered to be an ideological and historical vestige.
The Vatican protested vigorously against the persecution, but its efforts led to no relaxation.[31]

In 1923, the leaders of the Catholic hierarchy,
Bishop John Cieplak, Monsignor Constantine Budkiewicz,
and Exarch Leonid Fedorov, the head of the incipient
Russian Uniate Church, were arrested. Cieplak and
Budkiewicz were sentenced to death and Fedorov to
ten years' imprisonment. Cieplak's sentence was
changed also to ten years' imprisonment, but Monsignor
Budkiewicz was brutally executed. The Communists
then proceeded to liquidate the Russian Uniate Church
and to destroy the clerical leadership of the Latin

13

Catholic Church.  By the time of Lenin's death in
1924, only one bishop and several hundred priests
(down from about 900 at the time of the Treaty of
Riga) remained.[32]  The following year the League of
Godless (Militant Godless as of 1929) was organized
to conduct antireligious propaganda on a more systematic basis.[33]

There seemed to be some hope of relaxation in
1925 when the Jesuit bishop, Michael d'Herbigny was
permitted to visit the USSR to discuss Vatican-Soviet
relations.  At that time the Soviet leadership was
attempting to obtain diplomatic and economic support
in Western Europe, particularly in view of the signa-
ture of the Locarno Treaty, which embodied the principle of "collective security" and linked Germany, no
longer an outcast like the Soviet Union, as it had
been at the time of the Rapallo Treaty, with the
European victors of the First World War.  Bishop
d'Herbigny, during his visit, secretly consecrated a
new group of bishops; for this reason he was expelled
and most of the new bishops set upon.  The Pope endeavored to protect the bishops and denounced the
Communist tirades against religion.  In the early
1930s he called for a crusade of prayer against the
atheistic persecution of the Church.  A later instruction required that the special prayers, which
Leo XIII had introduced at the end of each Mass for
the liberty of the Holy See, should be offered throughout the world "for the conversion of Russia."  The
Catholic response, in the end, was without effect upon the Soviet government.  By the end of the 1930s,
the Catholic leadership in the Soviet Union was non-
existent.  All the bishops and most of the clergy
had been removed through exile, imprisonment, or
death.

Pope Pius XI issued in 1937 his Encyclical
Divini Redemptoris which, like many Papal pronounce-
ments before and since, roundly condemned Marxism-
Leninism.[34]  During the Second World War his successor,
Pius XII, did not alter this position; but he was
careful to observe impartiality between the belliger-
ents and never endorsed the Nazi invasion of the
Soviet Union.[35]

The political partition of Europe, after the
defeat of Nazi Germany in 1945, left almost half of
the Continent at the mercy of an atheistic power.
This was a new and painful situation for all the
Christian Churches in countries overrun by the Red
Army.  There was also a new problem in the formerly
occupied countries of Western Europe--Italy and France
in particular--owing to the increase of Communist

influence resulting from the Resistance Movements.
Five of the following chapters of this book describe
the impact of the Communist regime upon the Catholic
Church in Poland, Hungary, Czechoslovakia, Yugoslavia,
East Germany, Bulgaria, Romania, and Albania; the
vicissitudes of the thirty years' ordeal between the
Marxist rulers and the Catholic clergy and people;
the varying national situations which have affected
that ordeal, and the recent attempts of the Holy See
to establish a modus vivendi with their governments.
The identification of Catholicism with the whole
nation in the case of Poland, with a majority in
Czechoslovakia and Hungary, and a substantial part
of it in the other countries, excepting Albania and
Bulgaria, has compelled a certain prudence upon the
Communists while preoccupied with consolidating their
political power. But no such inhibitions affected
the treatment by the Soviet government of the Churches
in countries annexed, or reannexed to the Soviet
Union itself. Thus immediately after the war there
began a severe repression of the Catholic Church in
Lithuania, including massive deportation of the
intelligentsia, the Ukraine and Belorussia, as well
as harsh handling of the Lutherans in Latvia and
Estonia. The Red Army was also guilty during its
occupation of Slovakia of brutal attacks on priests
and religious, and local attacks on the Church in
Croatia and Slovenia, in the early days of Tito's
regime, were vicious. Between 1946 and 1949 the
Ukrainian Uniate Church in Galicia and Transcarpathia
was forcibly joined to the Russian Orthodox Church,
and this was specifically condemned by the Holy
See.[36] In 1948, the Romanian Uniate Church was forced
to merge with the Orthodox Church and, in 1950, the
same fate befell the Greek Catholics in the Ukrainian-
speaking Prešov area of Slovakia.[37]
 While Pope Pius XII continued to protest against
the oppression of the Church in Eastern Europe and
to maintain such contact as was possible with the
bishops and also encouraged opposition to the Communist Party in successive elections in Italy, it would
not be true to represent him as taking an active
part in promoting the political and military reaction
of the West to the expansion of Communist Russia. In
fact, though giving a friendly reception to Allied
representatives as he did to numerous other groups
of visitors to Rome, he was always most scrupulous
not to identify the Holy See with any partial coalition in view of its historical independence and its
concern for the great number of Catholics on the

15

other side of the "Iron Curtain." Most of the Papal encyclicals and allocutions of the 1940s and 1950s on social questions, following the doctrine of Pius XI's Quadragesimo Anno, were in fact positive expositions of the Church's social teaching on such matters as the rights and duties of individuals, the family, industrial relations, economic life, and the ordering of national and international society. The Church's opposition to socialist and revolutionary doctrines as well as to the evolutionary modernism associated with them, was developed in general terms, not referring specifically to Soviet Russia, Eastern Europe, or China, but addressed more obviously to considerable movements of intellectual opinion, especially in France, derived from the influence of such authors as Emmanuel Mounier, Jacques Maritain, and Teilhard de Chardin. The decree of July 1949, Responsa ad dubia de communismo, declaring that Catholics ought not to join or support Communist Parties was also mainly concerned with the same objectives. What was an outstanding historical development of the period in Western Europe was the rise and power of the Christian Democrats and similar parties in almost all the Continental countries which had been involved in the war (e.g. France, Germany, Italy, Belgium, the Netherlands, Austria) who were vigorously opposed not only to the encroaching Soviet power, but to Communism in their national life. Under leaders such as de Gasperi, Adenauer, and Schuman, they formed the core of NATO and the European side of the Atlantic.

By the spring of 1948 the Kremlin, moved by its fears of the Truman Doctrine and the Marshall Plan, and by its apprehension of Titoism spreading to the other satellites, implemented a ruthless policy to integrate the Eastern European countries into its totalitarian system.[38] Stalin's program included a violent, systematic determination to end the independence of the Catholic Church in Eastern Europe, to subordinate the Church to the puppet regimes, and, finally, to sever all ties between the Papacy and Catholics in Soviet-controlled territories with the exception of occupied Germany, where the Church's social base was undermined but where there were no vicious attacks.[39] The conquest of all continental China by the Communists in 1949 was an even more devastating blow to the Church than the persecution in Eastern Europe. Within a few years it virtually demolished the Catholic community of three million with its hierarchy, which had been the outstanding achievement of Pius XI's pontificate.

The early 1950s witnessed the high-water mark of the Communist world's foray against the Catholic Church. In the early 1950s, the final years of Stalin's despotism, the Church was buffeted with the arrest of clergy and attempts to split Roman Catholics, especially in Lithuania and Czechoslovakia, away from Rome.[40] Propaganda charging the Church and Papacy with fascist sympathies gushed forth from the Communist countries.[41]

In 1956, as the policies of de-Stalinization and "peaceful coexistence" took root, some relaxation of the oppression occurred. For example, Stefan Cardinal Wyszynski, the primate of Poland, who had been imprisoned in 1953, was freed. However, the improvement, as far as Catholicism in Eastern Europe was concerned, did not proceed much beyond the level of abandoning brutality and violence (the G.D.R., Poland, and Yugoslavia stand out as exceptions). Antireligious legislation and discrimination remained intact in all of the Communist countries and the various regimes all practiced, with varying degrees of intensity, such policies as blocking or hindering interminably the construction of new churches (especially in the new housing complexes in Eastern Europe); unreasonably taxing church property and personnel; limiting religious services and celebrations; restricting vocations and seminaries; prohibiting, in many cases, the organization of a hierarchy; cultivating pro-regime "peace priests;" interfering with religious publications; imposing atheistic education and opposing religious education; disallowing church organizations; discriminating against believers in jobs and schooling; and, finally, interfering in internal church matters, including the selection of priests and bishops and communications with the Holy See.[42] In the Soviet Union, at the end of the 1950s, Khrushchev reverted to more repressive and violent measures against religion.[43]

Given the consistent pattern of persecution in the Soviet Union and the Communist states of Poland, Hungary, Czechoslovakia, Yugoslavia, Romania, East Germany, Bulgaria, and Albania, it is not surprising that Pius XII justified the national Hungarian Rising in 1956 and denounced its suppression by the Red Army. Even though the persecution of the 1950s was nowhere as virulent in Eastern Europe as it had been in Stalin's day, the Church was pilloried and worse. The Papacy had practically no dealings with the Communist governments of Soviet Russia, Poland, Hungary, Czechoslovakia, Romania, Bulgaria, and

Albania. Diplomatic relations, however, existed with Yugoslavia until December 1952, providing the Holy See with a channel for vigorous support of the bishops in their grievances against Tito's Government. They were broken off by Belgrade after the announcement that Archbishop Stepinac of Zagreb was to be made a Cardinal.

NOTES

1. Bohdan R. Bociurkiw has provided an excellent analysis of Soviet religious policy in "The Shaping of Soviet Religious Policy," Problems of Communism (May-June, 1973), pp. 38-44ff. For the Catholic side, see Walter Kolarz, Religion in the Soviet Union (London, 1961) and this writer's The Catholic Church and the Soviet Government, 1939-1949 (Boulder, Colo., 1977).

2. For details on the struggle between Rome and Byzantium for the establishment of a Church in Kievan Rus, see Eduard Winter, Russland und das Papsttum 3 vols. (Berlin) 1: 19-44. The effects of the Schism of 1054 on Vatican-Russian relations are described on pp. 45-68.

3. For details on the growth of Catholicism in Lithuania, see ibid., pp. 111-32. On the consequences of the Florentine Union, see pp. 133-43; also see Joseph Gill, The Council of Florence (Cambridge, 1959).

4. On the Union of Brest, see Oscar Halecki, From Florence to Brest (1439-1596) (New York, 1958), and Winter, Russland, pp. 253-73. In 1646 at the Uzhhorod Union the diocese of Mukachevo (Carpathian Ukraine) was brought into union with Rome.

5. Ivan III improved his claim to the title by marrying a niece of the last Eastern Roman Emperor of Byzantium.

6. Winter, Russland, pp. 147-70.

7. Dmitri Stremoookhoff, "Moscow the Third Rome: Souces of the Doctrine," Speculum 28 (January 1953): 84-101.

8. For a good study on the relations between Nicholas I and the Ukrainian Uniate Church, see Wasyl Lencyk, The Eastern Catholic Church and the Czar Nicholas I (Rome-New York, 1961). For an overall view of Russian-Catholic relations, see the first chapter of James J. Zatko's Descent into Darkness (Notre Dame, 1965) and Dunn, Catholic Church and Soviet Government, pp. 1-15.

9. Zatko, Descent, pp. 26, 58-59. For a biography of Leonid Fedorov, see Diakon Vasilii, OSBM, Leonid Fedorov, Zhizn' i deiatel'nost (Rome, 1966).

18

10.  See Bohdan R. Bociurkiw, "The Uniate Church in the Soviet Ukraine: A Case Study in Soviet Church Policy," Canadian Slavonic Papers 7 (1965): 89-113.

11.  Jean-François Revel, "The Myths of Eurocommunism," Foreign Affairs 56 (January 1978): 297.

12.  The Christian Science Monitor (Midwestern edition, U.S.A.), May 8, 1978.

13.  Richard Pipes, "Liberal Communism in Western Europe?" Orbis 20 (Fall 1976): 598.

14.  Ibid.

15.  The Christian Science Monitor, June 13, 1977.

16.  For a compilation of Marx's views on religion, see Karl Marx and Frederick Engels, On Religion (New York, 1964).

17.  Lewis S. Feuer, ed., Marx & Engels: Basic Writings on Politics and Philosophy (New York, 1959), p. 263.

18.  Ibid., p. 240.

19.  Frederick Engels, Anti-Dühring (New York, 1966), pp. 345-46.

20.  Karl Marx and Frederick Engels, Harold J. Laski on the Communist Manifesto (New York, 1967), p. 147.

21.  In Marx's "Critique of the Gotha Program," he did declare that the workers' party ought "to liberate the conscience from the witchery of religion." See Robert C. Tucker, ed., The Marx-Engels Reader (New York, 1972), p. 397.

22.  For the most complete collection of Lenin's writings on religion, see V.I. Lenin ob ateizme, religii i tserkvi (Moscow, 1969). For a good, although somewhat dogmatic and occasionally distorted, treatment of Lenin's views on religion, see M.I. Shakhnovich, Lenin i problemy ateizma (Leningrad, 1961). For a review of Soviet antireligious legislation, see V.A. Kuroedov and A.S. Pankratov, eds., Zakonodal'stvo o religioznykh kultakh (Moscow, 1971). The best Western analysis remains Bohdan R. Bociurkiw, "Lenin and Religion" in Leonard Schapiro and Peter Reddaway, eds., Lenin: The Man, the Theorist, the Leader. A Reappraisal (New York and London, 1967), pp. 107-34.

23.  Bociurkiw, "Lenin and Religion," pp, 107-134.

24.  Ibid., pp. 110-11; Shakhnovich, Lenin, p. 13; Erwin Adler, "Lenin's View on Religion," Studies on the Soviet Union 10 (1970): 11.

25.  V.I. Lenin ob ateizme, pp. 72-73.

26.  Dunn, Catholic Church and Soviet Government, pp. 45-81.

27. See Francis McCullagh, The Bolshevik Persecution of Christianity (New York, 1924), pp. 159, 210, 233.

28. See Alexander Solzhenitsyn, Gulag Archipelago [Part I] (New York, 1973), pp. 343-47.

29. See Alexandre Bennigsen, "Modernization and Conservatism in Soviet Islam," and Andrew Blane, "Protestant Sectarians and Modernization in the Soviet Union," in Dennis J. Dunn, ed., Religion and Modernization in the Soviet Union (Boulder, Colorado, 1977), pp. 243-45 and pp. 396-97 respectively.

30. See Bociurkiw, "Soviet Religious Policy," pp. 38-39, and Kolarz, Religion, pp. 176-77.

31. See this writer's "Pre-World War II Relations Between Stalin and the Catholic Church," Journal of Church and State 15 (1973): 193-204. Also see Kolarz, Religion, pp. 198-99.

32. Zatko, Descent, p. 183.

33. For details on the history of the Militant League of Godless, see Joan Delaney, "The Origins of Soviet Antireligious Organizations," in Richard H. Marshall, Jr., Thomas E. Bird, and Andrew Q. Blane, eds., Aspects of Religion in the Soviet Union 1917-1967 (Chicago, 1971), pp. 114-29.

34. For the Communist view of Pius XI, see Zdenko Roter, Katoliška cerkev in država v jugoslaviji (Ljubljani, 1976), pp. 196-97, and M.M. Sheinman, Ot Piia IX do Ioanna XXIII (Moscow, 1966), pp. 82-102.

35. See this writer's "Stalinism and the Catholic Church During the Era of World War II," The Catholic Historical Review 59 (1973): 404-28. The Vatican has published 9 vols., to date, on its policies during World War II. See Pierre Blet et al., eds., Actes et documents du Saint Siège relatifs à la seconde guerre mondiale (Citta Del Vaticano, 1965-76).

36. For documents on the suppression of the Ukrainian Uniate Church, see Diiannia Soboru Hreko-Katolyts'koi Tserkvy, 8-10 bereznia 1946, u L'vovi (Lvov, 1946); Bociurkiw provides an excellent analysis of this event in his "The Uniate Church in the Soviet Ukraine," pp. 104-7. On events in Czechoslovakia, see T. Zubek, The Church of Silence in Slovakia (Whiting, Indiana, 1956), pp. 29-30; and Ludwig Nemec, Church and State in Czechoslovakia (New York, 1955), pp. 202-18.

37. Bociurkiw, "The Uniate Church," p. 111; First Victims of Communism (Rome, 1953), pp. 58-59; Svetlo Pravoslavia, No. 1-2 (1950), pp. 1-27; Zhurnal Moskovskoi Patriarkhii (Zh.M.P.), No. 7 (1950),

pp. 40-53; P. Cârnatiu and M. Toderiniu, "Calvarul
Bisericii Unite," in Biserica Română Unită Două Sute
Ani de Istorie (Madrid, 1952), pp. 275-365; Radu
Florescu places the Romanian Uniate Church in its
historical context in "The Uniate Church: Catalyst
of Rumanian National Consciousness," The Slavonic and
East European Review (July 1967), pp. 324-42.

38. For an excellent analysis of the Kremlin's
post-war thinking, see Adam Ulam, Expansion and
Coexistence: Soviet Foreign Policy 1917-1973 (New
York, 1974), pp. 378-496.

39. For good, general accounts of the post-war,
religious conditions, see Albert Galter, The Red
Book of the Persecuted Church (Westminster, 1957);
Robert Conquest, ed., Religion in the USSR (New York-
Washington, 1968); Walter Kolarz, Religion in the
Soviet Union (New York, 1962); Institute for the
Study of the USSR, Religion in the USSR (Munich,
1960); Gary MacEoin, The Communist War on Religion
(New York, 1951); G.W. Schuster, Religion Behind the
Iron Curtain (New York, 1954); Robert Tobias, Commu-
nist-Christian Encounter in Europe (Indianapolis,
Indiana, 1956); Paul Mailleux, S.J., "Catholics in
the Soviet Union," and V. Stanley Vardys, "Catho-
licism in Lithuania," in Marshall, Aspects of Religion, pp. 357-78 and pp. 379-403 respectively.

40. Dunn, Catholic Church and Soviet Government, pp. 132, 166-67.

41. See Sheinman, Ot Piia IX, pp. 103-29; and
Dunn, Catholic Church and Soviet Government, pp.
134-37 passim.

42. For a good summary of Church-State problems
in Eastern Europe, see Bohdan R. Bociurkiw, "Religion
in Eastern Europe," Religion in Communist Lands
1 (July-October 1973): 9-14.

43. Michael Bourdeaux, ed., Religious Minorities in the Soviet Union (1960-1970) (London, 1970),
pp. 3-6; Donald A. Lowrie and William C. Fletcher,
"Khrushchev's Religious Policy, 1959-1964," in
Marshall, Aspects of Religion, pp. 131-155.

# 2. Motivation

Following the death of Pius XII in late 1958 and the election of John XXIII, a change began to develop in Soviet-Vatican relations.  The alteration evolved against the background of Khrushchev's policies of de-Stalinization and "peaceful coexistence," and the prolonged example of Tito's diminutive ill-treatment of the Catholic Church in Yugoslavia. Since the Yugoslav-Soviet schism in 1948, Tito had been slowly, very slowly, diminishing his persecution of the Catholic Church in order to strengthen the internal cohesion of the Yugoslavs, particularly the Croatians and Slovenians, in the face of Soviet hostility.  In the Soviet Union, following Stalin's death in 1953, Khrushchev emerged as the new leader and was soon forced by popular unrest with the continuing severity of the Stalinist system and by the weakness of his own position (his rivals for Stalin's job remained on the Presidium) to initiate changes in Stalin's domestic and satellite policies.  It was simply impossible to sustain Stalinism in all of its manifestations when the new leadership was divided and unsure of itself and when some of the reasons for the system had disappeared:  no longer was the Soviet Union isolated and vulnerable and no longer was it economically, politically, and militarily weak as it had been immediately after the war.  Accordingly, there was widespread welcome (as well as shock) for Khrushchev's denunciation of Stalin's despotism at the 1956 Congress of the Communist Party.

But Khrushchev did not stop with measured, internal relaxation.  He was also determined to launch the policy of "peaceful coexistence" which announced that the inevitable war between Capitalism and Communism was no longer inevitable, that Communism would conquer the world without nuclear war.  Khrushchev's reasons for doing so were several.  The practical result of Stalin's aggressive policies had been the creation of NATO and the rearmament of Germany. It seemed evident that the thermonuclear war, which neither side wanted to risk, was no means of promoting the world revolution. The "Ban the Bomb" agitation directed against the United States was already making great progress among the Western democracies. It was therefore arguable that the cause of Communism could best be advanced, and greater technical and commercial advantages obtained for the Soviet Union and its satellites by the exploitation of peace. Further, "peaceful coexistence" provided an argument by which the USSR could refuse to develop the military (especially nuclear capability) and economic power of Red China--if there were to be no war with the Capitalists, there would be no need to build up China as a strong ally of the Soviet Union. Moscow, in other words, would maintain its position as the strongest Communist power and leader of the world Communist movement. The Chinese, of course, objected bitterly to the new policy and soon began to openly criticize it and Khrushchev. But the policy was soon defined as "the chief aim" of Soviet foreign policy and was officially adopted by the Congress of the CPSU in 1961. It is, as we have seen, designed to "develop the world socialist system" without provoking the capitalist states to war, and, secondly, to curb the ambitions of the Chinese. It supplies the motivation for the whole policy of détente from the Communist point of view.

In Eastern Europe, the policy of de-Stalinization led Khrushchev to attempt to change the base of the Communist parties' power from Stalinist terror to popular support. Initially, he seemed to think Tito could serve as a model of liberalization and an object of popular support which the Soviet satellites in Eastern Europe could emulate. In the process he jettisoned another of Stalin's fixed ideas, that of hostility to Tito. Some of the die-hard Stalinists in Eastern Europe were purged and other Communist leaders were urged to make changes. But following the Polish uprising and the Hungarian Revolution in 1956, Khrushchev's penchant for liberalization in Eastern Europe cooled as did his appreciation of Tito. While Khrushchev did not revert to Stalinism or even to estrangement from Yugoslavia, he now moved very cautiously on internal reform in the Soviet Union and the Soviet bloc. In 1957 his "harebrained" policies united a majority of the Politburo against him, including his once bested rivals for power, Malenkov and Molotov. The First Secretary outfoxed his opponents, however, and with the support of the army and the Central Committee, maintained his position and replaced his adversaries with friends.

Despite the consequences of his policies, particularly of de-Stalinization in Eastern Europe, Khrushchev was still committed to attempt to garner popular support for the Communist regimes. He was determined to pursue the policy of "peaceful coexistence" with the West, and friendly ties with Tito. All these policies were opposed eventually by the Chinese who saw any understanding between the West and Moscow, such as existed in Yugoslavia, as extremely threatening to their interests--hence their strange alliance with Albania. Not only would it mean, as we have already seen, that the Soviets would have less need of a strong Communist ally in Peking and, thus, reduce their technological, economic, and military aid, but also Soviet abandonment of the revolutionary campaign against imperialistic capitalism. The rift with the Chinese was a source of great agitation to Khrushchev, but it still did not lead him to abandon his policies, part of the motivation for which, as the Chinese feared, was to prevent the development of a strong Communist China, independent from and equal to the USSR.

Since Khrushchev wanted both better relations with the West and popular support for the Communist regimes in East Europe, the Catholic Church became a natural object of his interest. This is not to say that the Catholic Church was at the center of Moscow's political objectives, but that because of its importance as an institution in Eastern Europe, especially in Poland, Hungary, Czechoslovakia, Yugoslavia, and Lithuania, and in the West, it had to be taken into consideration. John F. Kennedy, a Roman Catholic, was a major candidate for president in the 1960 election in the United States and Konrad Adenauer, a staunch Catholic, was chancellor of the German Federal Republic. There were dangers in Khrushchev showing any consideration to the Catholic Church, the main one being vulnerability to the charge by ideological rivals that the Kremlin was emasculating Marxism-Leninism. These dangers were reduced within the Soviet Union itself by the fact that the Catholics were so few in number and by the revival, on a large scale, of the anti-God campaign since 1959.

John XXIII's pontificate, which began in 1958 and lasted until 1963, was in many ways the beginning of far-reaching change within the Catholic

Church. John not only decided to call the Second
Vatican Council, but also to experiment with the
Vatican's policy toward the Communist world. Undoubtedly influenced by Tito's qualified toleration of the
Church in Yugoslavia (John XXIII had spent a good
many years in southeastern Europe as a Papal diplomat)
and by the potentialities inherent in Khrushchev's
policies of de-Stalinization and "peaceful coexistence," Pope John was ready to see if a bridge could
not be built to the Communist East. Accordingly, in
1962, the Vatican invited the Russian Orthodox Church
to send observers to the opening session of the
Second Vatican Council. This development served as
the first concrete step in détente between Rome and
Moscow.[1]

Khrushchev, of course, was certainly by 1962
quite ready to inaugurate contact with the Vatican.
Pope John impressed him as a man with whom Khrushchev
could communicate.[2] He was, as Khrushchev was later
said to have remarked, a simple peasant like himself.[3]
With Kennedy's election victory, the Vatican must
have seemed more important to Khrushchev. Though he
almost certainly exaggerated the influence of the
Papacy in Washington, the ideological nexus between
John XXIII and a Catholic President seemed a significant fact and, thus, elevated the Vatican in importance in his eyes. Additionally, Khrushchev was
probably persuaded that Pope John could influence
Adenauer.[4]

Early in 1961, Pope John published the encyclical
Mater et Magistra in which he had much to say on
social ethics. In a passage referring to the inter-
dependence of citizens the word socializazione, used
in the Italian translation, gave rise in press commentaries to the inaccurate notion that the Pope was
referring favorably to the growth of socialism. For
the Communists, this perhaps indicated that the new
Pope would be receptive to a new relationship, an
impression reinforced in 1963 by his further encyclical Pacem in Terris, with its eulogy of the United
Nations in which the Soviet Union was developing an
almost proprietary interest.

The contact between Rome and Moscow, enjoined by
the presence of Russian Orthodox Church observers at
the opening session of the Second Vatican Council,
took an unexpected turn in late October 1962 as the
Cuban missile crisis unfolded. At the height of the
Cuban crisis, a Prelate of the Secretariat of State
at the Vatican asked Norman Cousins, the editor of
Saturday Review, to relay to Moscow the desire of the
Pope for peace and, at the same time, to inform

25

Khrushchev that the Vatican was ready for an improvement in Papal-Soviet relations. The fact that Cousins was an American may have underlined for Khrushchev the value of the Catholic Church in the United States as a lever for influencing Kennedy. Possibly as a litmus test of Khrushchev's intentions, Pope John, at the suggestion of the Ukrainian Uniate bishops attending the Council, instructed Cousins to ask Khrushchev to release the long-imprisoned primate of the Uniate Church, Metropolitan Josyf Slipyi.[5] The Vatican also asked the Russian Orthodox Church observers to intercede for the Metropolitan. In early 1963, Khrushchev granted the Pope's request, evidently under certain conditions,[6] and Metropolitan Slipyi took up residence in Vatican City. In March 1963, Khrushchev sent his daughter and son-in-law, Aleksei I. Adzhubei, then editor of Izvestiia, to Rome to visit Pope John and his cordial reception of them was taken as a symbol of the prospect of friendly relations with the Communists, if not compromise with their doctrines.

At a very elementary level, Khrushchev and Pope John launched the process of a Soviet-Papal rapprochement. The Vatican was well aware of the fact that the key to a general understanding with the Communist states of East Europe, exclusive of Yugoslavia and Albania, was an improvement of relations with the Kremlin, and that once the leading Communist state demonstrated a willingness to improve, the other Communist regimes in Eastern Europe would follow suit or, at least, re-evaluate their ties with the Catholic Church.[7] In that sense, the activity of the Pope and the First Secretary of the CPSU stimulated a general relaxation of tension (to use the Russian expression for détente) in Catholic-Communist relations in East Europe and--what became no less important and soon of more danger to the Church--an encouragement to the growth of Marxism among the Catholic clergy and laity of Europe and the Americas.[8] Brezhnev and Pope Paul VI continued the new policy and expanded the contacts to international affairs and ecumenical relations between the Vatican and the Russian Orthodox Church. The change in the Vatican's attitude toward the Soviet Union and other Communist states of East Europe synchronized with a remarkable improvement in relations with Marshal Tito. In fact, in Yugoslavia, as we shall see, the Church's Ostpolitik enjoyed its greatest successes.

To date, with the exception of Yugoslavia, Papal-Communist détente has not led to any very dramatic

26

changes. Nonetheless, there have been some very
important alterations and they could have either
favorable or adverse consequences. The new relationship has been characterized by: (1) an improvement
in the treatment of the Catholic Church, in comparison with the Stalinist period, by the Communist governments of Eastern Europe with the exception of the
Soviet Union and Albania;[9] (2) dialogues and exchanges between Papal and Communist officials and
Orthodox dignitaries; (3) a diminution in the Vatican's anti-Communist propaganda and the Communist
regimes' (again, excepting Albania) anti-Vatican
propaganda; (4) the agreement on, at least, two general international goals: stability in East Europe,
and avoidance of nuclear war; (5) a sense of betrayal
and isolation among many Catholics in East Europe,
especially in the Ukraine and Lithuania, as well as
by many Catholics of Eastern and Central European
origin in the United States and Canada; (6) the
strengthening of "progressive" and Left Catholics;
(7) finally, the release of some imprisoned clerics,
including Metropolitan Josyf Slipyi in 1963, Archbishop Joseph Beran from Czechoslovakia in 1965, and
the long-tormented "illegal" Uniate bishop, Vasyl
Velychkovsky, in 1972. Before an attempt is made to
analyze why the Vatican and the Kremlin as well as
the Soviet satellites and Yugoslavia would be interested in improved relations, it is useful to identify
the framework in which the policy evolved.

The Vatican officers, aside from Pope Paul,
directly involved in the new policy included Arch-
bishop Agostino Casaroli, Secretary of the Council
for Public Relations, Cardinal Johannes Willebrands,
Archbishop of Utrecht and President of the Secretariat for Christian Unity, Cardinal Franz Koenig,
Archbishop of Vienna and President of the Secretariat for Dialogue with Unbelievers, Cardinal Jean
Villot, Secretary of State of the Vatican, Father
Pedro Arrupe, S.J., the Jesuit Superior General,
Monsignor Luigi Poggi, Apostolic Nuncio for Special
Missions and leader of the Holy See's delegation for
permanent working contacts with the Polish Govern-
ment, Bishop Ramon Torrella Cascante, Vice-President
of the Secretariat for Christian Unity, Father John
Long, Head of the Eastern Churches Department at the
Secretariat for Christian Unity, Monsignor Andre-
Marie Deskur, Secretary of the Papal Commission for
Public Information, and Fr. John Bokovsky and Mon-
signor Gabriel Montalvo, both members of the Vatican's
Council for Public Relations. Other Church leaders
who undoubtedly played a role in the new policy

27

included Cardinal John Krol, Archbishop of Philadelphia and member of the Sacred Congregation for Eastern Churches and a frequent visitor to Poland, Cardinal Franjo Seper, President of the Congregation on Doctrine and Faith and the first East European bishop to head a Vatican Congregation, and Archbishop Joseph Schroetter, Secretary of the Congregation of Catholic Education. Other groups which surely provided advice or attempted to affect policy included the superior generals of religious orders and congregations with religious members in Eastern Europe (Marians of the Immaculate Conception, Basilians, Dominicans, Congregation of Missionaries, Brothers Hospitallers of St. John of God, etc.), the various foreign national colleges in Rome (for example, the Russicum), the representatives of respective National Bishops' Conferences (for example, the Poles, Romanians, etc.), and the East European national Catholics in Rome. Naturally, the Pontifical Institute for Oriental Studies has been participating in the Vatican's Ostpolitik.[10] As a rule, the East European Communists preferred to go over the heads of local bishops and deal directly with the Holy See and, in that sense, the Communist regimes became a provider of information, however distorted, to Rome.

The officials of the Papal Secretariat of State concerned with the Soviet Union and the other Eastern European states are few in number; and, while the Holy See is certainly the recipient of a great bulk of information on religious conditions in those countries and the policies of their governments, its analysis and use of this information is open to criticism. For the East European bishops the details of the Church's life and vexations, such as restrictions on the number of churches open, on religious teaching, or on the ability of the clergy to carry on their pastoral duties, are the most important aspects of Church-State relations. How can such practical details be dealt with in the broad picture of such relations with which Vatican diplomacy is concerned? There remains also the problem of the institutionalized advisers, such as the consultatores of the various Congregations and Papal Offices, who wish to prove their knowledge by interpreting the facts. They are often accused of interfering with information and research, so that what data reaches the Pope and his immediate assistants may have been altered because it does not agree with the policies or suffered expertise of these consultants. The Vatican also seems to ignore much of the research carried on outside of Church institutions.

28

As for the Soviets, the Soviet satellites, and Yugoslavia, the Vatican dealt with an array of government and religious officials and institutions. In the USSR, the Vatican, as with any foreign institution, had contacts with the Foreign Ministry, including Foreign Minister Andrei Gromyko. It also had relations with the Council on Religious Affairs, presently under the chairmanship of Vladimir Kuroedov. This body, responsible to the Council of Ministers of the USSR, controls and regulates the activities of organized religion and, in the words of Vladimir Kuroedov, "contributes its aid to religious organizations in their international relations."[11] It evidently works closely with the Department of External Relations of the Moscow Patriarchate. The Committee of State Security or the KGB also had a major interest in Vatican-Soviet relations not only because the Church was an international force, but also because not a few Soviet citizens looked to Rome for religious leadership.[12] Recently, large numbers of Catholics, especially in the Lithuanian S.S.R., protested against Soviet religious restrictions and paid dearly for their courage. In a vague defense of the crackdown against these and other dissidents, Iuri Andropov, head of the KGB, argued that it was only natural for the state to move against individuals who had committed "anti-Soviet activities."[13] The Vatican also had contacts with the Russian Orthodox Church, including Patriarch Pimen of Moscow and All-Russia, Metropolitan Yuvenaliy of Tula and Belev, Head of the Department of External Relations of the Moscow Patriarchate, and Metropolitan Nikodim of Leningrad and Novgorod, Chairman of the Holy Synod Commission on Christian Unity and Inter-Church Relations and Patriarchal Exarch to Western Europe. The Catholic Church also had relations with the so-called Berlin Conference (BK) of Catholic Christians from European States-- an international organization of the "progressive" Catholic clergy and laymen, mainly from the Soviet bloc[14]--, the Christian Peace Conference, the Soviet "peace" movement, and various international and domestic conferences whose purpose was to rally ecclesiastical support for the current Soviet policy aim.[15]

In the East European states, as in the Soviet Union, the Vatican was involved with the leaders of the Communist parties, foreign ministers, the various "peace" groups, the state security organs, and the ubiquitous office of religious affairs. Details of these relationships will be given in subsequent

chapters, but, in general, it is doubtful that the
Communist regimes were following a monolithic direction, prescribed by Moscow, in their relations
with the Vatican.  There is, of course, the overriding strategy of the ruling Communist Party of
employing "peaceful coexistence" as a means of promoting the victory of socialism in the world, a
policy in which the courting of the Christian Churches
now plays no inconsiderable part.  Certainly the
East European church legislation was written with
Soviet advisers, but it differs from country to
country and from the model of the USSR.  The Kremlin
has had to adjust to the nationalism and indigenous
traditions of the East European countries, and, of
course, in Yugoslavia and Albania, the Soviets have
had virtually no influence over the government's
religious policy.  The fact is that Church-State
relations in Eastern Europe are complicated arrangements with, at least, a triangular framework involving in the case of Poland, for example, relations
between Warsaw and Rome, Moscow and Rome, and Moscow,
Warsaw, and Rome.

PAPAL MOTIVATION

> In the social sphere the Christian
> doctrine has many common aspects with
> the social divisions of Marxism and
> other progressive movements which ought
> to allow the formation between them of
> solid and organic links in many domains.
>           Archbishop Casaroli, l'Unita, April 6, 1974

A major reason why the Vatican was ready to
welcome the opportunity of a dialogue with the Communist governments of East Europe and the Soviet Union
was that the Church in Lithuania,Latvia, Hungary,
Czechoslovakia, Romania, and Bulgaria was, by the
beginning of the 1960s, structurally weak as the
result of the repression from which it suffered.
Bishops, above all, were desperately needed, particularly in Czechoslovakia and Hungary.  In February
1973, Pope Paul VI explained to newly ordained
priests from Czechoslovakia that "after many dealings
and much study we have succeeded in consecrating four
bishops in Czechoslovakia.  Czechoslovakia was on the
point of losing its hierarchy which almost did not
exist."[16]  The Holy See is not seeking diplomatic
relations with the Communist countries, only relations, "because they make possible a closer and more
continued contact."  Diplomatic relations are not

30

that important, but the Vatican will establish such ties, according to Archbishop Casaroli, if such associations will serve the Church, the nations, and the community of peoples.[17] After years of estrangement from the Communists and witnessing the erosion of the Church's bases in East Europe, the Vatican was ready to try the tact of dialogue to arrest that process of erosion.

A second advantage in seeking a modus vivendi with the Communist states of East Europe and the Soviet Union is that good relations are seemingly better than bad relations for maintaining the high standards of Catholicism in those areas of East Europe where the Church is a powerful factor in the national life, namely in Poland, Croatia, and Slovenia. The Catholic Church today is more vigorous in those areas where it feels and withstands persecution than in other parts of the world. Poland, for example, has more vocations for the priesthood than any other European country, and Zagreb in Croatia was the scene of an international Mariological and Marian Congress in 1971. It would be illlogical to assume that the Vatican is conducting detente with the Communist governments of these regions in order to weaken the present position of the Catholic Church where it is in a strong position. The Polish bishops, particularly their leader, Cardinal Stefan Wyszynski, are quite opposed to any Vatican-coordinated change in Church-State relations in Poland precisely because they fear the Papacy will undercut them and make too many concessions to the Communists.[18] It is not that the Polish bishops are against change per se, but, rather, given the Church's strength in Poland, they deem it best to take a hard line to force the government into concessions.[19] From their point of view, any circumscription of the Polish Church would not lead to real concessions elsewhere in East Europe because the Vatican would no longer have the leverage to persuade Moscow to make adjustments.

Another factor in the Papal-Communist détente is that the Papacy is convinced that the division of Europe into opposing political, ideological, and military camps is unnatural and arbitrary, and believes that it is now in the process of being transformed back into a single cultural unity, politically naïve as this seems to many observers. Although the Church recognizes the many differences among the peoples of Europe, it views them all, East and West, as sharing a common Christian heritage, and, thus, united in a real sense.[20] For the Church,

31

Christianity is the basis of Western civilization, the dynamic of the European spirit, and, accordingly, the Vatican has a very special role, now that "detente" is the order of the day, to encourage dialogue between East and West, and to draw out the Christian spirit.  For Archbishop Casaroli, the key to opening Eastern Europe is to avoid conflicts and to find common interests.[21]  "It is my conviction," he declared, "that the human element--man's instinctive need for freedom and religion--will eventually triumph as the sense of truth imposes itself."[22]  It is time, he would say, to bolster any and every effort which reduces tension and promotes mutual advantages whether it be the Common Market, the Nuclear Test Ban Treaty, or the Helsinki Conference on European Security and Cooperation.[23]  The main criticism made of this prelate is his disregard of the avowed object of the "policy of peaceful coexistence" as defined by the ruling Communist Party of the Soviet Union, and his own belief in the compatibility of Marxism and Christianity.  In the Italian Communist paper l'Unita of April 6, 1974 there was, for instance, a report of a conversation of Mgr. Casaroli with a group of journalists during his visit to Cuba, which he has never denied or modified, in which he said:  "In the social sphere the Christian doctrine has many common aspects with the social divisions of Marxism and other progressive movements which ought to allow the formation between them of solid and organic links in many domains."  It is not surprising, therefore, that the diplomacy of the Vatican with which he is identified is so discredited among the Catholic clergy and faithful in Lithuania, the Western Ukraine, and other Eastern European countries who know what Communist persecution is.

Another important reason for the Ostpolitik of the Vatican is the strength of the Communist parties in Italy and France.  The possibility of Communist participation in a French government, despite the defeat of the Left coalition in the parliamentary elections in 1978, is in the cards; and the Italian Communist Party, being the second largest party in the country, found, after the 1976 election and the government crisis in early 1978, that the minority Christian Democrat government needed its parliamentary cooperation in order to survive.  Thanks to the support of the Socialist Party, its demands for inclusion in the government itself may well become irresistable (despite the Red Brigade's murder of Aldo Moro in May 1978), to the great discomfiture of the United States and most other members of NATO.

In France, though anticlericalism has much diminished, the hierarchy has long ceased to have any political influence, while the Catholics are acutely divided between Left and Right. In Italy, the Church retains more of its traditional authority in public life, but the Revision of the Concordat, now almost completed, will end its privileged position as the recognized religion of the country. In view of these developments, it seemed advantageous to the Holy See to be on good terms with the Soviet Union and the other Communist states of Europe; to examine more closely and objectively the nature and contemporary practice of Communism; to establish precedents, and to be in a position to avert or moderate any unfavorable alteration, should the P.C.I. come to power, of the Church's legal and cultural position in Italy. Of course, the Vatican has not yet come to the point of endorsing a Communist regime in Italy or anywhere else. In Portugal, the Church's influence in the defeat, by the great majority of the electorate, of the attempted Communist take-over was undoubtedly considerable.[24] One might even argue, though without much conviction, that the Church's Ostpolitik is only a temporizing tactic, geared to halt or at least dilute with Christianity some of the Communist inroads in Catholic countries until more acceptable leaders can emerge. The fact is that the Papacy has been taking steps, such as Pope Paul's reception of the Communist mayor of Rome in late 1976, to find a place for itself in Enrico Berlinguer's so-called "historical compromise." The Church is not yet ready to embrace Communism in Italy or France, but it is making preparations in case such an embrace proves unavoidable, and Ostpolitik is an important step in those preparations. The Vatican also had to respond to the rise of Left Catholicism in the West, a significant group of Catholics who feel that Catholicism and Communism can coexist and that "a system of free economy is of necessity ethically inferior to socialism."[25] Wilfried Daim, for example, a Viennese medical doctor, wrote that Pope Pius XII was "at best a dilettante" in dealing with Eastern Europe, that Polish Catholicism is "in its intellectualization more than a little retarded compared to that of other countries," that "the Soviets would have no objection whatever to an Orthodox-Catholic union, if the Catholic Church were willing to endorse socialism--if only in the sense of agreeing to the principle of public ownership of the means of production-- and thus to reach a decision against capitalism," and, finally, that Paul VI was "a second Pius XII."[26]

An additional argument for better relations is
that the Vatican has accepted the fact, probably soon
after the Soviet suppression of the Hungarian Revolution in 1956, that Soviet control of Eastern Europe is
a long term reality. Archbishop Casaroli has made it
clear that the Papacy now considers the political
and territorial changes in Europe, following World
War II, as facts of life which must be lived with.[27]
The Papacy, of course, wants to bridge the divisions
which have divided Europe into opposing camps, but it
clearly has accepted the territorial alterations that
occurred in Europe at the end of the Second World
War.[28] This fact must be supplemented by another.
Through the course of the 1960s, and especially in
recent years, it became obvious that Soviet military
strength, despite the fissiparous tendencies in the
Communist camp, was increasing and, perhaps, equaling
that of the United States. Further, the recent
Soviet naval build-up in the Mediterranean and the
Indian Ocean and the military and political successes
of Soviet-sponsored movements in Asia and Africa, in
particular the Communist take-over of all of the former Portuguesse territories in West and East Africa,
following after the Communist victory in Indochina,
have clearly altered the strategic balance of power in
the Soviets' favor. That has become a necessary deter-
minant of the foreign policy of Western Europe, as it
is of the United States. The U.S.S.R., in other words,
was the dominant European power and its status, whether
in Eastern or Western Europe or the world at large,
was ostensibly not about to alter, but, if anything,
was likely to be enhanced. To remain impervious to
that reality would be imprudent for the Vatican.
Throughout the centuries of its existence, the Church
has always been ready to adjust to man's sundry political systems, though it is not easy to see how this
adaptability can be applied to a formally atheistic
polity. As long as the state would permit the Church
to perform its spiritual mission of saving souls, the
Church could accept and has accepted polities that
vary from democracies to dictatorships. Archbishop
Casaroli declared that the Church's mission is universal and, accordingly, that the Church cannot be
tied to any one system or block of states.[29] Following this line of thinking, the Vatican can be said
to be consistent in warming to the Communist countries. In World War II, for example, it kept con-
nections with Great Britain, France, the United
States, Italy, Japan, and Germany, though this impartiality had no doctrinal undertone. The Communists, of course, are not permitting the Church to

pursue its mission without obstruction, and the Vatican is quite aware of this. In fact, Archbishop Casaroli is highly pessimistic about relations with the Communist states and the fruit of those relations.[30] Nonetheless, from the Papacy's vantage point, the effort is necessary because it could be the way to religious toleration in the Communist world. To those who see the Church as sacrificing its principles to realpolitik, the Vatican can only argue that anathemas did not work against Communism, it has grown and continues to grow, so it is time to try cooperation. Casaroli has made it clear that trading barbs with Communists produced no benefit for anyone, and that there is absolutely no substitute for his method of dialogue.[31] Historically, the Papacy can point to the fact that it maintained relations with Hitler's Germany even though the Nazis interfered with the Church's mission. This was done not because the Church condoned Nazism or Hitler, but because the opportunity to care for souls, however curbed, was still preferable to a complete break with the resulting likelihood of increased persecution and isolation for Catholics. The Communists, after all, can always make life more difficult for Catholics.

A further argument for the contact of the Papacy with the Communists is that the Church is always, but especially in the nuclear age, anxious to do everything possible to prevent war.[32] Vivid memories of the ravages of two World Wars and the efforts of the Popes to mitigate them impel the Holy See to leave no stone unturned to spare making a repetition of that catastrophe. In the second case, peace and security are the temporal conditions under which the Church can best carry out its spiritual mission. Because of the Papacy's propensity for tranquility, the Church wished to seek an end of the Cold War, as it is called, and, more specifically, to decrease the strains and divisions in Europe. Throughout recent history, the Papacy has been overwhelmingly an advocate of peace. Today, when the world is beset by the horrors of scientific and technological warfare, its advocacy of peace, as Archbishop Casaroli said, is "a preeminent duty."[33] The desire of the Vatican for peace, however, does not mean that it accepts Bertrand Russell's famous or infamous dictum of "better red than dead." Casaroli has stated that what concerns the Church is its spiritual mission and spiritual and moral reality.[34] Today the Papacy believes that peace is essential and that Europeans have more in common than they have causes of division.[35] Besides these considerations, the last war led to an expansion of anti-Christian Communism, and there is a good chance that another war might lead to further expansions of the anti-Christian philosophy. Without war, Communism is already making headway in Italy, France, Asia, and Africa. It is highly unlikely that another war would witness the defeat of Communism. Given such factors, the best strategy for the Church is to work for peace and to try to change the antireligious nature of Communism. Ostpolitik is a step in that direction. Such appears to be the reasoning which at present prevails in the Vatican. Of course, the Soviet Union and the other Communist states of East Europe fully exploit the Vatican's desire for peace to enhance their own policies of "peaceful coexistence" and "détente." The Russian Orthodox Church, the Christian Peace Conference, of which Metropolitan Nikodim of Leningrad and Novgorod is chairman, and, especially, the so-called Berlin Conference (BK) of Catholic Christians from European States constantly appeal to the Vatican to support Soviet foreign policy objectives.[36]

Another reason for the Church's rapprochement with the Communist regimes is linked to the occasional by-product of cooperation: character assimilation. The Vatican knows only too well that the Communists have ruthlessly persecuted religion and, in most cases, persist in harassing believers in one fashion or another. Through collaboration, the Church, however, hopes to reduce the persecution and, eventually, gain a foothold for its mission.[37] The Church aims at securing, at least, toleration, but it certainly plans for more through a modus vivendi, including conversion. The process of conversion is a gradual one and, in the case of the Communists, the ground floor would be the abandonment of official atheism. Will the Communists abandon atheism? If they do, they forsake their ideology and Leninist orthodoxy, though there are some leading Marxists today--Georges Marchais is one--who profess that the denial of the Christian faith is not essential to membership in the Party. On the other hand, the Soviets and East European Communists are politicians who have more than once temporarily sacrificed ideology for the sake of realpolitik. That no doubt led the late Pope Paul and his advisers to hope that the strength of religion in Eastern Europe will induce the regimes to find it an official place in Communist society. Of course, the Church also hopes for reunion with the Russian Orthodox Church, a vain hope which Moscow feeds by allowing theological dialogue between Orthodox and Catholic prelates.[38]

36

An additional reason for seeking a compromise
with the Communist world was tied to the evident
conviction of Paul VI that some socialist ideas were
worthwhile. In 1967, in his encyclical _Populorum
Progressio_, he indicated sympathy for a number of
socialist notions by decrying what was described as
the evils of unrestrained capitalism, including the
imbalance in the production and distribution of the
world's goods, and the tendency to place private
property above the "fundamental exigencies of the
common good." This encyclical, whose main theme was
the duty of the wealthy to come more generously to
the aid of the developing nations, was undoubtedly
colored with the prevailing anti-colonialism. It
was seized upon by the advocates of the "theology of
revolution" as reinforcement of their thesis. This
was done by taking out of context the Pope's refer-
ence to the use of violence which did not in fact
depart from the traditional teaching of the Church
which the Second Vatican Council had recently re-
affirmed. What he actually wrote was:

> Recourse to violence as a means to
> right these wrongs to human dignity is
> a grave temptation. We know, however,
> that a revolutionary uprising, save where
> there is manifest, long-standing tyranny
> which could do great damage to fundamental
> human rights and dangerous harm to the
> common good of the country, produces new
> injustices, throws more elements out of
> balance and brings new disasters. A real
> evil should not be fought against at the
> cost of greater misery.[39]

Though quarrying in Papal encyclicals to prove
one's point is a common occupation of Catholic contro-
versialists both of the Left and the Right, there is
no doubt of the propensity of Paul VI to have looked
for good among socialist ideas wherever it could be
found. In his letter _Octogesima Adveniens_ (May 14,
1971), issued to mark the eightieth anniversary of
Leo XIII's encyclical _Rerum Novarum_ on the social
question, he did, however, maintain all the historical
points of doctrine, as for instance the condemnation
both of the class war and of _laissez faire_ liberal-
ism. The most extreme example of the "lurch to the
Left" was the long letter of Cardinal Roy of Quebec,
written at the Pope's request, to the _Osservatore
Romano_ which went very far in aligning the Church
with the Marxist "liberation" campaign and described

class warfare as the fruit of "a lucid dialectic."[40]
What lends special cogency to the Vatican's search
for positive aspects of the socialist program is that
the "winds of change," to borrow a phrase from
Harold Macmillan, are plainly blowing in Latin America, Asia, and Africa in a leftist direction.  The
Catholic Church is predominant in Latin America;
it is by far the largest Christian body in Africa
south of the Sahara where, as in Asian countries,
the Communist exploitation of local nationalism
creates acute problems.  The Papacy seemingly feels
that if the Catholic Church is to hold its position
and, more importantly, given the priorities of a
Church which believes itself to be the true faith,
expand its influence, it must attune its message to
the developing nations of the "Third World."  Some
Catholic clergy in Latin America are working with
and leading socialist movements without incurring the
censure of the Vatican.[41]  Certainly the Church has
not embraced Communism or even publicly modified its
condemnations of Communism so often repeated during
the present century, but it does seem to be willing
to countenance the possibility of socialism's holding
an answer to the problem of inequality in the distribution of the world's wealth.[42]  The Communists of
Eastern Europe, of course, fully encourage the Vatican's direction through the use of "collaborationist"
clergy and laymen in the West, and the general argument that Communists and believers can work together
for social justice, providing the former's "leading
role" is accepted.[43]

A final and important argument for accommodation
is that the Vatican would have been isolated, politically and ecumenically, if it had not attempted a
new relationship with governments in the Communist
orbit.  To remain inflexibly anti-Communist while
the World Council of Churches, representing the
Orthodox and Reformed Churches, was in the opposite
camp and the governments of Europe and North America
adopted conciliatory policies toward the Soviet Union
would be imprudent from both a diplomatic and religious point of view.

COMMUNIST MOTIVATION

"One can be a Christian and a Communist.
This is not a contradiction."
Georges Marchais, La Croix, January 25, 1977

As the Catholic-Communist concurrence has here-
tofore evolved, it has been primarily an affair

38

involving the governments of the Soviet Union, Poland, Hungary, Czechoslovakia, Yugoslavia, Romania, East Germany, and Bulgaria, rather than the Communist world as a whole. Albania remains antagonistic because of the aggressive atheism of its ruler, Enver Hoxha, and its attachment to Maoist dogma; from the Maoist stand-point approving the policy of détente would involve the sin of Soviet "revisionism," and, possibly, assist Belgrade's inveterate design for a Yugoslav-controlled Balkans.

Among the governments which have searched for a modus vivendi with the Catholic Church, the motives have varied. Yugoslavia's desire for an agreement appears to be linked to two realities. In the first place, the Catholic Church is a significant voice in the multinational state of Yugoslavia, with the majority of the Croatians and Slovenians adhering to Catholicism. Tito's miracle has been his ability to hold together Yugoslavia's ethnic heterogenity. Part of the reason for his success has been his awareness that continued religious persecution would serve as a centrifugal force opposed to Yugoslav unity. Conversely, religious tolerance, Tito seems to think, has brought the Papacy to the support of the government and to the concept of a continuing, unified Yugoslavia.[44] Strong ties with the Vatican, at any rate, would dissipate Catholic alienation in Slovenia and Croatia, and rob nationalists there of Papal patronage and religious martyrs. Secondly, Tito, in his unique but isolated position as the maverick of international Communism, requires an economic and political locus standi in the West. The Holy See, at minimum, can provide Belgrade with a bridge to a number of Western powers, notably Italy.

Romania's wish for contacts with the Vatican are somewhat similar to Tito's motif. The Church can offer Bucharest a touchstone in the West where Nicolae Ceausescu has been seeking economic and political security from the Soviet bloc. At the same time, relations with the Roman Church emphasize Romania's claim to be a vestige of the erstwhile Roman Empire. The relationship is complicated, however, by the existence of the national Orthodox Church and its hostile and repressive attitude to the Uniate Church in which the government, of course, concurred.

The willingness of the Soviet Union, Poland, Hungary, Czechoslovakia, East Germany, and Bulgaria to pursue accommodation with the Catholic Church is connected to a multiplicity of reasons. First there is Moscow's desire to have the Vatican support the

policies of "peaceful coexistence" and "détente."
As Brezhnev declared in May 1977: "The cause of
peace and détente should be the business of every-
one."[45] Accordingly, Moscow openly courts the Vatican, sending its ministers to Rome, receiving Rome's
ministers, and inviting the Vatican to participate
in the Conference on Security and Cooperation in
Europe. The Holy See is now described as "realistic"
and "favorably disposed towards the principles of
peaceful coexistence and a relaxation of tensions."[46]
    Moscow also believes that the Church can help
in maintaining order in the Soviet Empire in Eastern
Europe. The Ukrainian Uniates, suppressed since
1946, remain a force of disruption in the USSR. There
is abundant evidence that the Uniate Catholic Church
continues to operate as an underground movement and
as a wellspring of Ukrainian nationalism--realities
that are anathema in the totalitarian society.[47]
Since the late 1950s, a "neo-Uniate" group called
Pokutnyky ("Penitents") has emerged, and significantly, in contrast to the other Uniates, it refused to
profess even outward loyalty to the Soviet regime.[48]
The group, however, is small, disorganized, and,
since the early 1960s, split from the main body of
Uniates. In addition to the Pokutnyky, hundreds of
Ukrainian Uniate émigrés keep the plight of their
Church in the Western news, and recently have demanded that the Vatican establish a patriarchate for
the Ukrainian Catholics, and name Cardinal Josyf
Slipyi, the head of the Ukrainian Uniates-in-exile,
as the Patriarch. Such irredentist activities ex-
pose the Achilles' heel of nationalism in the USSR,
and, accordingly, the Soviets have responded with a
revealing barrage of diatribes against the Cardinal
and the idea of a Uniate Patriarchate.[49] The Vatican has kept a very low profile on the problem of a
Uniate Patriarchate. There is evidence that Metropolitan Slipyi was released conditionally from a
Soviet prison in 1963 and that might explain partial-
ly Rome's reluctance to promote Slipyi and the idea
of a patriarchate. Of course, the Vatican might
also be reasoning that the situation of the catacomb
Uniate Church could always be worse, if the Holy See
were to complain publicly of persecution. Presum-
ably the Vatican's cautious approach to the Uniate
problem is pleasing to Moscow, although, if its
attacks upon the Uniate Church are evidence, it prefers the total abandonment of the Uniates by Rome.
In May 1976, for example, the Russian Orthodox
Metropolitan of Lvov and Ternopol, Nikolai, announced
that "The Catholic Vatican had for centuries a desire

to subject the entire Orthodox Church to its domination," but that "Uniatism has outlived its time and
is like a drowning person clutching at a straw."[50]
Radio Lvov in the Ukraine, in a more shrill tone,
declared that "The Uniate ravens dressed in black
cassocks will never again see the Soviet Ukraine, its
fields in blossom and its clear, blessed and cloud-
less skies. They will never see it as they cannot
see the backs of their heads."[51]

In addition to the Uniate Catholics, there are
Lithuanian, Latvian, Polish, German, Belorussian,
and Armenian Catholics in the Soviet Union. The
Lithuanian Catholics, particularly, are a numerous,
compact group with a strong nationalist-Catholic
tradition.[52] Since the late 1960s, they have become
one of the most vocal and active wings in the religious-nationalist agitation sweeping the USSR.[53] In
dealing with the Lithuanian Catholics, Moscow has
two major policies: (1) to dilute their concentration through the migration of Russian nationals into
and of Lithuanian nationals out of Lithuania (this
policy started with the deportation of large numbers,
particularly of intellectuals, in the early days of
the annexation to the Soviet Union [1945-50] but has
not yet been revived on a massive scale); and,
(2) to paralyze the structure of the Catholic Church
through indirect and, where necessary, overt forms
of persecution, such as arresting active laymen and
women, impeding the pastoral activity of remaining
bishops, and keeping the number of new priests below
normal replacement needs.[54] As a price for detente,
the Kremlin obviously desires from the Vatican a
policy of benign neglect. The Kremlin would like the
Papacy to treat the Lithuanian persecutions as if it
were a problem of Soviet internal affairs, but this
step the Vatican has not taken. The Kremlin undoubtedly hopes the Holy See will sustain the continua-
tion of Soviet domination in the Baltic region, and
terminate its diplomatic relations with the Lithuanian Government-in-exile. In the meantime, the
Soviets have deftly conducted relations with the Vati
can so as to discourage and confuse Lithuanian nation
alists who feel that the Church is selling them out
for no obvious gain.[55] The Papacy cannot plead ig-
norance to what is going on in Lithuania. The
Chronicle of the Catholic Church in Lithuania, a
samizdat* journal circulated since 1972, has made
that excuse impossible,[56] though the Vatican's
knowledge of Church affairs in Lithuania and

*Underground, multigraphed publication.

41

elsewhere in East Europe is by no means complete and though the Vatican and the world at large have been subjected to numbing Soviet propaganda which claims that there is religious freedom in Lithuania.[57] At best, the passivity of the Holy See can be understood on the grounds that it is convinced that the Communists will increase persecution in the satellites if it attempts openly to interfere in Soviet-Catholic affairs.

Besides the persecution of Lithuanian Catholics, other Catholics in the Soviet Union, including the Latvians, Polish, German, Belorussian, and Armenian Catholics, are also persecuted.[58] Details of their condition are virtually impossible to obtain, although quite recently German and Polish Catholics in the Moldavian SSR have documented persecution.[59] As with the Lithuanians, the Vatican is passive toward the plight of these Catholics.

In Eastern Europe, there is, as among national minority groups in the Soviet Union itself, widespread disaffection. The rebellions and uprisings which have occurred in Poland, East Germany, Hungary, and Czechoslovakia since the end of World War II have, of course, been linked to economic and political discontent rather than religion. But nonetheless, religion is a powerful arm of public persuasion and can be utilized to dampen political-economic disturbances. This was borne out, quite dramatically, in 1970, when one of Edward Gierek's first responses to the Polish workers' riots in the Baltic ports was to request the cooperation of the Catholic Church in restoring order.[60] In the ferment which has been rife in Poland since the authorities arbitrarily increased (and subsequently withdrew in panic) food prices in June 1976, the Catholic Church has shown itself to be a major defender of civil rights and a powerful mobilizer of public opinion.[61]

From the Catholic Church in Eastern Europe, the Soviets hope to gain what they tried to achieve at the end of World War II. Simply put, Moscow wants the support of the Catholic Church to facilitate its supremacy in Eastern Europe. As the dominant religion in Poland, Hungary, and Czechoslovakia, the Church could do much to reinforce the status quo, to legitimize the local Communist regimes, and to make them palatable to the people.[62] The Church's leverage in Poland, the kingpin of the Soviet Eastern European empire, is decisive, and there rapprochement with Rome holds out the hope of reducing, if not stifling, anti-Soviet, religious-nationalist feeling.[63] In the 1960s and early 1970s, the immediate goal of Papal-Communist détente in Poland was to obtain the Vatican's recognition of the boundary changes between Poland and Germany resulting from World War II.[64] More generally, with the Papacy as a friend, the Kremlin would go into the future with a surer hand on Eastern Europe. Furthermore, the various governments of Communist East Europe, especially Poland, prefer to deal with the Vatican on ecclesiastical affairs rather than work with local church leaders who are often uncompromising and more knowledgeable about the details of Church-State relations.

Another reason why Moscow is seeking a modus vivendi with the Church is that Catholicism, as a major religion in Spain and Portugal, Ireland, France, Italy, West Germany, Switzerland, Austria, Belgium, the Netherlands, and Luxembourg, can help win Western European acquiescence in the security goals of the USSR on its western borders.[65] In this regard, it is no less valuable to Moscow to have the goodwill of the Church in North America. The Vatican's support of the Soviet-originated Helsinki Conference of 1975 is no doubt seen as a step in that direction. The Church might be useful in preparing Europe for "Finlandization" or even for assimilation into the Soviet orbit if it could be detached from its defensive alliance with the United States. The Soviet military build-up is no doubt required to enforce the authority of Moscow within the "Socialist Commonwealth" which it already controls, as was accomplished in Czechoslovakia in 1968. But the Kremlin's military machine is so extensive and formidable, both in nuclear and conventional weaponry, that it could easily be used for a blitzkrieg. Even the threat of such a use of power could reap rich political rewards in the West, once it had been sufficiently softened up by détente. Historically, Russia has sought security through expansion. If Western Europe could be Sovietized or, at least, fitted into the Soviet sphere of influence somewhat akin to Finland, the boons to Moscow would be tantalizing: (1) such stimuli of anti-Sovietism as the contrasts between the Communist life style and Western freedoms would diminish on the borders of the Soviet Empire; (2) a rich store of economic, technological, scientific, and manpower resources would become available; (3) Marxism-Leninism could be once again advertised as the wave of the future; (4) finally, Moscow would gain strategic advantages against the United States and China. Granted these benefits represent maxima; the difficulties which the Soviets might encounter in trying to force Western Europe into its sphere of influence might be as great as the boons. Nonetheless, the historian must go with the record and conclude that, from Moscow's point of view, expansion is the best form of security. From that perspective, friendship with the Vatican is valuable because, at minimum, it removes a major enemy from the Western camp and tends to reduce fears of Soviet aggression.

Another Soviet motive for détente is related to the fact that the Catholic Church has great influence in Latin America, and also in the Middle East and Africa and Oceania.[66] As such, the Church can be quite useful to the Kremlin by giving the Soviet Communists a degree of acceptance among Catholics in those countries. This is quite important in Moscow's struggle with China for influence in the "Third World" and for control of the world Communist movement.

An additional reason is that an apparent agreement with the Vatican can be manipulated, as Russian Orthodoxy has been exploited, to belie the charge that the Communists persecute religion and suppress dissent and minority groups. Association with the Papacy can also improve the USSR's image among religiously-conscious people and help garner world opinion behind Soviet foreign policy goals.[67] Moscow shares, at least, two explicit international objectives with Rome, as mentioned earlier: the avoidance of nuclear war and stability in Eastern Europe. Radio Moscow, for example, on March 17, 1978 praised the Vatican as an institution which "pays great attention to the major problem of the times--that of peace and international security." Discussions between Andrei Gromyko, the Soviet foreign minister, and the Pope and Archbishop Casaroli invariably revolve around peace, disarmament, and European security.[68] It is logical that the Kremlin would search out backing for these designs in every sympathetic quarter, including Rome.

A further part of the explanation behind the Catholic-Communist cooperation is that the Church, since the Second Vatican Council, has emphasized ecumenism and understanding of nonbelievers and atheists. Soviet ideologues responded with some praise, some confusion, but, generally, with the conclusion that the Church was engaging in futile efforts to save itself from an inevitable demise.[69] Nonetheless, these new developments in the Catholic Church offered, at least, an excuse for a more friendly attitude toward Rome.[70] Besides, religious toleration in the West seemingly has led to a genuine religious decline and possibly the Soviets reasoned that

détente, if not toleration, might produce some of the
same consequences in their own bailiwick.  They are
forever commenting upon the "crisis of religion" in
the West (as well as in the East) and Vladimir
Kuroedov, the Chairman of the Council on Religious
Affairs, specifically emphasizes "the profound crisis
shaking the modern Catholic Church."[71]
     The Communists also have it in mind to undermine
the influence and power of the Church.  Obviously,
they hope to exploit the present influence of the
Church for their various designs,[72] but in the long
term, the Catholic Church, like religion in general,
must be overturned.  The Communists do not mince
words about the ultimate incompatibility of religion
and Marxism-Leninism and openly predict the demise of
religion.  In a recent article entitled "Religion and
Science" in Nauka i religiia, it is made absolutely
clear that there is a "profound and essentially
irreconcilable antagonism between the scientific
[read Marxist-Leninist] and religious philosophies"
and that this incompatibility "is based most of all
on their diametrically opposing philosophic principles and functions of class ideology; this is reflected in every part of the contemporary ideological
struggle."[73]  Vladimir Kuroedov declared that religion will soon disappear, the result of the "implacable, historical process of progress."[74]  We are,
thus, left with the paradoxical situation of the
Communists, on one hand, praising Catholicism as
"realistic," "tolerant," and "practical,"[75] but, on
the other hand, openly attacking the Church as "reactionary" and "counterrevolutionary,"[76] and attempting to undermine and compromise it through
collaborationist clergy and public association with
religious persecutors.
     The Communists, also, of course, wish to mani-
pulate the growth of Left Catholicism in the West
and "Third World" to further Soviet policy aims.  The
phenomenon of Western "Left Catholicism" is by and
large the result of the Church's desire, since the
Second Vatican Council, to concentrate on social
problems rather than spiritual and supernatural concerns and to reach a modus vivendi with the Communist states.  Ironically, the Communists now exploit
the Left Catholic movement to push the Vatican
further along in its Ostpolitik.[77]  In the Communist
countries of Eastern Europe, of course, there have
always been collaborationist clergy and laymen to
pressure the Vatican to reach an understanding with
the Communist governments and to rebut charges of
religious persecution.

A final factor could be that Moscow's overtures to the Vatican were a smoke screen to obscure a major, antireligious campaign which commenced in the USSR in 1959, and lasted until Khrushchev's demise.[78] They could have been part of the flurry of activity in 1961-62 which saw the Russian Orthodox Church and the All-Union Congress of Evangelical Christian-Baptists join the World Council of Churches.

## NOTES

1. Stanislaw Markiewicz, Kościół rsymskokatolicki a państwa socjalistyczne (Warsaw, 1974), pp. 106-110. Also see Zygmunt Tyszka, "Polityka wschodnia Watykanu," Zycie i myśl 21 (May 1971): 22.

2. Communist authors argue that what made better relations between the Vatican and the Communist governments possible was the advent of Pope John XXIII and the fact that he changed the Church's policy. See Markiewicz, Kościół, pp. 101-2; M.M. Sheinman, Ot Piia IX do Ionna XXIII (Moscow, 1966), pp. 133-41. For an interesting evaluation of Pope John's personality and Ostpolitik, see Giancario Zizola, l'Utopia di Papa Giovanni (Assisi, 1973). Also see the entire issue of Nauka i religiia, No. 6 (1963), and Literaturnaia gazeta, December 8, 1962.

3. Norman Cousins, "The Improbable Triumvirate: Khrushchev, Kennedy, and Pope John," The Saturday Review, No. 54 (October 1971), p. 30. More detail can be found in the same author's The Improbable Triumvirate (New York, 1972).

4. Markiewicz, Kościół, pp. 102-5.

5. Cousins, "Triumvirate," pp. 27, 34. Also see Jozef Mackiewicz, Watykan w cieniu Czerwonej Gwiazdy (London, 1975), p. 189.

6. M.A. Morozov and E.I. Lisavtsev, Aktualnye zadachi ateisticheskogo vospitaniia (Moscow, 1970), p. 17, claim that the Vatican has not fulfilled the agreement of Cardinal Slipyi's release "that he would not engage in political activities among the former Uniates." For details of the Cardinal's release and life, see Milena Rudnyts'ka, Nevydymi stygmaty (Rome-Munich, 1971).

7. Markiewicz, Kościół, pp. 11-36.

8. Lazar Velikovich, "Contrary to the Understanding," New Times (Moscow), No. 32 (August 1976), pp. 21-22; Juan Rosales, "Revolution, Socialism, Theology," World Marxist Review (Toronto), No. 6 (June 1975), pp. 80-90.

9. Albania, aligned with China, has claimed to be the first totally atheistic state. For comment,

see l'Osservatore Romano, April 26, 1973.

10.  Fr. Paul Mailleux, S.J., the rector of the Pontifical Russian College in Rome, has no doubt provided advice to the Vatican on Ostpolitik.

11.  V. Kouroiedov, L'Eglise et la religion en U.R.S.S. (Moscow, 1977), p. 41.

12.  According to a recent book by John Barron entitled KGB: The Secret Work of Soviet Secret Agents (New York, 1974), p. 140, the Council on Religious Affairs is "dominated by the KGB." According to the classified handbooks of the Council on Religious Affairs, the Vatican is both a powerful and dangerous foe. See V.A. Kuroedov and A.S. Pankratov, eds., Zakonodal'stvo o religioznykh kultakh (Moscow, 1971), pp. 302-3; K.Z. Lytvyn and A.I. Pshenychnyi, eds., Zakonodavstvo pro relihiini kulty (Kiev, 1973), pp. 226-27, 249.

13.  Moscow Radio, September 12, 1977.

14.  See Chronicle of the Catholic Church in Lithuania [hereafter CCCL], No. 19 (October 15, 1975), cited in ELTA, No. 2 (February 1976), p. 3; CCCL, No. 18 (1975), cited in ELTA, No. 10 (October 1975), p. 10; and Begegnung (East Berlin), No. 10 (1975), p. 17.

15.  Bohdan R. Bociurkiw, "The Catholic Church and the Soviet State in the 1970's," (Unpublished manuscript), p. 13.

16.  Radio Vatican, February 28, 1973.

17.  Private notes of Peter Hebblethwaite, former Jesuit and editor of the Jesuit periodical The Month (England).

18.  Peter Hebblethwaite, "The Vatican Power Game," The Observer (London), December 22, 1974), p. 9.

19.  Ibid.

20.  Archbishop Agostino Casaroli, "La Santa Sede e l'Europa," Civilta Cattolica (February 19, 1972), pp. 370, 376.

21.  Ibid., p. 377.

22.  Hebblethwaite, "Vatican Power Game," p. 9.

23.  Casaroli, "La Santa Sede," pp. 379-81.

24.  The Times (London), October 21, November 10, 1975.

25.  Wilfried Daim, The Vatican and Eastern Europe, trans. Alexander Gode (New York, 1970), p. 17.

26.  Ibid., pp. 74-75, 81, 173.

27.  Casaroli, "La Santa Sede," pp. 367-69.

28.  Ibid., pp. 367-71.

29.  Ibid., p. 370.

30.  Ibid., pp. 372-73.

47

31. Hebblethwaite, "Vatican Power Game," p. 9.
32. Casaroli, "La Santa Sede," p. 373. Also see Casaroli's interview with Otto Schulmeister, Die Presse (Vienna), December 21, 1974. For Soviet evaluations of the Church's position on peace, see I.I. Kravchenko, "Katolicheskaia traktovka sotisal'nykh otnosheniiv razvitykh kapitalisticheskikh stranakh," Voprosy nauchnogo atheizma, No. 6 (Moscow, 1966), pp. 270-306; L. N. Velikovich, "Voina i mir voitsenke sobora," Voprosy nauchnogo atheizma, No. 6 (Moscow, 1968), pp. 307-25; I. Iastrebov, Nauka i religiia, No. 1 (1970), pp. 49-50.
33. Casaroli, "La Santa Sede," p. 373.
34. Ibid., pp. 370, 379.
35. Ibid., pp. 376-81.
36. For details on the "peace" activities of the Berlin Conference and the Russian Orthodox Church, see their respective organs, Begegnung (East Berlin) and Zhurnal Moskovskoi Patriarkhii (Moscow).
37. See this author's "Papal-Communist Détente: Motivation," Survey, No. 2 (99) (Spring 1976), p. 145.
38. See the convenient summary of Catholic-Orthodox relations in The Journal of the Moscow Patriarchate (English edition), No. 7 (1976), p. 24.
39. For Soviet comment, see I.M. Kichanova, "Problema cheloveka," Voprosy nauchnogo ateizma, No. 6 (Moscow, 1968), pp. 268-69.
40. Cardinal Roy was the head of the Pontifical Commission on Justice and Peace.
41. See Rosales, "Revolution, Socialism, Theology," pp. 80-90; New York Times, September 19, 1969; Peter Hebblethwaite, The Runaway Church (London, 1975), pp. 157-60.
42. Giovanni Barberini, "Introduction," in Erich Weingärtner, ed., Church Within Socialism (Rome, 1976), pp. 2-3.
43. B. Strashun, "Socialist Democracy Triumphs," International Affairs, No. 1 (Moscow) (1977), p. 19.
44. Attacks upon clerics have continued, however, because the Catholic Church is viewed not only as a rival, but the backbone of Croatian nationalism. See, for example, Zdenko Antic, "Tension Between State and Catholic Church in Yugoslavia Continues," Radio Free Europe Research Report, No. 112 (July 1, 1975), pp. 1-9.
45. Radio Moscow, May 29, 1977.
46. See N.A. Koval'skii, Religioznye organizatsii i problemy Evropeiskoi bezopacnosti i sotridnichestva (Moscow: Znanie, 1977), p. 39; and Velikovich, "Contrary to Understandind," p. 21.
47. See Bohdan R. Bociurkiw, "Religion and Nationalism in the Contemporary Ukraine," in

48

George W. Simmonds, eds., <u>Nationalism in the USSR and</u>
<u>Eastern Europe in the Era of Brezhnev and Kosygin</u>
(Detroit, 1977), pp. 183-87;  Vasyl Markus, "Religion
and Nationality: The Uniates of the Ukraine," in
Bohdan R. Bociurkiw and John W. Strong, eds., <u>Reli-</u>
<u>gion and Atheism in the USSR and Eastern Europe</u>
(Toronto, 1975), pp. 107-18;  and Dunn, "Papal-
Communist Détente," p. 149.

    48.  See footnote #47 above, and <u>Liudyna i svit</u>,
No. 11 (1968), pp. 36-39.

    49.  Dunn, "Papal-Communist Détente," p. 149.

    50.  Radio Moscow, May 29, 1976.

    51.  Radio Lvov (Ukraine), February 2, 1978.

    52.  See V. Stanley Vardys, ed., <u>Portrait of a</u>
<u>Nation: Lithuania under the Soviets</u> (New York, 1965).

    53.  Bohdan R. Bociurkiw has provided an ex-
cellent analysis of this phenomenon in "Religious
Dissent in the U.S.S.R.: Lithuanian Catholics," in
James Scanlan and Richard DeGeorge, eds., <u>Marxism and</u>
<u>Religion in Eastern Europe</u> (Dordrecht, 1976),
pp. 147-75.  Michael Bourdeaux has provided a commentary and analysis of the <u>CCCl</u> in <u>Land of Crosses</u>
(London, 1978).

    54.  V. Stanley Vardys, "Catholicism in Lithu-
ania," pp. 393-403;  V. Stanley Vardys, "Geography
and Nationalities in the USSR: A Commentary," <u>Slavic</u>
<u>Review</u> 31 (September 1972): 546-70.

    55.  <u>CCCL</u>, No. 4 (1972), p. 10;  No. 9 (1974),
pp. 16-17;  No. 14 (1972), p. 10.

    56.  Thirty-one issues of the <u>CCCL</u> have reached
the West.

    57.  See, for example, Radio Moscow, November 23,
1976;  Radio Moscow, November 10, 1977;  Radio
Vilnius, April 20, 1978;  <u>Izvestiia</u>, January 31, 1976.

    58.  See Paul Mailleux, S.J., "Catholics in the
Soviet Union," in Marshall, <u>Aspects of Religion</u>,
pp. 359-78.

    59.  <u>Keston News Service</u>, Issue No. 49 (March 2,
1978), pp. 2-3.

    60.  <u>New York Times</u>, December 24, 1970.

    61.  Leszek Kolakowski <u>et alii.</u>, "The Polish
Resistance," <u>The New York Review of Books</u>, Nos. 21 &
22 (January 20, 1977), p. 61;  Adam Bromke, "A New
Juncture in Poland," <u>Problems in Communism</u> (September-
October 1976), pp. 11-12.

    62.  Koval'skii, <u>Religioznye organizatsii</u>,
pp. 36-37, 41-42;  Miklos Vetö, "Kremlin and Vatican,"
<u>Survey</u> (July 1963), pp. 163-72.  On Soviet postwar
goals in Eastern Europe, see Adam Ulam, <u>Expansion and</u>
<u>Coexistence: Soviet Foreign Policy 1917-73</u> (New
York, 1974, 2nd ed.), pp. 338-495.

63. Koval'skii, Religioznye organizatsii, pp. 33, 37; Stanislaw Staron, "State and Church Relations in Poland," World Politics 21 (July 1969): 580, 598-601; Hansjakob Stehle, "Vatican Policy Towards Eastern Europe," Survey, No. 66 (January 1968), p. 115. Cf. Henry Korotynski, "Church and State in Poland," New Times, No. 36 (September 7, 1966), pp. 14-16, and Eleonora Syzdek, "Gosudarstvo i katlicheskaia tserkov' v Norodnoi Pol'she," Politicheskoe samoobrazovanie, No. 4 (1966), pp. 138-44.

64. "Poland in the Vatican's Eastern Policy," Contemporary Poland 7 (October 1973): 20-23.

65. See M.P. Mchedlov, Sovremenniia bor'ba idei i religiia (Moscow: Znanie, 1977); Koval'skii, Religioznye organizatsii, pp. 14, 25, 33, 36; Sovetskaia Rossiia, August 27, 1973; Velikovich, "Contrary to the Understanding," pp. 21-23; Radio Moscow, January 7, 1971; Radio Moscow, January 27, 1972.

66. I.V. Lavretskii, "Nekotorye voprosy politiki Vatikana v Afrike," Voprosy istorii religii i ateizma 7 (Moscow, 1958): 105-29; V.U. Nunka, "Natsional' no-osvoboditel'noe dvizhenie i religiia," Novoe v zhizni nauke tekhnike (Moscow: Znanie, 1972), pp. 32-43; Rosales, "Revolution, Socialism, Theology," pp. 80-90.

67. Koval'skii, Religioznye organizatsii, pp. 8-9, 14, 25, 31-40.

68. Radio Moscow, June 29, 1975; New York Times, November 11, 1970; The Tablet (London), March 13, 1971; Sovetskaia Rossiia, February 22, 1974; New York Times, February 25, 1971.

69. See Mchedlov, Sovremenniia bor'ba; E.M. Babosov, Nauchno-teknicheskaia vi modernizatsiia katolitsizma (Minsk, 1971); M.P. Mchedlov, Katolitsizm (Moscow, 1970); M.P. Mchedlov, Evoliutsiia sovremennogo katolitsizma (Moscow, 1967), p. 45; N.A. Sadovskii, "Novye momenty v sotsial'noi doktrine katolicheskoi tserkvi," Voprosy filosofii, No. 1 (1971), pp. 87-89; "Vatikan pered vzovom ateizma," Kommunist (Vilnius), No. 9 (1974), pp. 78-87; L. Velikovich, "Catholicism and the Time," New Times, No. 48 (November 1972), pp. 18-20; N.A. Koval'skii, Katolitsizm i mirovoe sotsial'noe razvitie (Moscow, 1974), pp. 17-31, 57-83.

70. Velikovich, "Contrary to the Understanding," p. 21; Sheinman, Ot Piia IX, pp. 130-32, 135-38; Markiewicz, Kościół, pp. 111-36.

71. Kouroïedov, L'Eglise et la religion, p. 57. Also see Koval'skii, Katolitsizm, pp. 16-17.

72. Kommunist, No. 15 (1964), p. 88; Voprosy filosofii, No. 8 (1965), p. 115.

73. Vaclav Toufar, "Religiia i nauka," Nauka i religiia, No. 5 (1975), p. 85. Also see Sovetskaia Litva, December 19, 1963; Mchedlov, Sovremenniia bor'ba, pp. 49-50.

74. Kouroïedov, L'Eglise et la religion, p. 58.

75. See Koval'skii, Religioznie organizatsii, p. 39; Velikovich, "Contrary to the Understanding," pp. 21-22.

76. M.M. Sheinman, "Problemy sovremennogo katolitsizma," Nauka i religiia, No. 10 (1970), pp. 82-84; Koval'skii, Katolitsizm, pp. 57-83.

77. Koval'skii, Religioznye organizatsii, pp. 8-9; Rosales, "Revolution, Socialism, Theology," pp. 80-90. The final document of the Berlin Conference of European Communist Patries in 1976 noted that "Ever broader Catholic forces. . . play an important role in the struggle for the rights of the working people, and for democracy and peace."

78. For details see Lowrie and Fletcher, "Khrushchev's Religious Policy," pp. 131-55.

# 3. U.S.S.R.: Persistent Problems

The Vatican's Ostpolitik has been played out a-
gainst a background of continuing persecution in the
Soviet Union. The position of the Church, in fact,
has deteriorated since the Papal initiative. This
chapter will first describe the present distribution
of Catholics in the USSR and, then, proceed to outline the major developments in the Soviet-Papal détente.

## PRESENT STATUS OF THE ROMAN CATHOLIC CHURCH IN THE USSR

Latin rite Catholics in the Soviet Union represent a relatively small religious group, estimated
at over three to four million.[1] While they are
spread across the Soviet Union from Siberia to the
Baltic Republics, the bulk of them are located in
Lithuania and Latvia (especially the province of
Latgalia) and the western oblasti of the Belorussian
and Ukrainian SSRs. Ethnically, the Church is composed of Lithuanians (about 2.25 million or three-
fourths of the Republic's population[2]), Latvians
(about 269,000[3]), Poles (probably most of the
340,000 Poles living in Western Belorussia, and at
least one third of the 295,107 Poles in the Ukraine[4]),
Belorussians (several hundred thousands[5]), Germans
(mainly in Siberia and Kazakhstan to where they were
deported during World War II[6]), Hungarians (some
80,000 located in the Transcarpathian oblast of the
Ukraine[7]), Estonians (about 2,500[8]), and a very small
number of Ukrainians, Slovaks, and Czechs.[9] In
addition, several thousand Catholics of both the
Latin and Uniate Armenian rites live in Armenia and
Georgia.[10]

The Catholics, unlike the Russian Orthodox
Church and a few other religious organizations, have
not been allowed to create a central, ecclesiastical

authority. Only in Lithuania and Latvia have the
Catholics been permitted to organize into dioceses
with their own bishop and clergy. Elsewhere, Catholics
are without diocesan structure (Belorussia and the
Ukraine) or have been placed under the jurisdiction of
the Archdiocese of Riga (the Leningrad parish and the
two functioning Estonian parishes[11]) or the Archdiocese of Kaunas (the Moscow parish[12]). Hungarian Catholics in the Carpatho-Ukraine have been permitted to
keep a Vicariate General in Uzhhorod which included in
the late 1960s 26 churches and 22 priests.[13] The
Ukrainains and Belorussians seem to rely informally on
Riga for new clergy, although the Polish Catholic
Church continues to treat Roman Catholics there as
under its jurisdiction despite Soviet objections.[14]

According to official Soviet references, there
were in 1960-61, 1,235 Roman Catholic churches and
chapels in the USSR with some 1,270 clergy.[15] By
1966, the number of "working" churches dropped to
about 1,000.[16]

## LITHUANIA

In Lithuania, the Church has two archdioceses
(Kaunas and Vilnius) and four dioceses (Panevežys,
Vilkaviskis, Kaišiadorys, and Telšiai and Klaipeda),
although none has a residential bishop and they are
presently managed as four administrative units.[17]
The episcopal duties of the two most popular bishops
(Julijonas Steponavičius and Vincentas Sladkevičius),
who have been confined to remote villages, have been
taken over by administrators chosen from the so-
called "progressive" clergy.[18] The diocese of
Telšiai and Klaipeda has been vacant since the death
of Bishop J. Pletkus in September 1975, while the
dioceses of Vilkaviskis and Kaunas are administered
by Bishop Liudas Povilonis, who took over for retired
Bishop J. Matulaitis-Labukas in the spring of 1976.
The see of Panevežys is managed by Bishop Romualdo
Krikščiunas.

In 1972, the six dioceses included fifty-four
deaneries and 662 parishes (sixty-one of these have
no priest), down from sixty-two deaneries and 717
parishes in 1940.[19] The official Vatican yearbook,
Annuario Pontificio, listed 884 priests in Lithuania
in 1971 (down nearly 40 per cent since 1940),[20] but
other sources claim that ninety-seven of these priests
were not permitted to carry out pastoral duties,
sixty-two totally disabled, and 105 pensioned.[21] The
median age of the Lithuanian priests (fifty-five in
1971)[22] has been increasing and their number regularly

53

dropping because of an intentionally small numerus clausus prescribed by the government on the only remaining theological seminary in Kaunas.  The supply of priests is growing into a sharp problem for the Church in Lithuania:  between September 1960 and June 1974, only 110 priests were ordained while during the same period 269 priests died.[23]  A number of priests have been covertly trained and consecrated, but they do not come close to filling the need.[24]

The Church in Lithuania, in contrast to the Russian Orthodox Church and a few other religious organizations, has not been able to publish its own periodical and has been acutely limited in preparing essential liturgical and religious books.  Accordingly, Catholics have had to rely for such texts upon clandestine publication works run by devoted laymen.[25]  The Church has also, again unlike the Russian Orthodox Church, not been able to keep monasteries, but small underground convents persist in Lithuania, with the "illegal" nuns doing most of the work in religiously educating the young.[26]  As in other areas of the Soviet Union and the Communist bloc, the socialization of minors has continued as the central confrontation between the atheist government and the Church.  While compelling antireligious instruction for school children, the Lithuanian regime has been especially strict in imprisoning and fining nuns and priests charged with teaching religion to the young.[27]

Because of the deteriorating condition of their Church, the Lithuanian Catholics mounted, beginning in 1967, a rather massive campaign to publicize the Soviet Government's infringement of its own laws and of its asphyxiation of religious worship in general. Such agitation is unquestionably essential for the survival of the Church and the Lithuanians know it. Space does not permit an extensive treatment of this protest, but its implications for the future of the Soviet Union should not be underestimated.[28]  Between 1968 and 1972, Latin Catholics in Lithuania restricted themselves to clerical and lay petitions requesting, generally, the Soviet government to abide by its own legislation on religion, to halt arbitrary interpretations of religious laws, and to curtail all forms of religious persecution.[29]  Some of the protest documents also reproved the Kremlin's restrictions against Lithuanian culture, continued suppression of the Uniate Church, and, increasingly, the Vatican's Ostpolitik.[30]

The Soviet rulers did not respond to the various petitions addressed to them (despite their legal duty to do so within a month), but, instead, moved to crush the growing challenge in Lithuania. Some of the clerical leaders were incarcerated on the charge of illegal religious instruction of the young (Article 143 of the Lithuanian Criminal Code).[31] Their plight, in turn, precipitated lay protests which soon culminated in the appearance in 1972--over the heads of submissive ecclesiastical leaders--of a samizdat publication, the Chronicle of the Catholic Church in Lithuania. Modeling itself after two earlier samizdat journals--the Chronicle of Current Events and the Ukrainian Herald--, the CCCL proposed to report on "the situation of the Catholic Church, the nation's heritage, the arbitrary actions, repressions and other discriminatory means of the government organs. . . ."[32] In addition, the editors hoped to persuade the Vatican to reevaluate Ostpolitik by presenting accurate information on the Church's position in Lithuania.[33] They feared that the Holy See was being duped, or worse, that it was abandoning them. In common with Lithuanians in the United States, they were particularly irritated by the report which Father Pedro Arrupe S.J. made on his return to Rome from a visit to the USSR in September 1977, that he had found the religious situation improved since his last visit six years before and had been invited to speak in an Orthodox Church. The Chronicle warned its readers not to be deceived by a temporary relaxation of persecution. "The Soviet government is not acting in good faith. The diminution of the persecution of the Church is merely a tactical maneuver by the Communist Party."

The themes in the CCCL range from reports of Soviet truculence against Lithuanian Catholics, with some mention of Ukrainian and Belorussian Catholics, to Soviet maltreatment of Lithuanian intellectuals and nationalists. It is a solid, factual publication which, despite intense KGB efforts at eradication, has persevered.[34] In August 1972, the Vilnius daily, Sovetskaia Litva, urged caution in responding to the Catholic protest movement,[35] and, to be sure, the Soviet government has made some concessions to reinforce the hand of the "loyalists" among the bishops and clergy. In December 1969, it agreed to the consecration of two new bishops (Povilonis and Krikščiunas) and is apparently ready to accept another bishop providing he is selected from among the collaborationist clergy.[36] Kaunas Seminary was allowed to accept fifty applicants (up from the 1966 quota of thirty) by the 1974-75 academic year. But at the same time, the authorities moved with massive force to single out the leaders of the Lithuanian dissent movement, to scare off their followers, and especially to close down the Chronicle and other underground publications.[37]

Beginning in November 1973, a dragnet swept through Lithuania. Priests and laymen suspected of participating in the dissent movement were arrested. Five laymen (Petras Plumpa, Povilas Petronis, Jonas Stasaitis, A. Patriubavicius, and Virgilius Jaugelis) were tried in December 1974 and given sentences ranging from one to eight years of "corrective labor" for "illegally multiplying and distributing publications containing fabricated, provocative rumors, slanderous attacks on the Soviet state and social system," as well as for "sending abroad part of these publications."[38] Arrest and imprisonment have become the lot of not a few Lithuanian Catholics. At the same time, the authorities attempted to undermine the credibility of the Chronicle,[39] and to balance it with the collaborationist clergy who claimed that the Lithuanian Church was free and that the dissidents were spreading "disinformation" about the Church's position for their own political, anti-Soviet motives.[40] To improve the image of Soviet religious policy in the eyes of Roman Catholics outside of the Soviet Union, the regime permitted Cardinal Alfred Bengsch of Berlin to pay a visit to the Lithuanian Church in August 1975, a sojourn that was managed by the "progressive" clergy and kept the Cardinal far removed from any contact with the dissident clergy.[41]

The most disturbing aspect of the persecution of the Lithuanian Church has been the silence of the Vatican. The Chronicle has repeatedly emphasized that point:

. . . while defending victims of discrimination all over the world, [the Holy See] barely recalls the 'Church of Silence and Suffering,' does not bring up and does not condemn covert and overt persecution of the faithful in the Soviet Union.[42]

Dialogue, it seems, is useful to [the Communist regime] only so that the Vatican will keep silent about the persecution of Catholics in the Soviet Union. . . .[43]

There are four possible motives which, singly or in combination, might explain the Holy See's position. The Papacy might be assuming the attitude

56

which it adopted toward Nazism in 1942.
Then Myron Taylor, President Franklin D. Roosevelt's
personal envoy to the Holy See, requested that the
Pope condemn Hitler's atrocities, especially his
persecution of the Jews.[44] Cardinal Maglione, the
Papal Secretary of State, responded that His Holiness
had, on numerous occasions, decried all governments
which mistreated peoples and individuals, but that
the Pope could not descend to particulars for this
course of action "would immediately draw His Holiness
into the field of political disputes, require documentary proof, etc." The Cardinal protested that
"people have short memories in matters of this kind
and that many would have the Pope speak out daily in
denunciation of these evils."[45] The Vatican, in
other words, might feel that it has already clarified
its position on Communist persecution, as expressed,
notably, in the encyclical Divini Redemptoris and by
the frequent protests of the late Pope Paul against the
denial of fundamental human rights, and particularly
religious liberty, in general terms. Such a stance
leaves much to be desired not only because the
Chronicle of the Catholic Church in Lithuania has
provided "documentary proof" of persecution, but precisely because people do have short memories and a
principal duty of a moral leader, such as the Pope,
is to abhor consistently and vigilantly injustice
and immorality. Catholic doctrine does not allow
for relative morality or subjective truth and, thus,
if Cardinal Maglione's explanation is behind Papal
inaction, it would seem to represent a patent in-
consistency in Catholic principles.
    Moreover, the Vatican might be convinced that
any attempt to interfere with Soviet policy toward
Catholics would worsen an already bad situation.
The Soviets, from this point of view, might react to
Papal involvement by increasing persecution. The
Vatican might be quite persuaded that quiet diplomacy
is the best way of handling the Lithuanian problem.
It might even argue that the modicum of religious
life which the Lithuanians do have is the result of
its Ostpolitik. That position, though, would seem
somewhat cavalier, since the position of the Lithuanian Catholics has declined since rapprochement.
If the Papacy is privately objecting to the oppression in Lithuania with success, its successes have
remained hidden.
    Is the Papacy ignorant of the details of the per-
secution in Lithuania? While it would be difficult
to believe, as mentioned earlier, that the Vatican is
generally unfamiliar with current events in the

57

Lithuanian SSR because of the documentation readily
available in the CCCL, it is quite conceivable that
the Vatican is not well equipped either in terms of
personnel or organization to digest and analyze the
information.  Further, some lower echelon bureaucrats
might be hindering consciously or subconsciously some
important information from reaching the Pope himself.
In such cases as these, the inevitable result in terms
of Vatican policy is inertia, or at best, indecision.
     A fourth possibility is that the Vatican, while
not ignorant about the Lithuanian developments, is
uncertain how to react so that the position of the
Lithuanian Catholics or any other Catholic group
could be bettered.  This quandry goes to the heart of
a problem which has confronted leaders as diverse as
Franklin D. Roosevelt and Adolph Hitler:  is there
an open sesame for handling the Soviets?  While it
would be absurd to pretend that there is one master
key which would explain and simultaneously provide a
policy response to Soviet activities, the strategy of
reciprocity--give or take no more or no less than the
Kremlin proffers or gains--has proved again and again
to be an effective basis upon which to start working
with the Russians.  The Soviets do not respond to
unilateral concessions, but rather interpret them as
a sign of weakness.  Unfortunately this policy leaves
the initiative for change in Soviet hands, but there
it must rest; for it is the Soviets who started the
hostilities against the Church and they alone can
reduce or terminate them.  Such a diplomatic maneuver
as reciprocity assumes that the two parties involved
have both rewards and punishments which they can
administer to one another.  The Soviets' penalties
and concessions are obvious, but so are the Vatican's
to anyone who studies the issues.  The Papal ledger
of assets and debits has already been outlined in the
previous chapter, and provides the explanation for
why the Kremlin is willing to engage the Vatican.
The Holy See has substantial power of persuasion in
Eastern Europe, Western Europe, and around the world.
This power can be brought into play through exhortations, decrees, encyclicals, diplomacy, and example.
It can be wielded as a pro, con, or neutral tool in
the Catholic Church's relationship with Moscow.  If
it is used deftly, it could lead to an improvement
in the position of Lithuanian Catholics.  Of course,
the Church's power of persuasion is not an absolute,
but rather is intimately tied to the perception of
the Papacy's position.  If the Church appeared hesi-
tant to take a clear, public, even bold stand against
gross assaults on human rights and dignity, it would

be in danger of losing its influence.  Moscow would
then have no use for the Catholic Church; and the
plight of Catholics everywhere under Soviet domination
could only become worse.  Silence, in the face of injustice, has uncontrollable consequences.

THE ROMAN CATHOLIC CHURCH IN OTHER REPUBLICS

In Latvia, the Roman Catholic Church is a minority and, although certainly sharing in the torments af-
flicting the Lithuanian Catholic Church, a dissent
movement has not grown around it.  In 1974, according
to the Vatican's Annuario Pontificio, the Archdiocese
of Riga and the diocese of Leipaja embraced 178 parishes administered by 133 diocesan and 13 religious
priests with 18 seminarians at Riga seminary,[46] as
against 216 churches and chapels, 166 parishes, 190
clergymen, and 31 seminarians in 1940.[47]
The Latvian Catholics have no periodical and,
like the Lithuanians, seriously lack religious texts
and prayer books.  They were permitted once, in 1967,
to produce a prayer book and small missal.[48]  The
Church is led by Bishop Julijonas Vaivods, now in his
eighties, who holds the title of Apostolic Administrator of Riga and Leipaja.  He is helped by Bishop
Valerians Zondaks (b. 1908), former rector of the
Riga seminary and consecrated bishop in November
1972.[49]  Kazimirs Dulbinskis, the senior Latvian
bishop, after his return from a long imprisonment in
the Komi ASSR and exile in Belorussia, was confined
in the 1960s to a rural village and proscribed from
saying mass in public.[50]  In the latter part of 1975,
5,043 Latvian Catholics petitioned the Soviet Government not to demolish their church.[51]
Information on the position of Roman Catholics
in Belorussia and the Ukraine is extremely limited.
At the end of World War II, over 500,000 Catholics
were taken by the Soviets from West Belorussia and
West Ukraine and resettled in Poland, mainly in the
Oder-Neisse Territories which Poland had been allowed
to annex from Germany.[52]  In addition, the Soviets
ceded the Belostok region of Belorussia to Poland in
1945 and there were about 478,000 Catholics living
there.[53]  Today, Roman Catholics constitute a sizeable minority in the Belorussian SSR, located primarily in the Grodno oblast where, according to Soviet
sources, there were at minimum 176,000 "active Catholics" in the early 1960s.[54]  Most of these Catholics
are Poles.  The churches, numbering 154 in 1959,
were reduced during the Khrushchev antireligious
campaign to somewhere between sixty-five and one

hundred churches,[55] and most of these are located
in the Grodno oblast,[56] where the Poles represent
over thirty per cent of the population.  According
to a report by Dr. Federico Alessandrini, the Vatican's press officer, there were eighty priests
active in Belorussia in 1971,[57] and most of these
were Poles.[58]  The number of priests and faithful
continue to decline, as do the number of churches.[59]
The Vatican and the Soviet Government were reportedly
on the verge of agreeing to the consecration of a
Belorussian bishop a few years ago, but were frustrated by opposition from both the local Polish
clergy and Cardinal Stefan Wyszynski who wanted a
Polish candidate to be the bishop.[60]
     In the Ukraine, like in Belorussia, details
about the small Catholic Church are difficult to obtain.  Of the 132 Catholic churches officially
reported in 1961,[61] perhaps only some forty remain
open today.[62]  Apart from the Hungarians and Hungarian priests in Transcarpathia, most of the Catholics are Poles, administered to mainly by Polish
priests, some of whom were trained at the Riga
seminary.[63]  The operating churches are found primarily in the old Polish regions east of the 1939
Soviet-Polish border, especially in the Vinnytskia
and Khmelnytskyi oblasti.  There is a church in
Odessa, on the Black Sea coast, and its pastor also
serves some distant priestless churches.[64]  The
Ukrainian-language atheist monthly, Liudyna i svit,
has attacked the zeal and popularity of some of the
clergy.[65]  In the summer of 1974, Fr. Bernard
Mickiewic (Mickevicius) of Stryi, Galicia was tried
by a Lvov court for religious instruction of youth,
"performing actions directed at arousing supersti-
tion and religious fanaticism," and teaching "slanderous fabrications about the Soviet system."[66]
     In early 1978, two samizdat documents reached
the West from Polish and German Roman Catholics in
the Moldavian SSR, a republic wedged between Romania and the Ukrainian SSR.  These documents reported that there are 15,000 Catholics in Moldavia,
but that the Soviet authorities have closed all the
Catholic churches, except for one small chapel in
the cemetery at Kishinev.  There is only one registered priest, Fr. Vladislav Zavalnyuk, but he is
severely hampered in his ministry.  It was also reported that the authorities refused to register
groups of believers and have demolished a church
in the small town of Rashkovo which the Catholic
had built themselves.  Finally, the Catholics
pledged their loyalty to the Holy See and begged the

Pope to intervene on their behalf and support them
against the Council on Religious Affairs.[67]

## THE UNIATE (GREEK CATHOLIC) CHURCH IN THE UKRAINE

The Ukrainian Uniate Church remains a cryto-Church,
having been forcibly merged, officially, in the Russian Orthodox Church in 1946 in the West Ukraine and
in 1949 in Transcarpathia. The members of this largest "illegal" Church in the USSR are concentrated in
the oblasti of Lvov, Ternopol, Ivano-Frankivsk, and
Transcarpathia. Because of migration, exile, and re-
settlement, there are also Uniates located in the Central and eastern Ukraine, northern Kazakhstan, and
western Siberia.[68] It would be wishful thinking to
contemplate that the Kremlin might someday return the
legal life of the Ukrainian Uniates or, indeed, that
the Vatican is making any endeavor to bring this about.
The Communists would not countenance such a development because of its fear of inflating Ukrainian nationalism. But, at the same time, the Uniate affiliation
is a source of inspiration for the Ukrainian believers,
for few other faiths have been subjected to the total
abrogation of their institutional framework.[69]
The suppression of the Uniate Church has led
to a number of distinct responses by the Uniates.
Some have accepted official Orthodoxy in the hopes
of injecting it with Ukrainian national values
and traditions.[70] Others, probably the majority
of the "reunited" clergy and believers, still
consider themselves to be Uniate Catholics, but,
in order to practice their religion openly, attend
Orthodox churches. They would join the Greek
Catholic Church if it were legalized again, but for
the moment prefer to keep the faith and national
identity alive by existing within a legal framework.[71]
Still others reject the Russian Orthodox Church
as Russian-controlled and "schismatic" or compromised
because of its subordination to the atheist regime.
Most of these believers depend upon the "catacomb"
Church for religious needs. The underground Uniate
Church recognizes the authority of Cardinal Slipyi
and is reported to have 300-350 priests and three
or more secret bishops.[72] As mentioned earlier,
Vasyl Velychlovsky, one of the "catacomb" bishops
who had been incarcerated, was released from prison
in 1972 only to die in Canada in July 1973. It seems
the authorities know who are the bishops and
priests of the "catacomb" Church, but, while harassing them, usually stop short of arresting them

61

unless they move beyond administering to a small group of friends in private dwellings.[73] Younger priests, trained in the underground Church, are replenishing the ranks of the older priests and they are likely to be more militant than their predecessors.[74] A final faction which emerged in the 1950s, is the so-called "Penitents," a neo-Uniate group mentioned in the previous chapter which refuses to recognize the legitimacy of the Soviet Government.[75]

Since 1968, Uniate Catholics have become quite demonstrative in challenging their Church's "illegality," in petitioning for legalization of their Church, and in taking possession of churches closed or vacated by the Orthodox Church.[76] The regime has responded to the increased Uniate activity by sharpening its attack upon Uniate activists and launching a visceral propaganda campaign against this "bourgeois nationalist Church" which "was forever rejected by the Ukrainian people."[77]

The Uniate cause has been supported by dissident Lithuanian Catholic clergy, by the broader Ukrainian dissent movement, and recently by a leading Russian Orthodox dissenter, Anatolii Levitin-Krasnov, who appealed to Sakharov's Human Rights Committee in Moscow to defend the Uniates and other persecuted religions. "The Union in the Western Ukraine," wrote Levitin-Krasnov, "is a massive popular movement. Its persecution means not only religious oppression, but also restriction of the national rights of West Ukrainians."[78]

## VATICAN-KREMLIN RELATIONS

The real and immediate significance of the contact between the Vatican and the Soviet government has not been any measurable betterment in the treatment of Soviet Catholics. It was, rather, the beginning of a dialogue between the Holy See, the Soviet government and the Russian Orthodox Church, and, more importantly, the opportunity for the regularization of relations between the Catholic Church and the East European Communist states where the Church has a large following.

The initial steps in the rapprochement took place on a church to church basis. In 1962, Bishop Willebrands, on behalf of the Holy See, invited the Russian Orthodox Church to send representatives to the opening session of the Second Vatican Council.[79] In a surprising shift of policy, undoubtedly caused by pressure from the Kremlin, the Russian Orthodox Church accepted the Papal invitation and sent two envoys, Archpriest Vitali Borovoi and Archmandrite Vladimir Kotliarov, to the first session of Vatican Council II in October 1962.[80] (They were recalled to Moscow in January 1963 and debriefed.) This was the beginning of a concerted dialogue and exchange program between the two churches. In July 1963, after the death of Pope John XXIII, Pope Paul sent two emissaries to the eightieth birthday celebration of Patriarch Alexei.[81] The Pope also praised, at the same time, the American-British-Soviet test-ban treaty on nuclear weapons.

The Russian Orthodox Church continued to thaw when, at the Central Committee meeting of the World Council of Churches at Rochester, New York, in August 1963, Metropolitan Nikodim paid tribute to Pope John for his "realism," his "interest in all mankind," and credited the Second Vatican Council for a "better feeling of brotherhood" between the Russian Church and the Roman Catholic Church.[82] On September 15, 1963, Nikodim paid a courtesy call on Pope Paul and for the first time made his personal acquaintance.[83] In that same month, the Russian Orthodox Church decided to send representatives to the second session of the Second Vatican Council.[84] Early the next year, Cardinal Heenan, the British Catholic leader, was received by Nikodim in Moscow.[85] In February, the Russian Church leader called for a "dialogue" with Rome.[86]

Khrushchev's fall from power and his succession by Brezhnev in 1964 did not affect the new policy. In late 1964 Kommunist, the theoretical organ of the Soviet party, published an article entitled "Religious Renewal in a Situation of Stress." The author was M. Mchedlov, a Soviet correspondent in attendance at the Second Vatican Council, and his basic thesis was to urge the cooperation of Communists and left-wing Christians, especially Catholics in capitalist countries. He decided, in somewhat of a revisionist vein, that the Vatican was merely a tool of imperialists, notably the West Germans and the Americans. He was profuse in his praise of Popes John and Paul as "renovators" and had kind words for Pope John's encyclical Pacem in Terris.[87] The next year Voprosy filosofii, the chief philosophical journal announced:

> While recognizing the profound ideo-
> logical differences between Marxism and
> Catholicism, Communists consider that this
> should not be an obstacle to the joint
> struggle of atheists and believers in

defense of the fundamental interests
of the workers.[88]

The articles did not signal a change in Kremlin
policy--Moscow had always encouraged cooperation
between foreign Christians and Communists--but they
did at once reveal that Moscow was planning to exploit the Catholic Church to support "peaceful coexistence." It was precisely at this time that the
so-called Berlin Conference (BK) of Catholic Christians from European States was organized to encourage
and persuade the Holy See and Catholics to support
Soviet foreign policy aims.
　　It is also in the light of "peaceful coexistence"
that Moscow's sudden interest in direct contact with
the Vatican becomes understandable. Accordingly, it
should not have been a surprise when Soviet Foreign
Minister Andrei Gromyko made it a point to meet Pope
Paul during the latter's visit and appeal for peace
at the United Nations in 1965. The next spring the
Pope welcomed Mr. Gromyko at the Vatican. This was
soon followed by another significant meeting. On
January 30, 1967, in the first encounter ever between
the Pope and a Soviet head of state, President
Nikolai Podgorny was received by the Pope and discussed, among other things, the status of Catholics
in the USSR. No agreements were reached except to
continue the discussions, but Pravda reported the
colloquy on the first page.[89] This was a firm indication of the seriousness and importance with which
the Kremlin viewed an understanding with the Vatican.
L'Unità, the organ of the Italian Communist Party,
concluded that the tete-à-tete had "great significance" and that it "will contribute to a considerable
extent toward the development of better and wider
contacts between the Catholic Church and the socialist world."[90] In August 1967, Cardinal Franz Koenig,
head of the Vatican's Secretariat for Non-Believers,
maintained that the Soviet government was showing
signs of easing restrictions, although it was still
administratively hindering religion.[91] What the
Cardinal referred to was the fact that in December
1965, the seventy-year-old Monsignor J. Labukas-
Matulaitis was consecrated bishop of Kaunas in Rome.
He then returned to Lithuania to administer the dioceses of Kaunas and Vilkaviskis. Also in 1966 the
Soviet authorities allowed the publication of an
hymnal, rubrics for sacramental administration, and
a missal in Lithuanian.[92] However, the number of
clergy in Lithuania continued to decline as did the
number of churches.

One of the major developments in 1967 was a five-day meeting between theologians of the Roman Catholic and Russian Orthodox Churches in Leningrad. The Roman Catholic delegation was headed by Bishop Willebrands of the Secretariat of Christian Unity. Among the Russian Orthodox participants were Metropolitan Nikodim, Professor L. Voronov, and Professor Dmitri Ognitsky. Full details of these talks have not been revealed, but the press release from Tass declared that the discussions covered the following areas: the competence of the Church in the social field; the relationship between the individual and society, with emphasis on man's rights and duties; the development of the teaching of the Roman Catholic Church on property; Christian duty toward one's neighbor in diverse social systems; the inner peace and spiritual richness of the human being in relation to social justice; and international peace.[93] It was during this year that Pope Paul also issued, in March, his encyclical Populorum Progressio, which reflected, according to the New York Times, a "strong leftist--almost Marxist--tone."[94] This was an exaggeration; but the anti-colonialist and anti-capitalist phrasing of the encyclical is undeniable.

From the point of view of the Ukrainian Uniates-in-exile, the Vatican-Soviet relationship, by 1967, had gone far enough and cried out for comment. In fact, tension had been building up between the Ukrainian hierarchy-in-exile and the Vatican for a number of years. In January 1967, Metropolitan Slipyi broke the silence he had maintained since his release from the USSR in 1963 by signing with sixteen other Eastern Rite bishops an open letter to all other Catholic bishops. The bishops regretted that they were introducing a discordant note into the warm atmosphere following Vatican II, but they declared: "In the name of truth we must express out sorrow and at the same time give some clarification regarding the destruction of our Catholic Church in the Ukraine."[95] They went on to describe the events of 1946, to attack the role played by the Moscow Patriarchate, and to state that what occurred was totally against the will of the local clergy and people. They were, therefore, seeking support in their efforts to make it possible for the people of the Western Ukraine to determine their own religious future. The question began to turn on whether Archbishop Slipyi had patriarchal rights and responsibilities over the Ukrainian diaspora and Ukrainian bishops in partibus (i.e., in other countries outside of the Ukraine). He already had the title of

Archbishop-Major which canonically gave him the same rights as a partiarch in his own territory, but now the Uniate leader wanted to consolidate his position and that of Uniate Catholicism by extending his jurisdiction to include all Ukrainian bishops and Catholics throughout the world. The Vatican, knowing full well that such a development would be considered provocative by Moscow and that it would be a canonical anomaly--there had never been an Ukrainian Patriarch--soft-pedaled the issue, and for the next two years, it received little public attention. The Vatican would soon learn that the same traits of determination and stubbornness which enabled Metropolitan Slipyi to exist in prison and to vex the KGB would also torment it.

The Soviet invasion of Czechoslovakia in August 1968 did not halt the Vatican's Ostpolitik. To be sure, the Pope objected to the rape of Czechoslovakia by the armies of the Warsaw Pact countries, but it did not treat it as a major issue. In fact, on September 20, Cardinal Koenig called for a "dialogue" between Christians and non-believers and announced that the Church in Czechoslovakia enjoyed the same liberty as before the Soviet invasion.[96] That might have literally been true at that time, although the potential for improving the Church's position was indisputably greater before than after the Soviet occupation. One significant development was that the Uniate Church in Czechoslovakia, which had been re-established during the "Prague Spring," was not forced to merge again with the Russian Orthodox Church.

It was also in 1968 that two priests of the Russian Orthodox Church came as post-graduates to the Collegium Russicum in Rome. For long this institution had been considered in the Soviet Union as the place where "Vatican spies" were prepared for secret missions in Russia. Nothing more clearly designates the change in relations than the Soviet determination to breach this stronghold.[97] It is ironical that precisely at the time that Soviet-Vatican relations were becoming warmer, the Soviet regime suppressed political liberalization in Czechoslovakia and took drastic measures against Ukrainian Uniates. The Chronicle of Current Events, which appeared for the first time in 1968, reported that the police in October had searched the homes of ten priests of the former Lvov Greek-Catholic metropolinate and at the end of the year arrested the aged Bishop Vasyl Velychkovsky and two priests.[98] Perhaps the Soviets were concerned that the re-emergence of the Uniate Church in Czechoslovakia would serve as a source of religious irredentism for Ukrainian Uniates.

In Lithuania, in 1968, the Kremlin permitted the consecration of Msgr. J. Pletkus as bishop of Telšiai. The new bishop, though, did not represent a numerical gain for the Lithuanian hierarchy since he simply filled the vacancy created by the death of Bishop Petras Maželis. The number of Lithuanian clergy was slowly diminishing because, as mentioned, the authorities maintained a quota of students at the Theological Seminary in Kaunas which was below the clerical death rate. Furthermore, infiltration of the clergy by Soviet agents was a pronounced problem.[99]

The tension brewing between the leader of the Ukrainian Uniate Church-in-exile and the Vatican came to a head at the Fourth Synod of Ukrainian Bishops in 1969 in Rome, when Cardinal Slipyi raised the issue of the Uniate Patriarchate. The Vatican, however, turned a deaf ear to the Uniate leader and continued on with Ostpolitik.

On April 23, 1970, Cardinal Willebrands went to Moscow to attend the funeral of Patriarch Alexei. In November the Soviet Foreign Minister, Mr. Gromyko arrived in Rome. Pope Paul's discussions with him covered an array of topics, including joint efforts to prevent the proliferation of nuclear weapons, the Soviet proposal for a European Security Conference, the Middle East, the Vietnam war, and, finally, the position of Roman Catholics in the USSR.[100] No agreements, however, were divulged. Theological discussions between the Russian Orthodox Church and the Catholic Church continued in December, this time at Bari in Italy.[101] At the end of December, Pope Paul, in a possible test of his influence, sent a message to Moscow requesting clemency for two Jews sentenced to death for plotting to hijack an airliner.[102] Whether it was because of the Pope's request or the example of General Franco, who a few days earlier annulled the death sentences of some Basque terrorists in response to a Papal plea, the Kremlin, at any rate, commuted the death penalties to jail sentences.

Archbishop Casaroli traveled to Moscow in February 1971, where he was received by P.V. Makartsev, Vice-President of the Council on Religious Affairs, as well as by church leaders. Casaroli's official function was to deposit the Vatican's agreement to the Soviet-American-British nuclear test-ban treaty.[103] In addition, the Archbishop attempted to engage his hosts on the status of Roman Catholics in the Soviet Union. The Soviet officials, however, as reported later by Dr. Federico Alessandrini, the Vatican's

67

press officer, showed "a certain reserve" when the
Archbishop touched on purely religious matters. They
constantly, in contrast to Mgr. Casaroli, saw such
religious questions on a political plane. At first,
they refused to comment on the position of the Catholics in Belorussia, who, as pointed out previously,
had eighty priests but no bishop. They offered,
according to Dr. Alessandrini, an irrelevent reply
and then attempted to switch to another subject.
Nonetheless, Archbishop Casaroli believed that he
eventually had been able to put over the Vatican's
point of view, and he was confident that his arguments had been recorded.[104] Knowing the efficiency
of the KGB, the Archbishop's confidence was well-
founded.

Mgr. Casaroli, according to Professor Alessandrini, did not broach with the Soviets the plight of
Byzantine Rite Catholics which is surprising since
the Ukrainian Catholics, although their church is
suppressed, remain significant. Evidently he also
failed to mention Lithuanian Catholics, Armenian
Catholics, Latvian Catholics, and the five to seven
thousand Catholics scattered through eastern and
western Siberia and the regions of Central Asia.
In addition, the Archbishop did not consult with the
American Assumptionist chaplain who serves the foreign
embassy community in Moscow. In fact, no Papal
official, from the time that travels to Moscow became
commonplace, has ever to date inquired from this on-
the-scene observer what his opinion is of the Catholic Church in the USSR and of the Soviet government's
attitude toward Catholics.[105] In a somewhat sanguine
tone, Mgr. Casaroli summarized the results of his
talks by saying "we have the feeling there was a
spark and that they have accepted the idea of a
dialogue."[106]

The Ukrainian Uniates-in-exile, led by Cardinal
Slipyi, chafed under the growing contact between
Rome and Moscow. In 1971-72, they again pushed for
a Uniate Patriarchate, but ran up against a stone
wall. While the Ukrainian problem ebbed and flowed,
the Vatican persisted in its consultations with the
Kremlin and the Russian Orthodox hierarchy. In
June 1971, a new Russian Orthodox Partiarch, Pimen,
was elected, and Cardinal Willebrands attended the
ceremony at Zagorsk as Pope Paul's official envoy.
It was here, at this Local Sobor, that the Papal-
Communist detente reached shocking proportions.
When the Soviets claimed that the "Uniate Church
ceased to exist in the USSR," that it "voluntarily"
had ended its ties with Rome and that, "in accordance

68

with the freely expressed general will of its
believers," it had "reunited with the Russian Orthodox Church," Cardinal Willebrands failed to respond.
In the words of an eminent scholar on religion in the
Soviet Union, the Vatican's silent acquiescence was
"the most painful blow to the 'Catacomb' Church in
the Ukraine, and, possibly, the most important
achievement for the Kremlin and the Moscow Patriarchate. . . ."[107] The Vatican also did not issue an
official protest once its delegation had returned
from the Zagorsk Sobor.[108]

Relentlessly, détente went on. In February
1972, Pope Paul received a delegation of Russian
Orthodox officials. Their purpose was to work out
details for an exchange of theological students
between the two churches. In November, Archbishop
Casaroli, with the approval of the Soviet government,
consecrated the Most Reverend Valerians Zondaks to
serve as auxiliary bishop for the diocese of Riga and
Liepaja in Latvia. The latter event was noteworthy,
but pastoral care in Latvia was still far below
needs.[109]

It was also in 1972 that the Chronicle of the
Catholic Church in Lithuania began publication and,
as mentioned earlier, it attempted to make clear to
the Vatican the conditions under which Catholicism
labored in Lithuania. The first two issues, re-
porting the arrest and trials of two Lithuanian
priests, Fathers Juozas Zdebskis and Prosperas
Bubnys, reached the West against the background of
riots, street demonstrations, and the self-immola-
tion of a young man. The latter made it clear that
he was protesting not only against the lack of freedom for Lithuania as a national entity, but also
against the repression of the Roman Catholic
Church.[110]

The Lithuanian Chronicle continued to report
on religious persecution in 1973. At the same time,
the Papal-Russian dialogue advanced. In May, a
delegation of Vatican ecumenists, in Moscow to explore preliminaries for an ecumenical peace conference, signed a communiqué acknowledging that
"there is a strong tendency toward some form of
socialism in many parts of the world." The declaration hinted at an ideological swing toward the
left by the Vatican, but later one of the members of
the group stated in an interview given to Stampa,
a daily in Turin, that the Papacy's rejection of
Marxist ideology had not changed, but that collaboration with non-believers was desirable in certain practical matters, such as work for peace and

overcoming racial discrimination.[111]  In June the
Vatican formally accepted the invitation of the
Soviet Union to participate in the forthcoming
meeting of the Conference on European Security and
Cooperation in Helsinki.[112]  Moscow wanted the Vatican to participate because "the Church still has
large numbers of people under its influence in the
capitalist countries."[113]

With the dawning of the year 1974, the Vatican's
Ostpolitik, as it concerned the Soviet Union, now
clearly followed three lines:  exchanges and contacts
with the Kremlin and the Russian Orthodox Church,
relations with the Ukrainian Uniate Catholics-in-
exile, and, finally, its cautious interest in the
Catholics of Lithuania, as reflected in the pages of
the CCCL.  Another factor, more difficult to analyze,
was the effect which the Vatican's consorting with
the Soviet government had on its moral leadership
in the world, both in the East and the West.  A
famous exiled Russian author, Vladimir Maximov,
attacked the Holy See's Ostpolitik, in 1974, as
criminal, immoral, and misguided.  It can only gen-
erate disillusionment and bitterness, he asserted,
among those small Christian communities who must
lead a catacomb existence amid growing persecution
in the Communist bloc.  He criticized those "leading
princes of the Church" whose silence over this ill
accords with the blessing they impart to Communist
regimes that are endeavoring to strangle the renas-
cent Christian communities under their jurisdiction.
These leaders, the Russian writer stated, should
instead, and in virtue of their sacred duty and
authority, be the first to protest against those who
ever more and more are persecuting Christians.[114]
Some Catholics and non-Catholics in the West concluded that the Vatican was either ignorant of contemporary religious conditions in the Soviet Union or
that it was convinced that Russia had to be presented
and treated in a hopeful or, if one prefers, un-
realistic light.[115]  Whatever the case may be, there
is no doubt of the extension of Marxist influence in
Western Catholicism.  To what extent the Vatican's
Ostpolitik is responsible is a question for future
historians.  But certainly the Holy See must consider
its consequences upon all of Christendom.

In January 1974, Cardinal Willebrands reported
that broad ecumenical talks were being held with the
Russian Orthodox Church.[116]  In late February, the
Pope again received Andrei Gromyko.  Commenting on
the evolving talks between the Kremlin and the
Papacy, the CCCL reported that Lithuanian Catholics

70

believe that

dialogue is needed, but one should not
abandon oneself to illusions. Dialogue
can be useful only if the two parties are
fully led by good will. Concerning the
Communists' 'good will' witness the trials
against priests for teaching religion to
children, the prison terms imposed on the
faithful P. Pluira, P. Petronis, J. Stasaitis
for typing prayer-books and religious literature. . . . It seems to us that a dialogue
with the Church is needed by the Soviet
authority only so that the Vatican will keep
silent about the persecution of the Catholics
in the USSR in the hope of a betterment of
the faithfuls' situation. The dialogue is
being used to deceive the world public
opinion that in the USSR freedom of religion
is preserved.[117]

In 1975, the Soviet Foreign Minister was back
at the Vatican. His meeting with Pope Paul, on
June 28, was a prelude to the Helsinki Conference
which began in July. The talks lasted about an hour
and covered the position of the Catholic Church in
the Soviet Union, peace, disarmament, the Middle
East, and the forthcoming Conference on European
Security and Cooperation.[118] Earlier in the year,
Radio Moscow announced that the Vatican's politics
had become "more flexible" and "more realistic."[119]
In July, the Kremlin sent a group of Lithuanian Catholic clergymen, headed by the "progressive" bishop of
Panevezys, Romualdas Kriksciunas, to make a pilgrimage to the Vatican.[120]
Another theological conference was held in June
in Trento, Italy, between the Catholic and Russian
Orthodox Churches with Metropolitan Nikodim and
Archbishop Roger Etchegaray of Marseilles chairing
the sessions. The final declaration of the gathering
stated that "The Church, realizing that salvation in
a changing world means liberation from evil both
personal and collective, is striving to bring this
about by cooperating with all people of good will,
believers and nonbelievers."[121] All told, by the
end of 1977, the major accomplishments of the Catholic-Orthodox dialogue included the recognition of the
legality of mixed marriages between Catholics and
Orthodox believers (April 4, 1967), the admittance
of Catholics to Holy Communion in Russian Orthodox
Churches (December 16, 1969), theological student

71

exchanges (since 1968), and the personal exchanges
of messages between the Patriarch and Pope. In
addition, regular working contacts had been established between the Russian Orthodox Church's Department of External Relations and the Vatican's Secretariat for Christian Unity.

The CCCL reached twenty issues in 1975 and presented a dismal picture of religious persecution.
Chronicle 18 was particularly critical of the Helsinki Conference. The latter, of course, was the
highlight of Vatican-Soviet relations in 1975. On
his return from the Finnish capital, Archbishop
Casaroli, the head of the Vatican delegation, defended the conference against "pessimistic opinions."
He informed newsmen that, in his opinion, the efforts
of the conference for peace were "undoubtedly positive," not merely "empty words." He added, "I don't
believe that pessimistic opinions have foundation
inasmuch as they saw and perhaps still see in a
conference of this sort a peril to peace, through the
creation of an unjustified sense of security. . . .
At Helsinki the representatives of all participating
countries have taken on a commitment so solemn that
one has to think that they will try to hold themselves to it." The Archbishop termed Brezhnev's
speech "reassuring." He commented further that the
conference did not "consecrate the existing status
quo in regard to certain situations which some consider to be unjust. . . . I do not believe that the
efforts to guarantee the security and peace should
imply the sacrifice of rights which can be considered
just."[122]

The Helsinki Conference has been the highlight,
thus far, of Moscow's policy of "peaceful coexistence"
or, in the idiom of the day, "détente." It fully
appreciated the importance of having the Vatican
support Helsinki and wished to reinforce this direction immediately. Accordinly, a few weeks after
the conference, the Berlin Conference (BK) of
Catholics from European States, a collaborationist
group founded eleven years earlier, held an international conference at Riga in Soviet Latvia at which
it declared that détente must be made irreversible.[123]
Of course, as Pravda later made clear, "international
detente does not mean the renunciation of confrontation between two social systems representing the poles
of the basic contradiction of the present age
determining the course of world history." It is
simply "the result primarily of the great change in
balance of international power in favor of peace and
socialism and also of the persistent struggle of the

progressive forces of the present day against im-
perialist reaction."[124]  However, as for the Vatican,
the Soviets were content that it had accepted "the
objective processes of the reshaping of international
relations" and that it "was favorably disposed towards
the principles of peaceful coexistence and a relaxation of tensions."[125]  They were not so sure about
Cardinal Koenig, who in August 1975, published an
article in the Frankfurter Allgemeine Zeitung (West
Germany) in which he accused the Soviet Union of
being a "confessional state," officially propagating
the faith of atheism against religious believers.[126]
Vladimir Kuroedov declared that the Cardinal "is
blinded by hostility for the country of socialism."[127]
New Times, the Soviet journal, said "Cardinal Koenig's
Secretariat has gone in for blatant misinformation,
for spreading preposterous fictions designed to introduce an artificial tension into the ideological
contest between atheism and religion."[128]

The question of a patriarchate for the Ukrainian Uniates remained a focal point through 1975.
In July, over 3,000 Ukrainians, including sixteen
bishops and 102 priests gathered in Rome to celebrate
the Holy Year.  Pope Paul warmly greeted the Ukrainian Uniates and informed them that he was aware "of
how heroically they have born and are bearing their
share of the Cross of Christ."[129]  At the end of
July, though, Dr. Federico Alessandrini, the Vatican's
press secretary, announced that "a Ukrainian Patriarchate does not exist."[130]  The Soviets applauded
his stand.[131]

In 1976, the Russian Orthodox Church celebrated
the "30th anniversary of the reunion of West Ukrainian Greek Catholics with the Mother Church."[132]
The Holy See, in contrast, did not commemorate the
tragedy.  In June the Vatican was chided for adopting
an anti-Communist position in the Italian general
election and was warned that such a stance conflicted
"directly with the Vatican's proclaimed 'Eastern
policy' and. . . [was] designed to hold back the
process of détente."[133]  In June and again in September, the Berlin Conference (BK) of Catholics from
European States held conferences to support detente
and disarmament.  At the last meeting the symposium
adopted a resolution calling upon Catholics on the
Continent to join the world-wide movement for
détente.[134]  In September, a delegation from the
Secretariat for Christian Unity, led by Cardinal
Willebrands visited Moscow and Yerevan, capital of
Soviet Armenia, to join in celebrations marking the
twentieth anniversary of the Armenian Catholicos.[135]

The next year witnessed increased activity by the Berlin Conference (BK) as it announced its intention to intensify its cooperation with other peace forces and mobilize still broader circles of the public opinion and the Catholic Church in pursuit of detente, disarmament, and social justice.[136] In February, a BK delegation, led by Chairman Otto Harmut Fuchs, visited Spain and Portugal "in an expression of solidarity with all forces fighting for democracy and social progress."[137] In September, a meeting of the BK denounced the neutron bomb and called upon Catholics to increase their vigilence and to take action against "neo-fascist endeavors, which jeopardize the process of political détente."[138] At its Sixth Congress in November, the BK again denounced the neutron bomb and welcomed the Warsaw Treaty proposal on banning the first use of nuclear weapons.[139] In June, in Moscow, the Soviet government pulled off the so-called World Conference of Religious Workers for Lasting Peace, Disarmament, and Just Relations among Nations, at which the Holy See was represented by Fr. John Long of the Secretariat of Christian Unity. Vladimir Kuroedov declared that

> The conference attested vividly to the fact that the world religious public is getting widely involved in the active struggle for peace and security of nations. It is of particular importance now since the complicated international situation demands as never before the strengthening and continual developing of détente, and the expanding of all-round cooperation among nations.[140]

The issue of the Ukrainian patriarchate again surfaced in early 1977 but waned in the face of the Pope's intransigent opposition.[141] New issues of the CCCL arrived in the West with incremental evidence of Soviet persecution. In September, as mentioned earlier, Father Pedro Arrupe, S.J., announced after a visit to the Soviet Union that the religious situation in the USSR was better than since his last visit six years before. A month later a delegation of the Roman Catholic Curia, headed by Archbishop Jerome Hamer, was received by Patriarch Pimen and Metropolitan Yuvenaliy. They talked about peace and Patriarch Pimen's condemnation of the neutron bomb. Archbishop Hamer declared that "When I hear words about the need for peace, order, social justice and complete freedom for all people, my heart beats in

74

unison with those who say this, for I am a man and a Christian."[142]

On balance, one is constrained to conclude that, from the beginning of the rapprochement with Moscow into 1978, the Vatican has conceded more, either through omission or commission, than it has received in pursuing Ostpolitik. It is not a question of détente being wrong per se, but simply that there has not been reciprocity. To be sure, the "unofficial" Vatican position has not been as pacifying to Moscow as official actions and pronouncements indicate. Radio Vatican persists with its religious broadcasts for Soviet Catholics, including the Ukrainian Uniates, despite Soviet objections.[143] Annuario Pontificio perseveres in recording the Uniate dioceses in the USSR (as well as those in Romania and Poland).[144] And, confidentially, the Vatican continues to reassure the Uniates abroad that it has not forgotten their brethren in the USSR.[145]

Nonetheless, since Ostpolitik was put into practice, the Kremlin has not measurably reduced its anti-Catholic or antireligious propaganda and has even increased its repression of the Uniates. There also seem to be powerful forces within the Roman Catholic Church who are willing to sacrifice the Ukrainian Uniate Church in the hope of a reunion with the Russian Orthodox Church. It does not carry conviction to announce, as Pope Paul did in his Christmas address to the College of Cardinals in 1975, that the situation of the Catholic Church in the Communist countries is promising, or to understate the nature of the Communist persecution, again as he did in the same address, by observing that "situations of uneasiness" are still apparent in Czechoslovakia, Romania, and "certain regions of the Soviet Union."[146] Such euphemisms raise doubts about the Vatican's real knowledge of Soviet and Eastern European affairs.

## NOTES

1. A rough estimate based upon Bohdan R. Bociurkiw's calculations. See his "Catholic Church and Soviet Government," p. 4. Also see V. Stanley Vardys, "Modernization and Latin Rite Catholics in the Soviet Union," in Dunn, Religion and Modernization, p. 349.
2. Vardys, "Modernization and Latin Rite Catholics," p. 349.
3. Ibid.
4. The Soviet census has 340,323 Poles living in the oblasti of Grodno, Brest, and Minsk. See Itogi vsesoiuznoi perepisi naseleniia 1970 goda.

Vol. 4: Natsionalnyi sostav naseleniia SSR (Moscow, 1973), pp. 152, 196, 199-200.

5. Bociurkiw, "Catholic Church and Soviet Government," p. 4.

6. The 1970 has 858,077 Germans in Kazhakhstan, and sizeable concentrations in Western Siberia.

7. Mailleux, "Catholics in the Soviet Union," p. 366.

8. Nadeshda Theodorowitsch, Religion and Atheismus in der UdSSR: Dokumente und Berichte (Munich, 1970), p. 97.

9. Vardys, "Modernization and Latin Rite Catholics," p. 348.

10. Mailleux, "Catholics in the Soviet Union," p. 377, claims "the number of Armenian Catholics established in Armenia and Georgia is presently well over one hundred thousand."

11. Theodorowitsch, Religion und Atheismus, p. 97.

12. Ibid.

13. Mailleux, "Catholics in the Soviet Union," p. 366. See also I.N. Iablokov, Krizis religii v sotsialisticheskom obshchestve (Moscow, 1974), p. 49.

14. See J. Mirski, "Wrazenia z ZSSR 1970-1973," Kultura (Paris), No. 11/314 (1973), p. 57. Also see Bociurkiw, "Catholic Church and Soviet Government," p. 5.

15. See Robert Conquest, ed., Religion in the USSR (London, 1968), p. 98. Conquest cites two Radio Moscow broadcasts. Cf. Constantin de Grunwald, The Churches and the Soviet Union (New York, 1962), p. 108.

16. Spravochnik propagandista i agitatora (Moscow, 1966), p. 149.

17. Vardys, "Modernization and Latin Rite Catholics," p. 349; Bociurkiw, "Catholic Church and Soviet Government," p. 6.

18. Vardys, "Catholicism in Lithuania," p. 390. Also see CCCL #25.

19. See Annuario Pontificio per l'anno 1976 (Vatican City, 1976) and Annuario Pontificio per l'anno 1940 (Vatican City, 1940). Also see R. Krasauskas and K. Gulbinas, "Die Lage der Katolischen Kirche in Litauen," Acta Baltica 12 (1972): 446-67. An official Soviet source reported 630 "working parish churches" in 1971 and "some 850 priests." See J. Rimaitis, Religion in Lithuania (Vilnius, 1971), p. 18.

20. Annuario Pontificio, 1972.

21.  Bociurkiw, "Catholic Church and Soviet Government," p. 6.

22.  Lithuanian American Community, The Violations of Human Rights in Soviet Occupied Lithuania. A Report for 1971 (Delran, N.J., 1972), p. 36.

23.  Bociurkiw, "Catholic Church and Soviet Government," p. 7.

24.  Ibid.

25.  CCCL, No. 9 (1974), p. 4.

26.  Ibid.

27.  Bociurkiw, "Catholic Church and Soviet Government," p. 7.

28.  Bohdan R. Bociurkiw has provided an excellent, preliminary analysis of this event in his essay entitled "Religious Dissent in the U.S.S.R.: Lithuanian Catholics."

29.  See "Declaration by the Priests of the Catholic Church in Lithuania," (August 1969), addressed to the Chairman of the Lithuanian Council of Ministers and the Catholic Church leaders in Lithuania by forty priests of the Vilnius Archdiocese, published in Lituanus 19 (1972): 46-53.  Also see CCCL, No. 2 (1972), pp. 1-7, 10-15; No. 4 (1972), pp. 1-25; No. 5 (1973), pp. 29-41; No. 6 (1973), pp. 7-11; No. 7 (1973), pp. 1-5, 11-14; No. 9 (1974), pp. 1-13, 47-48.

30.  CCCL, No. 6 (1973), pp. 23-28, 35; No. 1 (1972), p. 53; No. 4 (1972), pp. 3-4, 10, 16; No. 7 (1973), pp. 18-19; No. 9 (1974), pp. 16-17, 34-35.

31.  The arrests included: in the summer of 1970, Fr. Antanas Seskevicius (b. 1914), S.J., of Dubingiai; in the summer of 1972, Frs. Juozas Zdebskis (b. 1929) of Pienai and Prosperas Bubnys of Girkalnis.  All were found guilty and sentenced to one year in prison.

32.  CCCL, No. 7 (1973), p. 56.

33.  Ibid., No. 4 (1972), pp. 4, 10.

34.  The KGB has worked overtime to complete Case 345, as the campaign to destroy the CCCL is called.  See CCCL, Nos. 13, 14, and 15.  Also see Bourdeaux, Land of Crosses.

35.  Sovetskaia Litva, August 12, 1972.

36.  The CCCL, No. 10 (1974), p. 2, listed a group of episcopal choices reportedly favored by the authorities.  Included were Msgr. C. Krivaitis, Msgr. B. Varauskas, Canon I. Andrikonis, Rev. V. Butkus, and others.

37.  CCCL, No. 8 (1974), pp. 6-16.  Also see issues 9 through 20.

38.  Sovetskaia Litva, December 29, 1974. Cf. CCCL, No. 13, 1974.

39. CCCL, No. 16 (1975); cited in ELTA, No. 8-9 (August-September 1975), p. 9.

40. Bociurkiw, "Catholic Church and Soviet Government," p. 12.

41. Begegnung, No. 10 (1975), p. 30. Cf. CCCL, No. 19 (1975).

42. CCCL, No. 4 (1972), p. 10. More current criticism of the Holy See's Ostpolitik appears in CCCL, No. 18 (1975) and No. 19 (1975).

43. CCCL, No. 9 (1974), p. 17.

44. Pierre Blet et alii., Actes et documents du Saint Siege relatifs a la seconde guerre mondiale, 9 vols. Vol.5: Le Saint Siege et la guerre mondiale (juillet 1941-Octobre 1942) (Citta del Vaticano,1969), nrs. 472, 490, 374; Foreign Relations of the United States, Vol 3 (1942) (Washington D.C., 1956), pp. 775-76.

45. Memorandum, Conversation Between Maglione and Taylor, September 25, 1942, PSF 43, FDR Library (Hyde Park, N.Y.); also Sumner Welles to Taylor, October 21, 1942, PSF 43, FDR Library.

46. Annuario Pontificio, 1976, pp. 446-47.

47. Ibid., 1946, pp. 272, 205.

48. Mailleux, "Catholics in the Soviet Union," p. 365.

49. Annuario Pontificio, 1975, pp. 716, 784.

50. Ibid., p. 694; Mailleux, "Catholics in the Soviet Union," p. 365.

51. Radio Liberty, Materialy samizdata, No. 5/76 (February 13, 1976), as AC2412 (2pp.).

52. Leu Maroska, "The Roman Catholic Church in the Belorussian SSR," in the Institute for the Study of the USSR, Religion in the USSR (Munich, 1960), pp. 99-100.

53. Ibid., p. 99.

54. R. Platonov, Vospitanie ateisticheskoi ubezhdenosti. Propadanda nauchnogo ateizma v sisteme ideologicheskoi deiatelnosti partiinykh organizatsii Belorussii 1959-1972 gody (Minsk, 1973), p. 120.

55. Ibid.: also see Akademiia nauk Belorusskoi SSR, Institut filosofii i prava, Prichiny sushchestvovaniia i puti preodoleniia religioznykh perezhitkov (Minsk, 1965), p. 107. According to Mailleux, "Catholics in the Soviet Union," there were about sixty-five churches and sixty-five priests in Belorussia in 1967.

56. Akademiia nauk SSSR--Institut nauchnogo ateizma; Akademiia obshchestvennykh nauk pri TsK KPSS--Institut nauchnogo ateizma, Stroitelstvo kommunizma i preodolenie religioznykh perezhitkov (Moscow, 1966), p. 60. Also see Platonov, Vospitanie,

p. 120.

57. Tablet (London), March 13, 1971, p. 4;
The Guardian (London), March 3, 1971.
58. See "Koscio Zapomiany," Na Antenie, Vol.
13, No. 143, pp. 13-17; and No. 144, pp. 13-18,
supplement to Orze Biay (March-April 1975).
59. Mirski, "Wrazenia," pp. 58-59.
60. Bociurkiw, "Catholic Church and Soviet
Government," p. 15.
61. Ukrainska Radianska Entsyklopediia, Vol. 6
(Kiev, 1961), p. 253.
62. Bociurkiw, "Catholic Church and Soviet
Government," p. 15.
63. Mirski, "Wrazenia," p. 57.
64. Vardys, "Modernization and Latin Rite Catholics," p. 349.
65. D. Koretskyi, "V kostioli ta navkolo nioho,"
Liudyna i svit, No. 1 (1974), pp. 47-49.
66. Religiia i ateizm v SSSR, Nos. 9-10 (83-84
September-October 1974), p. 5.
67. Keston News Service, Issue No. 49 (March 2,
1978), pp. 2-3.
68. Bociurkiw, "Catholic Church and Soviet
Government," p. 16.
69. See Bociurkiw's "Religion and Nationalism
in the Contemporary Ukraine," pp. 81-93; and his
other study, "The Uniate Church in the Soviet Ukraine:
A Case Study in Soviet Church Policy," pp. 89-113.
70. See Bohdan R. Bociurkiw, "The Orthodox
Church and the Soviet Regime in the Ukraine, 1953-
1971," Canadian Slavonic Papers 14 (Summer 1972):
191-211.
71. See Lvivskyi, "Tserkva v Ukraini--Iak tam
spravdi?". Ukrainski Visti (Edmonton, Alberta),
September 5, 1974.
72. Bociurkiw, "Catholic Church and Soviet
Government," p. 18.
73. Lvivskyi, "Tserkva v Ukraini."
74. "Peresliduiut sviashchennykiv u Kvovi,"
Ukrainski Visti, February 20, 1975. Also see
Bociurkiw, "Catholic Church and Soviet Government,"
pp. 18-19.
75. For a Soviet account of the "Penitents,"
see Liudyna i svit, No. 11 (1968), pp. 36-39.
76. Bociurkiw, "Catholic Church and Soviet
Government," pp. 19-20.
77. Ibid., p. 20.
78. Ibid., p. 21.
79. Zh.M.P., No. 11 (1962), p. 13; Markiewicz,
Kościół, pp. 106-11.
80. Zh.M.P., No. 11 (1962), p. 13. Cf. Le

Monde, October 12, 1962.
    81.  New York Times, July 14, 1963.
    82.  Ibid., August 31, 1963.
    83.  Ibid., September 16, 1963.
    84.  The Times (London), September 28, 1963.
Cf. New York Times, October 2, 1963.
    85.  Markiewicz, Kosciól, p. 113.
    86.  Zh.M.P., No. 1 (1965), pp. 8-9;  Ecumenical
Press Service, February 11, 1965, p. 9.
    87.  Kommunist, No. 15 (October 1964), pp. 88-
98.
    88.  Voprosy filosofii, No. 8 (1965), p. 115.
    89.  Pravda, January 31, 1967.  Cf. Izvestiia,
January 31, 1967; Radio Vatican, January 31, 1967;
l'Osservatore Romano, January 30, 1967.
    90.  L'Unita, February 1, 1967.
    91.  New York Times, August 26, 1967.
    92.  Vardys, "Catholicism in Lithuania," pp.393-
394.
    93.  BBC Central Research Unit Talk, No. 216/67,
December 20, 1967, p. 1.  Also see Markiewicz,
Kosciot, pp. 115-16.
    94.  New York Times, March 29, 1967.
    95.  America (New York), September 16, 1967,
p. 262.
    96.  New York Times, September 22, 1968.
    97.  William C. Fletcher, Religion and Soviet
Foreign Policy 1946-1970 (London, 1973), p. 109.
    98.  Peter Reddaway, ed., Uncensored Russia
(London, 1972), p. 332.
    99.  Vardys, "Catholicism in Lithuania," pp, 394-
397.  For details on the number of priests, ordina-
tions, and seminarians, see the table in Michael
Bourdeaux's Land of Crosses.
    100.  New York Times, November 13, 1970.
    101.  Zh.M.P., No. 1 (1971), pp. 7-8; No. 5
(1971), p. 1.
    102.  New York Times, January 1, 1971.
    103.  Radio Moscow, January 7, 1971, praised the
Vatican's action.
    104.  Tablet (London), March 13, 1971, p. 4;
The Guardian (London), March 3, 1971.
    105.  Interview with J.R., December 1975.
    106.  Tablet (London), March 13, 1971; The
Guardian (London), March 3, 1971.  Cf. New York
Times, March 1, 4, 1971.
    107.  Bociurkiw, "Catholic Church and Soviet
Government," pp. 23-24.
    108.  Ibid., p. 24.
    109.  V. Stanley Vardys, "The Roman Catholic
Church in the Soviet Union,"  (Unpublished report

80

prepared for the British Council of Churches in 1973,
Keston College, England.)

110.  "Recent Events Among Lithuanian Catholics,"
Radio Liberty Research (46/73), February 15, 1973,
p. 1.
111.  The Christian Science Monitor, July 21, 1973.
112.  New York Times, June 23, July 5, 1973.
113.  Radio Moscow, January 25, 1972.
114.  Vladimir Maximov, "Wir leben am Vorabend,"
Deutsche Zeitung, June 22-28, 1974.
115.  See, for example, A.E. Levitin-Krasnov,
"The Situation of the Russian Orthodox Church," in
Gerhard Simon, Church, State and Opposition in the
U.S.S.R. (Berkeley and Los Angeles, 1974), pp. 188-
201.  Also see the controversial study by Herve Leclerc (pseud.), Marxism and the Church of Rome (London, 1974), and A.E. Levitin-Krasnov, "Open Letter to
Archbishop Casaroli," Religion in Communist Dominated
Lands 16 (1977): 174-77.
116.  l'Osservatore Romano, January 19, 1974.
117.  CCCL, No. 9 (1974), pp. 14-15.
118.  Radio Rome, June 28, 1975.
119.  Radio Moscow, March 5, 1975.
120.  Ibid., July 7, 1975.
121.  For comment, see Radio Vatican, July 8,
1975; and Radio Moscow, July 8, 1975.
122.  Ulisse A. Floridi, Mosca e il Vaticano
(Milan, 1976), pp. 120-21.
123.  Radio Moscow, September 5, 1975.
124.  Pravda, September 24, 1976.
125.  Velikovich, "Contrary to the Understanding,"
pp. 21-23.
126.  Frankfurter Allgemeine Zeitung, August 16,
1975.
127.  Izvestiia, January 31, 1976.
128.  Velikovich, "Contrary to the Understanding,"
pp. 22-23.
129.  l'Osservatore Romano, July 24, 1975.
130.  Floridi, Mosca e il Vaticano, p. 315 n. 78.
131.  Koval'skii, Religioznie organizatsii, p. 40.
132.  Journal of the Moscow Patriarchate (English edition), No. 9 (1976), pp. 9-25.
133.  Radio Moscow, June 23, 1976;  Radio Moscow, May 26, 1976;  Velikovich, "Contrary to the
Understanding," p. 23.
134.  Radio East Germany,"Voice of the GDR,"
June 1, 1976;  Radio East Germany, September 4, 1976.
135.  Radio Vatican, September 25, 1976.
136.  Radio East Germany, January 27, 1977.
137.  Ibid., February 23, 1977.
138.  Ibid., September 22, 1977;  also see

Begegnung, No. 9 (1977).
  139. Radio East Germany, November 26, 1977; also see Begegnung, No. 1 (1978), pp. 1-2.
  140. The Journal of the Moscow Patriarchate, No. 8 (1977), p. 58.
  141. Letter from Cardinal Slipyi to Pope Paul VI, Vatican City, April 14, 1977.
  142. Radio Moscow, November 22, 1977. My italics.
  143. Bociurkiw, "Catholic Church and Soviet Government," p. 24; also see Radio Vilnius, May 17, 1977; Velikovich, "Contrary to the Understanding," pp. 22-23.
  144. Bociurkiw, "Catholic Church and Soviet Government," p. 24.
  145. Ibid., pp. 24-25.
  146. New York Times, December 23, 1975.

# 4. Yugoslavia: The Model of Papal Ostpolitik?

The Catholic Church in Yugoslavia is treated after the Soviet Union not because the Church there is the strongest in Eastern Europe, but because Yugoslavia served as a concrete example of a Communist regime and the Catholic Church coexisting. The fact that a modus vivendi had been established in Yugoslavia surely influenced the Vatican in believing that an understanding was possible elsewhere in Eastern Europe and in the Soviet Union. Yet, whether or not Church-State relations in Yugoslavia served as a prototype, the dynamics of rapprochement in Yugoslavia bear primary and close examination for what they can reveal about how détente can be achieved and/or not achieved.

The major Yugoslavian officials who became involved in Catholic-Yugoslav relations, aside from Tito, included Milos Minic, Vice-President of the Yugoslav Federal Executive Council and Federal Secretary for Foreign Affairs, Milan Vukasovic, member of the Federal Executive Council and Chairman of the Commission for Relations with Religious Communities, Istvan Straub, Vice-Chairman of the State Office for Church Affairs, Zdenko Svete, Yugoslav Ambassador to the Holy See (as of April 1977), Stane Kolman, Chairman of the Slovene Commission for Relations with Religious Communities and former Ambassador to the Holy See (left ambassadorial post in December 1975), and Ivan Lalic, Chairman of the Commission for Religious Communities of the Executive Council of the Republic of Croatia. The Vatican officials involved, aside from those listed previously, included Mgr. Michele Cecchini, Papal Pro-Nuncio to Yugoslavia and Mgr. Mario Cagna, former Pro-Nuncio to Belgrade. The Vatican also certainly called for advice from the Bishops' Conference of Yugoslavia, presently chaired by Mgr. Franjo Kuharic,

Archbishop of Zagreb.

Yugoslavia's relations with the Catholic Church are different from the other Communist states examined in this book. Although there are still indications of antireligious activity, [1] Yugoslavia has been, since the mid-1950s, relatively free of strident persecution. Recent demands for more hostility to the Church seem to stem from nationalist than from ideological motives. Why is Yugoslavia unique and how has this affected Papal Ostpolitik?

Yugoslavia's distinctive character is not of recent origin. It has been generally out of step with the other Communist states on religious issues almost from the beginning. Immediately after the war, when the other Communists in East Europe were eschewing overt antireligious militancy, Tito launched, as early as 1944, a veritable war against religion, especially the Catholic Church. He was in line with the other Communist parties in 1948 when they initiated their antireligious crusade, but, by 1951 he was slowing down his campaign and, from 1953 on, practiced, in contrast to the other East European Communists, a policy of growing religious toleration. The Catholic Church and the other religious bodies were not able to recoup everything which they had lost during the preceding decade of persecution, but they were able to regain some losses and, today, the Catholic Church in Croatia and Slovenia is thriving.

At the end of the war, there were two main reasons for the difference in policy toward Catholics between the Yugoslav and other East European Communists: one was the experience of World War Two, the other the personality of Tito. Yugoslavia is a multinational state. Today the country, with a population of over twenty million, is composed of six republics, five different nations (the Moslem Slavs are emerging as a sixth), and a dozen different national minorities. The major national groups are the Serbs (41.7%), Croats (23.5%), Slovenes (8.8%), Macedonians (5.3%), Montenegrins (2.7%), Moslem Slavs (5.9%), Albanians (4.5%), Hungarians (3.0%), and Turks (1.5%). The republics, ranked in order of homogeneity, are: Slovenia (96.5% Slovenes), Montenegro (86.6% Montenegrins), Croatia (79.6% Croats), Serbia (73.8% Serbs), Macedonia (66.0% Macedonians), and Bosnia-Hercegovina (44.4% Serbs). [2] The national divisions are characterized by an array of languages and religions. [3] The major faiths are Orthodoxy and Roman Catholicism and there is a significant Moslem population. Serbia, Macedonia, and Montenegro are

the chief geographical homes of the Serbian Orthodox
Church and, as a rule of thumb, to be Serbian or
Macedonian is to be Orthodox.[4]  Croatia and Slovenia,
on the other hand, are overwhelmingly Catholic, al-
though spotted with important Orthodox settlements.
Bosnia-Hercegovina is a mixture of Catholic Croats,
Serbian Orthodox, and Slav Moslems.

The different nationality groups and particularly
the major ones--Serbs and Croats--have a history of
difficult and often acrimonious relations which extended into and was reflected by their religious
differences.  When the Kingdom of the Serbs, Croats
and Slovenians, which later took the title of Yugoslavia, emerged as an independent state from the
fallen Hapsburg empire at the end of the First World
War, many Yugoslav intellectuals hoped, in vain as
it turned out, that the religious and national divisions among the South Slav peoples could be bridged.
The country, however, in the interwar period, remained disjointed.  Instead of a conciliatory policy,
the government pursued a greater Serb dictatorial
policy which alienated the Croats.  World War II
brought new strains which unleashed a bitterness
which has yet to abate completely and which, at the
same time, partly explains why Tito and the Yugoslav
Communists initiated their persecution against
Catholicism earlier than other East European Communists.

In 1941, Germans, Italians, Hungarians, and
Bulgarians invaded Yugoslavia.  Under their tutelage,
an Independent State of Croatia was chiseled out of
Croatia, Bosnia-Hercegovina, and a small strip of
Dalmatia (most of Dalmatia, to the bitter disappointment of the Croats, was annexed by Italy).  A Nazi
puppet government was established in Serbia proper
and the rest of the country was partitioned among
aggressors.  Ante Pavelic, the leader of the new
Croatian state, set up a fascist government.  Its
power base was the Ustasa Party, an extreme nationalist group.  It was the Ustasa squads which perpe-
trated the massacres of Serbs and Jews.[5]  The Croatian people at first welcomed the Pavelic regime,
believing that independence would be a panacea for
their many problems and, that it was preferable to
Serbian hegemony.  The regime tied itself to Catholicism and proclaimed a virtual crusade against Orthodox Christians and, by extension, Serbs.  In the ensuing years, it is estimated that the Pavelic government in Croatia killed thousands, and coerced a great
number to convert to Catholicism out of a total population of approximately two million Serbs.  Among

85

the executed were three bishops and close to 220 priests. Two other bishops were exiled, one imprisoned, and about 330 priests expelled or forced to flee.[6]

The Roman Catholic Church was generally accused of supporting the Pavelic regime and a number of its clergy were active in the Ustasa Party, with some priests and friars actually participating in the murders. Archbishop Stepinac of Zagreb, the head of the Catholic bishops, objected to the atrocities in private meetings with Pavelic and, later in the war, publicly condemned the violence inflicted on the Serbs, the Jews, and Gypsies. But the Archbishop, like many Catholic Croatians, was plagued by ambivalence: on the one hand, they wanted a truly independent Catholic Croatia, but, on the other hand, they were increasingly repelled by the methods of the Ustasa.[7]

Needless to say, the willingness of some leading Catholics like Archbishop Šarić of Sarajevo, to associate themselves with the Nazi cause indeed compromised Catholicism and made it an easy prey to retaliatory attacks once Tito's partisans had taken over the country. Tito was able to exploit the resentment of many Serbian patriots over Catholic behavior and the traditional ill-humor of the Orthodox for Catholicism, and so obtain support for a frontal attack upon the Catholic Church.[8] It was no wonder then that Tito, in contrast to the other East European Communists, immediately launched that attack. However, although the equivocal role of Catholicism during the war played a part in determining the date as well as the motivation of persecution, Tito's independence and his own Communist ideology were the deciding factors.

Tito was a dedicated revolutionary. Obsessed by the vision of the Communist revolution sweeping across Europe and shattering the capitalist world order, Tito, at the end of the war, was ambitious and impatient, flushed with missionary zeal. For him the defeat of Germany was the prelude to the collapse of capitalism which Communists had been predicting since 1917. He could see no reason why the Communist powers, at the end of the war, should not simply advance westward, providing the jolt which would tumble capitalism over the precipice. Soviet Russia, the leading Communist state, from Tito's point of view, was the predominant military power and the capitalist states of the West, singularly or in combination, were hardly barriers to the realization of the Communist millenium. How could it be otherwise? History,

Tito was sure, was on the side of Communism and, for him, it made sense to adopt aggressive policies to precipitate the worldwide Communist revolution. The times dictated action. The topsy-turvy milieu of postwar Europe was exploitable. It was not a period for patience.

Implicit in his impatience was Tito's expectation that his own power was about to expand. Power, ultimately, as for Stalin and other Communist true believers, was at the center of Tito's outlook and policies. He lusted for power. Power explains his insatiable appetite for land (he wanted to take Albania, Greek Macedonia, Bulgaria, and part of Italy, Hungary, and Austria), and, also why he broke with the Soviets and they with him. It is clear that what bothered Stalin the most about Tito was his independence from Moscow. Tito had a power base of his own in Yugoslavia, because of his iron grip over the Yugoslav Communist party and his popular image as a war hero. He obviously had learned well the mechanics of power during his stay in the USSR before the war. Adam Ulam has provided a brilliant analysis of Tito and Titoism and, at the same time, of the fatal flaw in the whole concept of international communism, the "inherent self-contradiction of its expansionist and missionary goal."

> An ideology which in its essence is nothing but a worship of power by its very victories must endanger the power system which propagates it. Because Tito and his group were devout Stalinists, they could not part voluntarily with their rule, even when threatened with the hostility of the very people they had worshipped. And in their rebellion they demonstrated that, for the rulers of Russia, the Communist fanaticism of their foreign colleages is a poor substitute for a purely mechanical system of controlling the Communist parties abroad. The latter, and especially those in power, present the rulers of Russia with a veritable dilemma. A strong Communist regime is not unlikely to develop the virus of Titoism, which is nothing but Stalinism transplanted to a foreign soil.[9]

Tito's ambition and his revolutionary impatience were apparent as early as 1945. For example, in April 1945, unrestrained by total dependence upon Moscow, Tito unilaterally decided to send his partisans into the Italian province of Venezia Giulia and

Trieste, to which the Slovenes and the Croats had
some historical claims.  He certainly believed that
his actions would enrich him and Communist Yugoslavia
and, of course, have the full support of Moscow.
Field Marshal Alexander, the Allied commander in
Italy who had jurisdiction over Trieste and its en-
virons demanded that Tito retreat forthwith, but to
no avail.  The Western leaders refused to accept
Tito's expansion and in fact, Churchill contemplated
direct retaliation.  Stalin, fearing that the crisis
over Trieste might harden the Western position on
Eastern Europe where he was attempting to carve out
his empire, expostulated with Tito, with the result
that, under protest, the Yugoslav partisans pulled
back from Trieste.  The schism between Tito and
Stalin had commenced.  As Ulam declared, "The Yugoslavs. . . could not understand why the all-powerful
Soviet Union would not risk a war on behalf of her
Yugoslav co-believers."  And "it was a first intima-
tion to the Russians of how their erstwhile docile
agents, once they became masters in their own
countries, could be transformed into troublesome
allies."[10]

At the end of the war, the determination of Tito
to bring down capitalism and create a Yugoslav Communist empire was duplicated in domestic policy.  He
was preoccupied with quickly fashioning a Communist
society in Yugoslavia, much like Stalin in Russia
during the five-year plans before the war.  Collectivization (never completed) and nationalization of
industry became objectives.  The determination to
create a Communist society involved an all-out persecution of religion, particularly of the Catholic
Church.  The Catholic Church was singled out, not
only because of the wartime events cited above, but
because it was the best organized religious institution, had ties with Italy, and was the backbone of
Slovene and Croatian nationalism.  The beginning of
the campaign against Catholicism was violent and
ruthless.  It began in 1944, shortly after Tito set
up a government in Belgrade.  The Agrarian Reform
Law passed in 1944 broke up the Church's landed es-
tates and, in the following year, the regime nationalized the Church's buildings, real estate, and
businesses.  The Church was thus almost immediately
without the major source of its income.[11]  The government eventually stepped in with a subsidy; it
provided Yugoslavia, like all other East European
Communist states except the USSR and Albania, with
financial leverage over the Church.  By the early
1950s the Church had lost, either through

nationalization or dissolution, all of its welfare
institutions, including nursing homes, hospitals,
and orphanages.[12]  The Church was also deprived of
its publishing houses and printing facilities.  By
1953 only five Catholic publications were extant out
of a total of 100 in 1944.[13]  Catholic schools were
nationalized and religious instruction was restricted
eventually to church premises and special catechism
centers.  Private or uncertified religious instruction was denounced and punished.[14]  The antireligious
onset was most severe in the treatment of clergy.
From 1944 onwards many Catholic priests were shot
without a trial.  Hundreds of others, through the
remainder of the 1940s, were imprisoned, beaten,
and prevented from fulfilling their functions.  Between 1945 and 1952 more than half of the entire
Catholic clergy had been imprisoned at one time or
another.  In 1952 there were still more than 200
priests in prison.[15]  The highlight of the anti-
Catholic campaign came early, with the trial in 1946
of Archbishop Stepinac of Zagreb, head of the
Catholic Church in Croatia.  He was charged with
supporting the Pavelic regime, the Nazis, and encouraging outrages against Serbs and Jews.  There
was no real evidence that he had backed the fascists,
and substantial proof that he had often opposed
them; no evidence that he had sanctioned atrocities
against Serbs and Jews, and significant proof that
he had protected many of them in jeopardy.  But he
was an unreformed antagonist of Communism, and "it
is for that sin that he received a sixteen-year
prison sentence."[16]
     The trial of the Archbishop was accompanied and
followed by continuous persecution of the Church in
Croatia and Slovenia; crude and brutal beatings of
priests and religious became commonplace.[17]  A
change came only with the Tito-Stalin break, but
even then it was some three years before a shift in
Tito's policy toward religion could be observed.
The time lag was attributable to the momentum which
had built up against Catholicism, to the uncertain-
ties and outcome of Yugoslavia's expulsion from the
Cominform and the good graces of Stalin, to Tito's
desire to fashion a Communist society, to the persistent passion of revenge for Catholicism's wartime role, and to the desire to suppress Croatian
and Slovenian nationalism.  But operating against
continued persecution and slowly but surely forcing
a cautious liberalization upon the regime, in economic policy as well as religious policy, was Tito's
realization that his country was now threatened by

89

the Soviet bloc. He had no choice but to seek
Western support, particularly in Italy and the
United States. A consequence of that strategic development was a necessary modification of his antireligious policies, particularly against the Catholic
Church which had strong support in the West. Even
more significant, in mollifying religious persecution, was Tito's perception that ultimately it would
be up to the Yugoslavia to convince the Soviets that
"administrative action" to resolve the heresy of
Titoism would be met by a unified and resolved Yugoslav people. Tito needed unity and popular support.
In other words, he had to initiate liberalization,
to a point, to bridge the passions of the war, the
alienation of the intellectuals, and the fissiparous
consequences of religious repression. Persecution,
desirable as it might be as a policy to instill Communism and as a means of destroying the institutionalized form of Catholic nationalism in Slovenia and
Croatia, tended, at the same time, to tear the
country apart, pit one national group against another,
and, ultimately, encourage centrifugal movements
which an unscrupulous opponent might exploit.

In December 1951, Tito started the process of
religious relaxation by releasing Archbishop
Stepinac from prison and allowing him to return to
his home village under supervision. The policy of
religious laxity was not uniform and attacks upon
the Catholic Church and its bishops and priests persisted until 1954. But the process of mitigation
had begun and proved to be the trend.

At the end of 1953 Tito ruled that physical
abuse of bishops and clergy was against the law and
unworthy of a socialist state. In the same year the
Law on the Legal Status of Religious Communities was
promulgated, allowing the churches a legal ground for
protecting their rights.[18] This policy of moderation was temporarily retarded when the Pope made
Archbishop Stepinac a Cardinal in 1953, a gesture
which Tito interpreted as an affront to his government and over which he broke diplomatic relations
with Rome. But improvement went on, nonetheless,
and it went on because Tito needed it.

There can be little doubt, as stressed above,
that the gradual relief of religious life in Yugoslavia played a central role in the Vatican's
Ostpolitik. Here was evidence that Communists could
change and that Catholicism could coexist with Communists, and in fact, grow in a Socialist state.
It would not be too much to say that Yugoslavia was
the decisive influence in Pope John XXIII's policy

of moving from "anathema to dialogue" with the Communist world. As such the Yugoslav situation merits close scrutiny. The essential fact is that Tito needed liberalization.

Through the 1950s, as Tito's relaxation of repression proceeded, the Holy See remained as critical of Belgrade as it had been since the end of the war. The tolerant nature of the new policies were, as stated above, the result of changes in the international arena which, in turn, dictated alterations in domestic affairs. This did not mean, though, that the Vatican's coldness did not affect these alterations. If the Vatican had been friendly to Tito before or even during the granting of religious concessions, the Yugoslav leader would not have found it necessary to give concessions or to impose them. Tito was compelled to make a number of significant concessions to the Catholic Church in order to profit from the goodwill of the Holy See in his relations with the Western world and in reducing Catholic alienation in Croatia and Slovenia. The Vatican's ability to exert influence on Tito, and, for that matter, the other Communist governments in Eastern Europe, was and is restricted to what they believe to be its value in support of or in opposition to their domestic and/or foreign policy.

It may be argued that the Church's hostility was an important element in improving religious conditions in Yugoslavia and that anything less than opposition to a regime which persecutes religion is imprudent. On the other hand, after such a government makes concessions, the Holy See should be ready to respond in kind--as indeed it did gradually, culminating in Pope Paul's reception of Tito in 1970. It is ultimately a question of reciprocity. Accordingly, if the Yugoslav case is to have practical meaning to the evolution of Ostpolitik in East Europe, the Vatican's consorting with a government which patently emasculates religion has to be deemed self-defeating. Vatican diplomacy is open to the criticism that it missed the lesson of Church-State relations in Yugoslavia. What it did apparently take away was the conviction that Communism and Catholicism can coexist and, armed with this unrefined insight, it launched its policy of Ostpolitik in the hope of reproducing in the rest of East Europe the Yugoslav experience. Unfortunately, in the process--especially in regard to the USSR and Czechoslovakia--it has tended to quell Western enthusiasm for the plight of Catholics in East Europe, at a minimum confused those who were struggling to defend their faith, and,

finally, created the inevitable impression of weakness among the Communist governments which, taking
their cue from the Soviets, invariably interpret un-
reciprocal concessions or gestures of friendliness
as signs of weakness.  It must be remembered that
this applies not only to the few European states
with which these pages are concerned, but also to the
increasing number of countries over which Communist
rule has been extended in other continents and whose
governments reproduce, sometimes in extreme forms,
the anti-Christian features of the world revolution
which they have learned from Moscow.  In Vietnam,
Mozambique, and Angola, for instance, there are millions of Christians--Catholics for the most part--
whose plight is mutatis mutandis no less serious,
if not worse than that of their brethren in Lithuania
or Czechoslovakia, and for whose rights the Holy See
is under obligation to struggle.  In those parts of
the world, the equivalent of the Vatican's Ostpolitik
in Europe has been for some years the courting of the
anti-colonialism of the new rulers, a policy for
which success may be claimed in many independent
Asian and African countries, but which has so far
been a conspicuous failure in the former European
dependencies which have come under Communist control.
From the Communist vantage point, the correct response to Ostpolitik, or appeasement, is not to shore
up the failing fortunes of Catholicism through reciprocity, but to press their presumed advantage and to
help Catholicism "wither away" through continued
persecution.  At the risk of repetition, Yugoslavia
is not like the other Communist states; Tito initiated relaxation because he needed Catholic allegiance,
both internally and internationally.  The Vatican's
favorable reaction to Tito's changes, i.e., the
inauguration and elaboration of Papal Ostpolitik in
Yugoslavia, was and is justifiable, prudent, and
worthwhile for the Church has made significant ad-
vances.  This does not mean that Catholicism in
Yugoslavia is today free and uninhibited.  The
Church's social, educational, and charitable functions remain severely hampered.  And Yugoslavia is,
after all, a one-party state where Marxism-Leninism
is the official ideology. The government of Tito,
in fact, feels obliged to keep the ideology pure for
it is the basis of his and the Party's legitimacy.
The ideology, also, overrides the divisive national-
isms and, thus, is an important "cultural" cement
which, at least, symbolically unites the hetero-
genous peoples of Yugoslavia.  The ideology with its
antireligious dimension, thus, cannot be dismissed

and the Church cannot relax. If Tito should mend his
rift with the Soviets (highly unlikely), he naturally
would feel less inclined to tolerate a strong Catholic Church in Croatia and Slovenia. If he should
determine, furthermore, that the disadvantages of
religious toleration, especially its strengthening
of nationalism in Croatia and Slovenia, outweighed
the advantages, he would no doubt once again attack
religion forcibly. Likewise, if he should conclude
that the West would support him even though he dis-
continued religious relaxation, he might well renew
his campaign against Catholicism and, indeed, this
consideration, in addition to the growth of Croatian
and Slovenian nationalism, might have played a role
in the sporadic attacks upon Catholic clergy in the
1970s.

The general pattern of Church-State relations in
Yugoslavia since the death of Stalin has, however,
been one of moderation and improvement. By 1958 the
easing of tension had reached such proportions that
the Yugoslav authorities allowed Cardinal Stepinac's
funeral to be held in Zagreb Cathedral, and shortly
thereafter permitted the Yugoslav bishops to take an
active role in the Second Vatican Council. In 1962,
the first issue of Glas Koncila (Voice of the
Council) appeared. It was intended by the Archbishop
of Zagreb to be a source of information on the proceedings of the Council, but it quickly developed
into a highly respected biweekly with a circulation
of over 180,000 and is now the best Catholic periodical in Eastern Europe. Other Church publications
soon started with government approval and, according
to Professor Branko Bonjak, the yearly circulation
of Catholic publications had reached 8,200,000 by
1968.[20]

Direct talks to normalize relations fully between the Yugoslav government and the Holy See began in
1963 and, by 1964, Mgr. Casaroli was involved.[21]
The talks continued into 1965 and were accompanied
by a general relaxation of the antireligious laws.
As a sign of ameliorating conditions, Pope Paul VI
received in private audience Yugoslavia's ambassador
to Italy, Ivo Vejvoda, in January.[22]

Two years after negotiations began, a Protocol
was concluded between the Holy See and the Yugoslav
regime, and emissaries below ambassadorial rank were
exchanged. The document recognized Rome's jurisdiction over the Roman Catholic Church in ecclesiastical
and spiritual matters. It also guaranteed separation
of Church and State and freedom of conscience and
religion. The Holy See agreed that Catholic clerics

93

should not involve themselves in politics, and specifically condemned all acts of terrorism.[23]

Some Croatians and Slovenians objected to the document partly because it was negotiated over their heads and partly because it was a compromise. But the Protocol was quite unique in terms of the Vatican's relations with the Communist states of East Europe and there are indications that Rome would like to duplicate it throughout East Europe.[24]

At the same time that the Protocol was concluded, a Christian-Marxist dialogue was initiated with a public discussion between Professor Bosnak of the Philosophical Faculty of Zagreb University and Father T. Šagi-Bunić, a Franciscan from the Theological Faculty in Zagreb (the two Catholic Theological Faculties at Zagreb and Ljublijana were separated from their respective universities in 1952). The dialogue has persisted, although rising nationalism in Croatia has led to a pause in the dialogue in that region since 1971.[25]

In the new atmosphere of relaxation, younger people, mainly in the cities with substantial universities, have become quite interested in religion. In 1967 the Central Committee of the Union of Youth in Croatia dedicated an entire issue of its journal Nase Teme (Our Themes) to religion. In 1969 Skolske Novine (School News), an educational organ, organized a seminar on "Education, the School, Religion, and the Church," and published the proceedings. The Jesuit Church in Zagreb today offers a special "Mass for Intellectuals," and it is filled with students.[26]

This internal relaxation was matched by diplomatic exchanges. In June 1968, Pope Paul received in private audience the Yugoslav Premier, Mika Spiljak. Also in that year Cardinal Franjo Seper of Zagreb (made a Cardinal in 1965) was named Prefect of the Vatican's Congregation on Doctrine and Faith, the first East European bishop to hold an important Curial post. In August 1970 , a turning point was reached when Belgrade and the Vatican restored full diplomatic relations. In March of the following year, Tito visited Pope Paul, in the first public and official visit to the Vatican by a Communist chief of state. It was reported that they discussed at length the problem of peace in the world and the Arab-Israeli conflict.[27] In a public statement on that occasion, the Pope recalled Yugoslavia's great religious history, praised its constitutional principles, and guaranteed that the Church would not interfere with the government's proper authority. Tito commented that Yugoslavia respected the sovereignty

94

and independence of all peoples and hoped that all prejudice and exploitation could be discarded.[28]
The position of the Catholic Church grew stronger through 1971. The Franciscan seminary in Dubrovnik set up a dialogue with Marxists on Lenin and Religion to commemorate the centenary of Lenin's birth. Belgrade University, in the same year, held a group of four seminars at which Catholic, Orthodox, and Marxist scholars debated. A Marian Congress was organized in 1971 in Zagreb and the city officials helped facilitate its various activities.[29]
The 1970s have shown marked improvement in the Church's position, although there are indications that the regime feels that liberalization has gone far enough and needs to be rolled back. In 1971, the Roman Catholic Church had a total of 2,634 parishes organized into eight archdioceses, thirteen dioceses, and three apostolic administrations. By the end of 1977, there were over 4,000 Catholic priests, over 6,600 nuns, and 6,859,010 professing Catholics. There are Catholic theological faculties at Zagreb and Ljubljana which together in 1971 had 403 students. The eight major seminaries had in that year 477 students and the twenty-two minor seminaries 1,535 students. In addition, over 200 students and fifty priests studied abroad in 1971, mainly in Italy, Austria, and West Germany. Virtually every Catholic parish now has religious instruction for youngsters and the priests are frequently assisted by nuns. The Bible is readily available throughout the country. The Catholic press is widely available, although both the government and some of the more conservative Yugoslav bishops attack and occasionally censure issues which they deem threatening to their respective views and positions.[30]
In November 1977, Milos Minic was received by the Pope. He also met with various Vatican officials, including Mgr. Casaroli, Cardinal Villot, Mgr. Achille Silvestrini, Under-Secretary of the Council for Public Relations, and Mgr. Giuseppe Caprio, Deputy Secretary of State. In their discussions, according to the Yugoslav news agency Tanjug, the Yugoslav and Vatican representatives discussed some of the world's crucial issues, especially the problems of developement, the establishment of a new international economic order, disarmament, and security and cooperation in Europe. In addition, they agreed that Church-State relations in Yugoslavia were good and the Pope, according to Tanjug, specifically urged that the Church and Catholics in Yugoslavia be loyal citizens and contribute to the social progress

of the community in which they lived.[31] On November 21, Pope Paul, in a speech to the Yugoslav Episcopal Conference, said he was pleased with the vigor of the Yugoslav Catholic Church and urged the bishops to overcome remaining difficulties in the religious life of Yugoslavia, especially the spreading of "so-called" scientific materialism in the schools and publications.[32] Tanjug news agency, in December, in reviewing an extensive article on relations between Yugoslavia and the Vatican in the Belgrade Review of International Affairs, applauded the Holy See's increasing interest in the policy of non-alignment and reported that the Vatican knows that Yugoslavia wants "no confrontation and conflict with the Catholic Church in Yugoslavia, but, instead, co-operation and contacts." Furthermore, the news agency concluded that "good relations between the Vatican and Yugoslavia clearly reflect the actual state of affairs in the present-day world" and "can serve as an example of how the Church can and ought to be free in a socialist country."[33] In March 1978, Milan Vukasovic, the Chairman of the Commission for Relations with Religious Communities announced, among other things, at a news conference that Yugoslavia was asking the Vatican to use its influence to see to it that a number of émigré Yugoslav missionaries break their ties with terrorists and their activities against Yugoslavia.[34] In late April 1978, exchanges between Belgrade and the Vatican continued to grow with the arrival in Yugoslavia of Fr. Pedro Arrupe, General of the Jesuit Order.[35]

All is not right in Yugoslavia, needless to say. The regime continues to attack religion, particularly if there is any hint of support or involvement in the Croatian and Slovenian national movements.[36] In 1975-76, there was growing tension over new religious laws being drafted in the Republics.[37] The Catholic press continues to be subject to censorship. Furthermore, the authorities are disturbed at the influence of Catholicism among the youth, a development which threatens in the long run the Patry's future and its ideology.[38] All in all, though, Catholic-Yugoslav relations are good and Ostpolitik here has been a success. The reasons why it is successful, however, should clearly be understood. Both the Church and Tito's government have progressed on the basis of reciprocity. Without a quid pro quo foundation, there can only be disillusionment, disappointment, and, ultimately, persecution.

NOTES

1. See Zdenko Antic, "Tension Between State and Catholic Church in Yugoslavia Continues," Radio Free Europe Research (RAD Background Report/112) (July 1, 1975), 1-9; and Adenko Antic, "Attacks Continue Against Catholic Church in Yugoslavia," Radio Free Europe Research (RAD Background Report/23) (February 13, 1975), 1-6; Zdenko Antic, "More Strain Between State and Catholic Church in Yugoslavia?" Radio Free Europe Research (RAD Background Report/61) (April 1, 1975), 1-4. In a thoughtful essay, Stella Alexander puts recent developments in perspective: "Church-State Relations in Yugoslavia Since 1967," Religion in Communist Lands, No. 1 (Spring 1976): 18-27.
2. George Zaninovich, The Development of Socialist Yugoslavia (Baltimore, Md.: The Johns Hopkins Press, 1968), p. 170.
3. For a survey of the religions of Yugoslavia, see Zlatko Frid. ed., Religions in Yugoslavia (Zagreb, 1971).
4. Zaninovich, Yugoslavia, pp. 15-16; Trevor Beeson, Discretion and Valour (Glasgow: Collins Fontana Books, 1974), p. 257; Bogdan Denitch, "Religion and Social Changes in Yugoslavia," in Bociurkiw and Strong, Religion and Atheism, pp. 370-371.
5. Hugh Seton-Watson, The East European Revolution (New York and Washington: Praeger, 1956 reprint), p. 79.
6. Beeson, Discretion, p. 261.
7. Ibid., p. 262. For an excellent, fresh assessment of Archbishop Stepinac, see Stella Alexander, "Archbishop Stepinac Reconsidered," Religion in Communist Lands, No. 6 (Summer 1978): 76-88.
8. Seton-Watson, Revolution, p. 291.
9. Adam Ulam, Titoism and the Cominform (Cambridge, Mass.: 1952), p. 231.
10. Ulam, Expansion and Coexistence, p. 384.
11. Beeson, Discretion, p. 265.
12. Gerhard Simon, "The Catholic Church and the Communist State in the Soviet Union and Eastern Europe," in Bociurkiw and Strong, p. 196, 201.
13. Ibid., p. 201; Galter, Red Book, pp. 172-174.
14. Simon, "Catholic Church," p. 199.
15. Ibid., pp. 208, 218; Beeson, Discretion, p. 266.
16. Seton-Watson, Revolution, p. 291. Also see Alexander, "Archbishop Stepinac," pp. 83-84.

97

17. Beeson, Discretion, p. 266.
18. Ibid., pp. 266-67.
19. Ibid., p. 273. Also see Ivan Ceranić, "Religious Communities in Yugoslavia," in Frid, Religions, pp. 24-26.
20. Denitch, "Religion in Yugoslavia," p. 382.
21. Ivan Lazić, "The Legal and Actual Status of Religious Communities in Yugoslavia," in Frid, Religions, p. 71. Also see New York Times, January 15, 1965.
22. New York Times, January 15, 1965.
23. Lazić, "Legal and Actual Status of Religious Communities in Yugoslavia," pp. 72-77. Also see Ceranić, "Religious Communities," pp. 26-30.
24. Beeson, Discretion, p. 270. Also see Zdenko Roter, Katoliška cerkev in država v Jugoslaviji 1945-1973 (Ljubljana, 1976), p. 207.
25. Beeson, Discretion, pp. 275-76. Also see the two following interesting articles: T. Stress, "Liberation from a Value?" Družina (Ljubljana: June 19, 1977), p. 3, and Vladimir Marković, "Dialogue in Belgrade," Blagovest (Belgrade: February 1977), pp. 35-36 in Religion in Communist Dominated Lands 16 (1977): 187-90. Also see Vjekoslav Bajsić, "The Standpoint of Christians Towards a Dialogue with Marxists," in Frid, Religions, pp. 146-53; Zdenko Roter, "The Sense of the Dialogue Between Marxists and Christians," in Frid, Religions, pp. 154-162. Dialogue has also commenced between the Catholic and Orthodox Churches. See Tomislav Šagi-Bunić, "Catholic Church and Ecumenism," in Frid, Religions, pp. 107-19, and Čedomir Drašković, "Orthodoxy and Ecumenism," in Frid, Religions, pp. 120-31. Also see Radio Vatican, October 6, 1976.
26. Beeson, Discretion, pp. 271, 276.
27. New York Times, March 30, 1970.
28. Beeson, Discretion, p. 271.
29. Alexander, "Church-State Relations," p. 22.
30. Beeson, Discretion, pp. 258-59, 271, 273-275, 277-79. Also see Radio Vatican, May 16, 1978.
31. Tanjug News Agency, November 15, 16, 17, 1977.
32. Radio Vatican, November 21, 1977.
33. Tanjug News Agency, December 2, 1977.
34. Ibid., March 6, 1978.
35. Ibid., April 19, 1978.
36. Ibid., March 6, 1978; Radio Belgrade, April 28, 1976.
37. Tanjug News Agency, March 6, 1978 and August 18, 1976.

38.  Antic, "Attacks Continue Against Catholic Church in Yugoslavia," Radio Free Europe Research, pp. 2-3;  "Review of 'Religious Affiliations,'" Aktualnosti Krscanske Sadasnjosti (AKSA) (Zagreb: February 6, 1976) in Religion in Communist Dominated Lands 16 (1977): 78-79.

# 5. The Polish Church: Distrust of Vatican Diplomacy

In December 1970, the Polish workers in the
Baltic seaports organized a strike which soon precipitated riots.  The immediate cause of the unrest
was the government's tactless raising of food prices
on the eve of the Christmas holidays.  So overwhelming was the discontent that Wladyslaw Gomulka,
the head of the Polish Communist Party and the responsible authority, had to step aside in favor of
Edward Gierek.  At the same time Piotr Jaroszewicz
replaced Josef Cyrankiewicz as premier.  Without
wasting time, the new leadership sought the support
of the Catholic Church in defusing the riots, stating
that the government was ready to work for the normalization of Church-State relations.  Jaroszewicz made
the offer real by spelling out the initial concessions he was prepared to give.  They included giving
the Church full title to the ecclesiastical land in
the territory taken from Germany at the end of
World War II.
Cardinal Stefan Wyszynski, a man whose influence
with the Polish people is second to none, and the
Polish bishops immediately called for calm and peace
throughout the country, making clear, however, their
sympathy with the workers and their reprobation of
the brutality of the police in suppressing the
strike.[1]  This sequence of events underscores the
nature of Church-State relations in Poland.  Formally, all the power is with the Party but the
Church has more influence on Polish thought and
feeling.  The Party is suspect as the surrogate of
Moscow, but the Church represents Poland in the minds
of the Polish people.  It is a question whether it
is altogether healthy for the Church to be quite so
clearly identified with any one nation but the fact
is that the influence of the Church is so great, that
the Party has to take it into account.

From the late eighteenth century onward,
Poland's history has been a chronicle of tragedy.
Although Prussia and Austria were hardly friends of
Poland, the principal enemy of the Polish nation, at
least in the eyes of the Poles, was Russia.  For
nearly a hundred and forty years or so that the tsars
dominated the largest part of Poland, from the Par-
titions to World War I, the Poles were constantly
at odds with the Russian government, sometimes violently so as in 1830-31 and 1863-64.  With the
Russian Revolution and the end of World War I, Poland
regained its independence but relations between the
Poles and the Revolutionary government remained
acrimonious and soon led to hostilities.  In 1920,
the Red Army was defeated at the gates of Warsaw.
It was forced to retreat, leaving, by the Treaty of
Riga (March 1921), the Western Ukraine and western
Belorussia under Polish sovereignty.  When the
Second World War commenced, Poland soon found itself
partitioned by the Molotov-Ribbentrop Pact and, then,
abandoned to Soviet hegemony by the Teheran, Yalta,
and Potsdam Agreements.  By 1945, Poland was clearly
doomed to be a satellite of Moscow once again.
Through all of Poland's hardships, particularly its
subjugations to the Russian tsars, the Catholic
Church represented Polish identity and pride.  In
the days of independence between the wars, the Church
was the center of national life, enjoyed constitutional guarantees of its privileged position, and
controlled an extensive and well-knit ecclesiastical
organization, together with schools, numerous chari-
ties, and an influential press.[2]  After the war,
strengthened by a notable religious revival and able
to claim the adherence of about 95% of the population as a result of territorial changes, the Church's
influence was staggering.  The Polish Communists,
as proponents of Moscow and Marxism-Leninism, were
cast from the beginning as the bogies of Polish
nationalism.
     Once in power, the Communists were determined
to prevent the Church from regaining its prewar
position and, at the same time, to bring it firmly
under its control.  They were shrewd enough to
realize that they must be careful because of the
Church's indigenous strength and their own weakness
in the hearts of the people.  But certainly the
Communists never throught that after some thirty
years in power the Church would be stronger and they
would be still, in the final analysis, dependent
upon Moscow for their position.[3]
     Church-State relations in Communist Poland have

been a tug of war.  Five major phases in this relationship can be distinguished.  The period from
1944-45 to 1947 was one of relative toleration, although certainly not amiability.  During this time,
the Polish Church resumed its charitable and social
activities, reopened the Catholic University at
Lublin as well as numerous schools and seminaries,
and began publishing an array of journals and newspapers, including the influential Cracow weekly,
Tygodnik Powszechny.  In addition, the land holdings
of the Church were exempted from the land reform
announced in January 1946; money was appropriated
for the reconstruction of war-damaged churches; and
the prewar ruling on mandatory religious instruction
in all public schools was maintained.[4]  Throughout
this period, the Church was adamantly anti-Communist
and openly supported Mikolajczyk's opposition party
in the 1946 election in which the Communists won an
"overwhelming victory."
    There were some problems, however, through the
early transitional phase and they did not augur well
for the future.  The regime repudiated the 1925
Concordat with Rome,[5] and launched a vicious propaganda campaign against the Vatican.  No doubt the
government believed that the Papacy supported the
Polish hierarchy's unfriendly attitude and attacks
on the Vatican were a veiled threat to the Polish
Church.  In addition, the Papacy balked at recognizing
the new Polish government, refused to appoint permanent bishops for the Oder-Neisse region until a
German peace treaty was concluded, and had not re-
voked the jurisdiction of the Polish bishops in the
lands annexed to the Soviet Union.[6]  Besides the repudiation of the Concordat and the fulminations
against the Vatican, the regime also sponsored, in
the fall of 1945, a group of lay Catholics under the
leadership of Boleslaw Piasecki, once an extreme
right-wing politician who had made his peace with
the KGB by means which can only be guessed.  The
group, called Pax, demanded complete cooperation between Catholics and Communists in the building of a
socialist society.  The organization was obviously a
fifth column which the government hoped to use to
split the Church and challenge the authority of the
bishops.[7]  Piasecki was re-elected as Chairman of
Pax in January 1976.
    The second phase in Church-State relations covers
the era of "high Stalinism," from 1948 to 1955.  Propaganda against the hierarchy, often imputing pro-
Nazi sympathies, now became commonplace.  Simultaneously, the government backed a small group of

priests who opposed episcopal policy and wanted to collaborate with the government on its terms. In 1949, a decree permitting religious and antireligious activity was implemented and church hospitals were nationalized. The next year, Caritas, the Church's welfare organization, was put under government supervision, and Church lands, with the exception of a small acreage farmed by parish priests, were confiscated. Nonetheless, a nineteen point Agreement between the Church and the State was reached on April 14, 1950. Its provisions appeared to guarantee freedom of worship and to grant the Church autonomy to teach religion in the schools, to run a press, welfare organizations, and educational institutions, including the Catholic University of Lublin, and to sanction religious associations and orders. It also allowed some Church ministrations in the army, prisons, and hospitals. However, the government interpreted the document differently from the bishops and soon demanded, as the latter's obligation under the agreement, complete support by the Church of the government's political and economic policies. On July 22, 1952, a new Constitution was enacted; it established separation of Church and State and, in theory, made the Church subject to government decree. On February 9, 1953, a law was passed which made all Church appointments, promotions, and transfers subject to government consent. Censorship of the Catholic press was stepped up. Tygodnik Powszechny was suspended in March 1953, and then reappeared in July, under the editorship of Catholics supportive of the regime. By 1953, the five hundred and sixteen Catholic publications of 1947 had been cut to forty-five.[8] Attacks upon the Vatican were crude and profuse.

The Polish hierarchy fought back through sermons, episcopal letters, editorial commentaries, and mass protests by the faithful. Arrest of a number of bishops commenced in 1952, including Bishop Kaczmarek of Kielce. Cardinal Wyszynski, who had replaced Cardinal Hlond as the Primate of the Church after the latter's death in 1948, was removed from office and confined under guard in a monastery at the end of September 1953. With their leader gone, the Polish bishops soon gave way to the increasing pressure of the government and took a loyalty oath on December 17, 1953.

With the hierarchy silenced for the moment, the government moved quickly to attempt to control the Church. The government-controlled publishing house, Pax, put out a stream of books explaining the

compatibility of Marxism and Catholic dogma and it
began to serialize sermons to ensure acceptable
preaching. Simultaneously, Catholic institutions
of higher learning were closely supervised. In
December 1954, a new Academy of Catholic Theology,
headed by a collaborationist priest, Father Czuj,
was started in Warsaw. Promoted as a concession, it
was in fact a move to gain leverage over the teaching of theology, since the new faculty replaced the
theological faculties of the Cracow and Warsaw
Universities. But the attempt was not entirely successful, and by the 1960s, the Academy was on
working terms with the bishops. The curriculum of
the Catholic University of Lublin was also curtailed.
By 1956, only the faculties of philosophy and the
humanities remained, while the faculties of Law and
Social Sciences and Theology and Canon Law were dis-
continued. Some of the social sciences were later
revived. Seminaries, previously ninety strong, had
fallen to twenty by 1956. Taxation on Church property was severe with even church collections being
assessed. The regime also kept the number of churches
below needs by refusing to grant building permits,
particularly in new industrial centers. At the end
of 1955, the teaching of the catechism was abolished
in all schools.[9]
    The next period from 1956 through 1958 has been
called the "liberal" phase because the Church had
some of its earlier freedoms restored.[10]  In the
climate of de-Stalinization and the subsequent unrest in Poland, Cardinal Wyszynski was released and
allowed to resume his post. Formal religious
teaching was also restored in the schools for those
parents who requested it (in writing) for their
children. Since most did, more than 90% of the
children attending school soon received religious
instruction.[11]  A new organization of lay Catholics,
called the Znak Group, also appeared in 1956. Its
ideological stand, as contrasted with Pax, was gen-
uinely Catholic in a non-Marxist way, and its basic
platform was to urge cooperation between Catholics
and the government simply out of pragmatic concerns.
It placed much hope in the fact that Gomulka, who
had a reputation for being a Polish patriot, would
put Polish interests ahead of ideology.[12]
    The basic inspiration of Znak has been the hope
of encouraging the Communist government to accept a
just, humane, and pluralistic society in Poland. Today the head of Znak is Professor Stanislaw Stomma
and the Chairman of the Znak Catholic Deputies in the
Sejm is Janusz Zablocki. The number of seminaries

104

also increased during the "liberal" phase, reaching by 1967 seventy.[13]

The fourth period from 1958 to the fall of Gomulka's regime in 1970 saw a return to hardline policies but without the venom and violence of the last years of Stalinism. The old problems, such as the Vatican's unwillingness to recognize the government, and to change the episcopal administration of the Oder-Neisse territories and the regime's refusal to grant building permits for churches and its high taxes on church property, helped to poison the air and produce the new round of Church-State antagonism. The Gomulka regime was determined to gain more control over the Church and to curb its influence, especially with the children.

The policy of rapprochement, although already set in motion by the exchanges between Khrushchev and Pope John XXIII in 1963, was not paralleled, in any meaningful way, in Poland until the 1970s. Starting in 1958, the government launched an attack upon religious instruction and soon banned it in most schools. At the start of the school year 1959-1960, religion was still being offered in 21,500 schools (out of a total of 28,000), but at the close of the 1960-61 school year, in only 6,500 schools.[14] Then, in July 1961, the government ordered that all religious instruction be taught in catechism centers outside of school property. The hierarchy resisted this move but, once implemented, it strove to prevent the government from controlling the catechism centers. These were supposed to be registered and subject to the inspection of the Ministry of Education in return for government financing, but countless unregistered centers, especially in rural areas, were set up. At the same time, the regime continued to attempt to weaken and challenge the hierarchy's authority by supporting such groups as the Pax Society and collaborationist priests. It also persisted in refusing, as mentioned above, to grant church building permits. Other disagreements included the government's ban on extensive religious publications, interference in religious holidays, processions, and pilgrimages, and its intolerable intrusion into church personnel matters, including the staffing of seminaries and the appointment of bishops. The government continued to inveigh against the Vatican.

The Church, however, maintained its highly disciplined, tightly knit, and extensive organization. In 1967, the country had twenty-five bishoprics (including five archdioceses, seventeen dioceses,

105

and three diocesan curiae) and 6,334 parishes. The Church controlled 13,273 places of worship. The bishops, under the leadership of the Primate of Poland, Cardinal Stefan Wyszynski, numbered over sixty and the priests 17,986. There were also 3,275 lay brothers and 27,975 nuns, and over 4,000 students in the Church's seventy seminaries. The bishops also did not hesitate to criticize the government in sermons, particularly on items which touched the issues of religious education, church taxes, new church buildings, and church personnel, especially the appointment of bishops.[15] By the end of 1977, there were seventy-seven bishops, 19,865 priests (19,456 at the end of 1976), about 30,000 nuns, and 5,058 seminarians studying for the priesthood. In the years 1970-76, Roman Catholic parishes increased from 6,376 to 6,716 and the number of churches and chapels went from 13,392 to 14,039. By the beginning of 1978, some 1,007 Polish missionaries of both sexes were involved in missionary work abroad, mainly in Asia, Africa, and Latin America.[16]

In short, Church-State relations by the beginning of the 1960s were strained, but in spite of the coercive weapons at its disposal, the government had been unable to control the Church in essentials. The relationship had become more or less stable by the start of the Second Vatican Council, however, and especially following the earlier described policies of Khrushchev, the Polish regime endeavored to undertake a new tactic to circumvent the Polish Church: dialogue with the Vatican. The Polish Church did not oppose the concept of such a dialogue, providing it was conducted on the basis of a realistic assessment of Church-State relations in Poland and had in view ultimately a normalization of such relations. The Polish hierarchy was, however, suspicious of Vatican diplomats negotiating with the Polish government on behalf of the Polish Church. The bishops' fear was the government's hope. A dialogue with Rome began shortly after the start of the Second Vatican Council, but it in no way lessened tension in Church-State relations in Poland for the next seven years or so.

The dialogue in Poland started in April 1963, when Cardinal Franz Koenig of Vienna, now head of the Vatican's Secretariat for Dialogue with Unbelievers and one of Rome's experts on Communist affairs, arrived in Warsaw for discussions. He met with Cardinal Wyszynski and Vice-President Podgorny and his expressed purpose was to begin negotiations for the improvement of Church-State relations.[17]

Cardinal Wyszynski received the visitor and soon afterwards he had a meeting with Gomulka, the head of the Communist Party and the government, their first in two years.[18] The talks, however, came to naught and quickly were replaced by a spate of reciprocal attacks and criticisms.[19]

The quarrel spilled over into 1964, and that year was marked by a continuous verbal feud between the Church and the government. In May, Cardinal Wyszynski was permitted to visit Rome and, in transit, he announced that religious training would continue in Poland despite the regime's threats of jail.[20] With the cardinal's return, the government increased its pressure on the Church by refusing to allow children at summer camp to attend church. In late August, the cardinal claimed that the Church was winning the struggle for survival in Poland and si- multaneously, denounced the Pax Society as a Commu- nist-front organization.[21] The government expressed, in October, disappointment in the attitude of the Polish Church, particularly in the light of the Vatican's moves toward "modernization." The Vatican, however, not about to be portrayed as standing against the Polish Church, quickly lined up with the Polish bishops by asserting that the Pax Society was attempting to "spread discord." On Christmas Day, Cardinal Wyszynski sent greetings to the government with the pointed request that the latter adhere to the Universal Declaration of Human Rights.[22] A hopeful sign, however, in the Church-State impasse did ap- pear toward the end of the year, when the Polish government showed a great interest in the accord on the filling of episcopal vacancies worked out be- tween the Vatican and Hungary.[23]

Relations in 1965 continued to show the ani- mosity that had become their characteristic feature. The year was rife with attacks and counterattacks by the Polish hierarchy and the government. The bishops scored the government for drafting seminarians into the army, for using public funds to spread atheism, for depriving Catholics of the right to attend paro- chial schools, for suppressing religious education, and for organizing public meetings on religious holidays. The government, in turn, charged the Polish bishops with meddling in politics and foreign affairs and with being too conservative. In November, there was a major government campaign to discredit the Church by asserting that the Polish bishops were taking a soft stand on German responsibility for the war and the Oder-Neisse boundary issue. The pretext for the campaign was the Polish "Bishops' Letter to

the German Episcopate," sent on November 18, 1965,
from Rome, by the thirty-six Polish prelates attending the final session of the Vatican Council, to
the German episcopate.  The missive touched at
length upon past Polish-German relations and concluded by invoking the spirit of the Gospel and prof-
fering  forgiveness and requesting to be forgiven
for the sufferings mutually inflicted.  It also invited the German bishops to attend the forthcoming
celebrations of the millenium of Catholicism in
Poland.  In the weeks that followed, the government
orchestrated a savage campaign in the mass media
which vilified the Polish bishops and questioned
their loyalty to Poland and the socialist society.[24]
    The new year brought no end to the Church-
State strains of 1965.  The antagonism circulated
around two major issues: the Polish bishops' conciliatory letter to the German bishops and the government's desire to play down the Church's celebration
of the millenium of Poland's conversion to Christianity.  The strife produced by these events led to
massive demonstrations throughout the year by the
Polish people in support of Wyszynski, whom the vast
majority felt was being victimized by the government.
The regime, in an attempt to curb the cardinal and
the Church's influence, claimed that the Primate
"wants to return to medieval principles of religious
intolerance," and inaugurated a massive poster campaign celebrating Polish patriotism in an attempt to
take the spotlight off the Church's millenium celebrations and to embarrass the bishops because of
their desire to open a dialogue with the German
episcopate.[25]  In addition, the government blocked
the planned visit of Pope Paul to Poland, and staged
the controversial play, The Deputy by Rolf Hochhuth,
which claimed that Pope Pius XII did not do enough
to try to prevent Nazi massacres in such countries
as Poland during World War II.  The East German
bishops who planned to attend the millenium celebration in Poland were denied visas.[26]  Cardinal
Wyszynski was also denied permission to travel to
Rome in January because, according to the government,
of the Polish bishops' letter and the attitudes it
reflected.[27]  By the end of the year, tension still
had not abated.
    But in the autumn of 1966, in Rome, Archbishop
Casaroli had opened preliminary talks on Polish
Church-State relations with Polish General Committee
member, Andrezej Werblan.  Archbishop Casaroli
arrived in Warsaw in February 1967, to begin a three-
stage tour of Poland in which he planned to obtain

on-the-spot information of church conditions.[28]  The
purpose of the Italian's visit implied that there was
another side to Church-State relations than the one
which Cardinal Wyszynski had painted.  Amidst rumors
of an impending Church-State agreement which the
Polish Episcopate's secretary, Bishop Choromanski,
branded as "gossip," Casaroli toured Poland and met
with Church and government officials.  If an agreement had been hoped for, none was reached.  In May,
the Vatican, as an obviously conciliatory gesture,
elevated the status of the four Polish bishops in
the disputed Oder-Neisse territories from vicar
generals to apostolic administrators, answerable to
Rome.  In June, Karol Wojtyla, the Archbishop of
Cracow, was named as Poland's second cardinal.[29]  However, no meaningful consequences followed these
events and, for the most part, the year was marred by
an exchange of charges between the Polish episcopate
and the government over such things as the loyalty
of Wyszynski, church building permits, and the
Church's "meddling" in politics.  As in 1966, the regime refused to allow Cardinal Wyszynski to travel
to Rome.[30]

The year 1968 started inauspiciously with an
attack by the Polish episcopate and the Vatican
upon Pax.  But soon, in the wake of Willy
Brandt's announcement in March that Germany was
ready to recognize the Oder-Neisse boundary, there
seemed to be a golden opportunity of reconciliation.
However, Church-State relations remained barren and
undeveloped.  The regime did, however, relax the
ban on Cardinal Wyszynski's travels and, in November,
the Primate went to Rome.[31]  The next year did not
witness much change in Church-State relations.  The
acrimony of previous years was missing but coolness
ruled.  In October, the government permitted Cardinal
Wyszynski to attend the Synod of Bishops in Rome, and,
in November, Casaroli had two days of long and detailed discussions with Herbert Wehner and Georg
Leber, German government officials, on the problem
of the ecclesiastical rearrangement of the former
German territories.[32]

In 1970, Church-State relations remained inim-
ical through most of the year, but in December, the
Gomulka regime fell in the wake of the strikes and
food riots in the Baltic ports.  The new government,
headed by Edward Gierek, immediately announced after
taking power that it would "strive for a full normalization of relations with the Church."[33]  The
announcement was quite conciliatory and marked the
beginning of a new period in Church-State relations

in Poland. The Ostpolitik of Willy Brandt and the Vatican demonstrated willingness to reorganize the Oder-Neisse territories in accordance with Polish preferences had already adumbrated a more relaxed relationship between the Catholic Church and the Polish government, but it only commenced in a serious vein in late 1970. Cardinal Wyszynski, on Christmas Day, decried the rioting in which many Poles were killed and hundreds wounded, but waited for concrete proof of the government's declared intention before using the influence of the Church publicly to seconding its efforts.[34]

At the beginning of the new year, with the Polish nation still reverberating from the uprisings which brought Gomulka's government down, the episcopate responded formally to the government's overture for better relations. The bishops initially criticized the government's handling of the demonstrations and charged that excessive force and intimidation were used. Then, the bishops declared that normalization could only come when the government recognized "the right to freedom of conscience and freedom of religious life together with full normalization of relations between the Church and State; the right of freely shaping the culture of one's own nation; the right to social justice. . . ; the right to truth in social life, to information according with the truth, and to free expression of one's views and demands; the right to material conditions which insure decent existence of the family, and of each individual citizen; and the right to such an attitude towards the citizens that they are not insulted, harmed or persecuted in anything."[35] The regime had obviously made the offer of "normalizing relations" to obtain Church support following the disorders and riots, but the bishops' response made it clear that the Church would offer itself as a buttress only when the government made some concrete concessions. From the bishops' point of view, a quid pro quo understanding was the only realistic approach to solving Church-State problems. The early January publication of the Vatican's yearbook, Annuario Pontificio, with the names of the former German bishops in the Oder-Neisse region deleted, served as an indication that the Vatican was ready to recognize the region as Polish territory and as an invitation to the government to make some concrete concessions to the Catholic Church.[36] The government soon acted. On January 20, Radio Warsaw broadcasted a very favorable commentary on the willingness of the Papacy to re-orientate itself toward the

socialist world and, then, on January 25, announced
that the government was setting in motion the
machinery to grant the Catholic Church full title
to church lands in the territory taken from Germany.[37] The bishops, meeting at the end of January,
welcomed the government's action and, in response,
called on the faithful "to fulfill their duty toward
the church in such a way as to help the fatherland
in its difficult conditions." At the same time, the
bishops commenced discussions with the government on
the full normalization of relations.[38] The bishops,
furthermore, in a letter read in every church in
Poland, called for civil concord and asked prayers
for Edward Gierek. The Pope, on February 14, requested Roman Catholics everywhere to pray for internal peace in Poland.[38] The regime appreciated
the stand of the Church and, again praised the
"positive Vatican reactions to the situation in
Poland," although its appreciation was mitigated by
criticism of its failure to name Polish "residential
ordinaries" in the Oder-Neisse territories.[39] Later
publications blamed the Vatican's reluctance on the
influence of the West German espicopate.[40] On
March 3, Premier Piotr Jaroszewicz met with Cardinal
Wyszynski for three hours and discussed, it was
reported, the problems of building permits for
churches, the promised granting to the Church the
ownership of the ecclesiastical buildings and real
estate in the former German lands, publishing an
independent church press, returning charity institutions to the church, and the reopening of the Church's
cultural and religious associations. Apparently this
meeting heralded the beginning of serious negotiations.[41] In April, the Polish Catholic press and
the Polish government press again commented favorably
about the progress of Church-State relations and the
Vatican's Ostpolitik.[42] The Vatican, withholding
the recognition of Polish boundaries until German
ratification of the Polish-German Agreement of 1970,
attempted to temper criticism by sending Cardinal
Koenig on a whirlwind tour of the Polish dioceses in
the Oder-Neisse region in April. The following month
witnessed the inception of talks between the Polish
government and the Vatican aimed at normalizing
their relations.[43] In June 23, the regime fulfilled
its January pledge and turned over to the Roman
Catholic Church full title to nearly 7,000 former
church buildings and 2,000 acres of land in the Oder-
Neisse territories. The church was generous in its
gratitude.[44] In the fall, Cardinal Wyszynski and a
number of other Polish bishops left for a Synod in

111

Rome. Radio Warsaw wished the cardinal well and hoped his participation in the bishops' conference would enhance the process of Catholic-Polish normalization. The Vatican was also praised by this and other broadcasts for its positive efforts in seeking an understanding and, in addition, for supporting the Soviet-sponsored European Security Conference.[45] In mid-October, the Vatican again won the acclaim of the Polish government by beatifying a Polish priest, Maximillian Kolbe, who died, as Radio Warsaw recorded, "a horrid martyr's death" in the Oswiecim-Auschwitz concentration camp. The government permitted a pilgrimage "of thousands" to attend the beatification ceremony in Rome.[46] Discussions on the improvement of ties switched from Rome to Warsaw with the arrival, on November 10, in Warsaw of Archbishop Casaroli, who by this time was being hailed as the Vatican's "Minister of Foreign Affairs" and, in some worldly circles, as a holy "Henry Kissinger." It was reported that the talks centered on the Vatican's ecclesiastical reorganization of the Oder-Neisse lands, the government's still prohibitive, although greatly relaxed, ban on church publications, and the Polish Church's desire to build more churches.[47]

The relaxation of tension, the mark of 1971, continued into 1972. On February 28, the government, in a major concession, ruled that the Church would no longer be required to submit reports on its income and expenditures or maintain records of its assets. Previously the Church had been forced to account for everything it owned from crucifixes to plows. The Polish hierarchy expressed its gratitude, but at the same time reiterated its previous requests that the government grant more building permits for churches. The government, for its part, demanded through the first part of the year that the Vatican make permanent the provisional ecclesiastical arrangements in the Oder-Neisse territories.[48] On June 28, the Vatican finally satisfied the demand of the Polish government and named permanent bishops (that is, changed the canonical status of the Polish Apostolic Administrators) for the Oder-Neisse region. Needless to say, the Polish government and episcopate were overwhelmingly grateful.[49] The year ended with a spate of acitivity. In early October, John Cardinal Krol of Philadelphia (a Pole) arrived in Poland to further Papal-Polish associations and, in late October, the Polish bishops asked the government to stop drafting seminarians for military service. In November, a delegation of Polish bishops, led by Cardinal Wyszynski, visited Rome to thank the Pope personally for altering the status of the Oder-Neisse dioceses. At the end of the year, the Primate declared that in 1972 there were 500 priests ordained, 2,981 students in the major diocesan seminaries, and 1,073 in the seminaries of religious orders (the largest monastic orders are the Salesians, Franciscans (Bernadines and reformed), Conventional Franciscans, Jesuits, and Capuchins). In that same year there were also 6,376 parishes, 18,151 priests, 13,392 churches and chapels, and 30,162 monks and nuns.[50]

In January 1973, the "leftist trend in the Church" was profusely commended in the monthly Polish journal, Ideologia i Polityka. From Cardinal Wyszynski's point of view, such pronouncements amounted to whistling in the wind and had no validity as either a description of Polish Church or Papal policy. However, if not reflecting reality, the description did provide insight into the government's frame of mind, assumed or real, on how the improvement of Church-State relations had to be explained. In February, the Vatican capped its process of normalizing the ecclesiastical status of the Oder-Neisse territories by naming Archbishop Boleslaw Kominek, the Wroclaw Metropolitan, a Cardinal.[51] Two problems, however, did cloud religious conditions during the year. The perennial grievance of the government refusing to grant building permits for churches agitated the Polish bishops throughout the year. Secondly, in October, the Government legislated a school reform which required busing of children from ill-equipped rural schools to the better equipped urban schools. The Catholic bishops, who agreed with the principle of the reform, opposed it however on the grounds that it was a subtle means to curb religious education by cutting the time after school available for religious instruction.[52]

Papal-Polish conversations, however, continued and, in November, the Polish Foreign Minister, Stefan Olszowski, was received at the Vatican. Radio Vatican declared that Olszowski's visit to Rome was "a kind of manifestation of respect for the Catholic community," and an important step in the normalization of Church-State relations in Poland.[53]

Archbishop Casaroli, leading a high level delegation, returned the foreign minister's visit in February 1974, and, according to Życie Warszawy, it marked another step toward world-wide détente and was a result of increasing normalization of Church-State ties in Poland. The mission included a prelate with the rank of Nuncio at the Vatican's

113

Council for Public Relations, Archbishop Luigi Poggi,
the Secretary of the Papal Commission for Public
Information, Monsignor Andre-Marie Deskur, and
Councillor of Legation of the Vatican's Council for
Public Relations, Monsignor Gabriel Montalvo. At a
dinner given in Casaroli's honor, Foreign Minister
Olszowski stated that Casaroli's visit was a part of
the general movement to find the best path toward
peace and international cooperation. Poland, he
declared, appreciated what John XXIII and Paul VI
had done toward ending conflict in the Middle East,
Vietnam, and the rest of the world. Poland had
always emphasized, the minister said, the role of
believers in implementing policy and that the normalization of Vatican-Polish relations could come about
through respect for Poland's socialist system.
Casaroli replied that the Church recognizes the need
to "seek existing covergencies, explore and foster
them, as well as to create new convergent planes."
The Church, in addition, according to the Archbishop,
had special obligations to work for peace and the
spread of truth, and justice. Following his discussions with the foreign minister, Casaroli stayed
on in Poland to meet Premier Jaroszewicz, Chairman
of the State Council Henryk Jablonski, and, eventually Cardinal Wyszynski.[54]

Poland and the Vatican seemed to be nearing the
stage of establishing diplomatic relations. When
Boleslaw Cardinal Kominek died in March, Premier
Jaroszewicz sent condolences to the Curia in Rome,
an unusual step since such messages are normally
sent only between governments having formal diplomatic relations.[55] With evidence mounting that
Rome-Warsaw ties might become formal, the Polish
bishops sought and received assurances from the Vatican that no Vatican-Polish government decisions would
be made without consulting the Polish episcopate.[56]
The Vatican's Ostpolitik with Warsaw seemed, by 1974,
to be nearing its climax. Reciprocal peregrinations
were frequent. The broader, political framework of
détente between East and West appeared irreversible
and, the Vatican's Ostpolitik seemed tied to the
forward motion which was crumbling the barriers of
the Cold War. Poland was gaining immensely, particularly in the economic field, from détente with the
West and it certainly was reasonable to hope that
economic détente would lead to a relaxation of the
ideological conflict between the East and the West,
and, in particular, between Catholicism and Communism
in Poland. But such was not the case.

As East-West economic détente evolved, the

114

Communist Polish United Workers' Party under Gierek
launched an all-out ideological offensive. In
February 1974, a new Institute for Basic Problems of
Marxism-Leninism was charged, under the leadership
of ideologist Andrezej Werblan, with the task of
developing the theory of Marxism-Leninism in Poland.
The next month, at a national gathering of ideological apparatchiks in Warsaw, Politburo member Jan
Szydlak stressed that East-West détente does not
diminish but, rather, exacerbates the ideological
struggle. He called for an intensive ideological
conflict whose objectives would be to bolster ideological bonds with the Soviet Union and to "unmask
the false image of capitalism by revealing its internal contradictions and the many manifestations of
its advancing crisis." An important element in the
campaign, was to lash out at Polish intellectuals
and the "reactionary" leadership of the Catholic
Church. Szydlak asserted that

> The main organized anti-socialist power
> in our country, a veritable center uniting
> all the anti-state currents while at the same
> time representing their last hope, is the
> reactionary wing of the Episcopate deriving
> its support from the institutional structure
> of the Roman Catholic Church. It is the
> only center of social rightist forces which
> has at its disposal a coherent philosophic
> outlook, a strong organizational base and
> numerous cadres. . . . Its political strategy
> is aimed, above all, at exploiting our
> difficulties and failures.[57]

Polish intellectuals struck back in 1974 by
raising the sensitive issue of the position of the
Poles in the Soviet Union and by demanding freedom of
religion, education, and culture for Soviet Poles.
In 1975, a letter by the popular Catholic author,
Stefan Kisielewski, published in the émigré historical journal Zeszyty Historyczne, charged that
". . . the study of recent Polish history is non-
existent. In its place there is a superficial and
one-sided compilation, artificially put together,
. . . geared to political propaganda, and exculsively
serving to mold the minds of the students in a way
desired by the party. The speciality of our system,
as Orwell envisaged it, is history in the service of
politics, adjusted and transmuted backward."[58]
The Catholic Church also retaliated. In a
series of sermons, in 1974, Cardinal Wyszynski

devastatingly fought the regime's ideological offensive.  He denounced the lack of building permits for
new churches, loyalty oaths for new priests, and the
severe taxation of the Church.  He feared that a
proposed educational reform would not allow suffi-
cient time for religious instruction.  He sharply
objected to the consolidation of all youth organizations into a unitary Union of Polish Socialist
Youth directly under the PUWP.[59]
     The cardinal also delved into politics.  He de-
clared that because of the historic role of the
Church in Polish history, it had a right to express
its opinion on critical questions affecting the
Polish people.  He demanded that the government respect basic freedoms: "A wise organization of society
precludes application everywhere of the same narrow
schemata; on the contrary, it provides the opportunity for free and unrestrained activity by
various social groups and strata. . . . This requires a courageous defense of the right to free
association as well as the rights to freedom of the
press, expression of opinion, and unrestrained
scientific research. . . ."[60]  In an ardent partiotic
sermon, the cardinal complained of the regime's
insistence that Poland's interests were identical
with those of the USSR:

> For us, next to God, our first love is
> Poland.  After God one must above all
> remain faithful to our Homeland, to the
> Polish national culture.  We will love all
> the people in the world, but only in such
> an order of priorities.
>      And if we see everywhere slogans advo-
> cating love for all the peoples and all the
> nations, we do not oppose them; yet above
> all we demand the right to live in accor-
> dance with the spirit, history, culture,
> and language of our own Polish land--the
> same which have been used by our ancestors
> for centuries.[61]

     Amidst the sparring of the regime with the
Polish Church and intellectuals, the Vatican proceeded with its Ostpolitik.  On July 5, 1974, Deputy
Foreign Minister Joszef Czyrek met with Casaroli and
they announced that the Vatican and the Polish government were establishing "permanent working contacts."  Kazimierz Szablewski was named the head of
the Polish working group and assigned to the Polish
embassy in Rome.[62]  The next year, between

116

February 25 and March 25, Archbishop Luigi Poggi, who had been named to lead the Vatican's delegation for "permanent working contacts" toured Poland and held prolonged discussions with Cardinal Wyszynski and Kazimierz Kakol, who had replaced Skarzynski as head of the office of religious affairs in May 1974. While the talks ranged from episcopal appointments to church building permits and education, no published, formal agreements were produced.[63]   It evidently, like Archbishop Casaroli's earlier sojourns, was a fact finding effort by the Vatican and a pro forma implementation of the accord on "permanent working contacts."   In July 1975, the Polish Foreign Minister, Stefan Olszowski and Mgr. Casaroli met at Helsinki during the Conference on European Security and Cooperation.[64]

Cardinal Wyszynski and the other Polish bishops had been concerned for some time that the Vatican might negotiate an agreement with the regime over their heads.[65] The Polish episcopate was entirely in favor of an understanding with the Polish government but they believed empirically that they knew church-state affairs best in Poland, at least, much better than the Vatican or the Polish Communists.  Accordingly, Cardinal Wyszynski felt obliged to prevent the Holy See from doing something which he considered stupid.  His attitude was clearly revealed, for example, at the Synod of Bishops held in Rome in October 1974, when he descended upon the head of Vatican Radio and informed him about what the radio should be broadcasting to Poland.  From the Cardinal's point of view, it was not a time for compromise with Marxism for that philosophy was bankrupt in Eastern Europe.  Instead the hour was at hand for the evangelization of Communist East Europe.[66]  In February 1974, the Pope removed Cardinal Mindszenty as Archbishop of Esztergom and declared the archdiocese vacant. Such an action appeared to those who were being persecuted in the name of Catholicism by the Communist governments of Eastern Europe a depressing indication of the Holy See's attitude to sacrifice religion to politics.  The circumstances of the Church in Poland and those in Hungary were, however, very different. Cardinal Mindszenty, honored as a martyr throughout the Catholic world, would not in any case have been allowed by the Communist government to exercise his pastoral duty in Hungary.  Throughout his long years of refuge in the American Embassy, the primatial diocese of Esztergom--in contrast to the situation in Poland--had been without an archbishop and the hierarchy of the country was disorganized.  The price

117

of securing governmental agreement to restructuring
the episcopal framework of the Church--always the
first consideration in the eyes of Rome--was to ordain bishops politically complacent to that government.  The spiritual work of politically complacent
bishops--of which there were many under the Old
Regime--is a matter of conjecture.  Fortunately, the
survival in Poland of a united and independent
episcopacy reduces the danger of such an unhappy compromise in that country.  But it would not be surprising if Cardinal Wyszynski were fortified, by the
Hungarian example, in his conclusion that it would be
dangerous to entrust the Polish Church to the diplomacy of the Vatican.
    By 1975, the polemics between the regime and
the Church and intellectuals escalated significantly.
The catalyst was the government's announcement that
it was amending the Polish constitution to enumerate,
inter alia, the "unshakable fraternal bond with the
Soviet Union," the leading position of the Communist
Party, and to make citizens' rights dependent upon
fulfillment of their duties.  The reaction to the
announcement was instantaneous.  On December 5, a
band of fifty-nine intellectuals, under the aegis of
the highly regarded economist, Professor Edward
Lipinski, petitioned the Sejm to include in the new
constitution a restoration of democratic liberties.
Invoking the Helsinki declaration on human rights, the
group requested that the constitution provide "freedom of conscience and religion, freedom to work,
freedom of expression and information, and freedom of
scholarly pursuit and learning."  Specifically, it
called for "admission of people with religious beliefs
into all state positions, independence for the trade
unions, the abolition of censorship, and autonomy
for the universities."[67]
    This petition was soon followed by countless
others from a broad spectrum of Polish life.  Protests were organized against the inclusion of the
regime's various amendments.  In January 1976, Cardinal Wyszynski endorsed the dissenters and in three
sermons in Warsaw complained vigorously against the
projected constitutional amendments.
    The authorities, shocked by the vigor of the
protests, watered down the new amendments to the
point where a virtual status quo was maintained, but
even then, Professor Stanislaw Stomma, the head of
the Catholic Znak group, abstained from voting when
the modified amendments were presented to the Sejm
for approval on February 10.  The Communists retaliated by conspicuously deleting his name from the

118

roster of candidates for the new parliament and, additionally, by taking administrative measures against some of the petitioners.

The retributory tactics of the regime negated its compromise on the constitutional amendments and further inflamed the opposition. In April 1976, the Polish bishops, in a strongly worded communiqué, which referred to the Helsinki Final Act, called for respect for the principle of national self-determination and human rights. It also cautioned the authorities against using administrative measures against the signatories of the various petitions.[68] More protests followed and the air in Poland was unsettling and rife with passion.

In this atmosphere, the regime, like Gomulka's in 1970, peremptorily and tactlessly raised food prices in June 1976. That development considerably deepened the political crisis in Poland by bringing the workers actively to the side of the intellectuals and the Church. Even more importantly, Gierek's credibility as a man who had pledged "constant, genuine dialogue with the people" was impaired irretrievably.[69] The riots and strikes which followed the increase in food prices simmered on despite the fact that the government at once cancelled the increases. Many of the strikers were jailed and dubbed "troublemakers" by the authorities. Twelve were imprisoned for up to five years. The Catholic Church and Poland's best-known writers and academics came to the defense of the workers and, by Christmas, the demonstrators were free. The intellectuals formed a "defense committee" for the workers and warned the regime that the only alternative to a more open society was violent demonstration. Cardinal Wyszynski pointed incisively to the anomaly of workers having to struggle for their rights against a workers' government.[70]

Against the background of rising tension, Ostpolitik pushed forward.[71] On February 9, 1976, Kazimierz Kakol received Archbishop Luigi Poggi and discussed "many problems of interest to both sides." On February 16, Foreign Minister Olszowski met with the archbishop.[72] At a meeting of the Polish Bishops' Conference in late April, Mgr. Poggi heard that the Church "urgently needed" about 500 churches and chapels, but that the authorities refused to grant building permits.[73] In June, Cardinal Wyszynski assailed forced work on Sunday. In late November, the Polish Primate detailed in a pastoral letter the threats which the Church faced in Poland. He discussed at length the problems of atheistic

119

propaganda, building permits for churches, and discrimination against believers in work and school.
He announced that "the hateful, ruthless campaign
against God's faith and the Church of Christ has not
abated."[74] In February 1977, the Polish bishops
denounced "unidentified persons" for putting out
forged sermons which undermined "the clear and clean
Catholic and social views of the Primate."[75]

Archbishop Poggi returned to Poland in March
1977, and met with Kazimierz Kakol and the new Polish
foreign minister, Emil Wojtaszek.[76] In July, Cardinal Karol Wojtyla objected to Sunday as a day of
work and Cardinal Wyszynski complained about the dem-
olition of chapels, theatrical productions in which
the Eucharest and Christian marriage were mocked, and
the general attitude of the communications media,
which were becoming increasingly hostile to the
Church.[77] On October 29, Edward Gierek and Cardinal
Wyszynski met and exchanged views "on the most important problems of the nation and the Church." The
Cardinal said the meeting "was dictated by the conscience of a Bishop and a Pole. It came about after
many years of reflection during which the needs and
interests of the Polish nation have always been
taken into consideration."[78] In mid-November,
Cardinal Wyszynski visited the Vatican and informed
the Pope that the Church's unity and vitality in
Poland were strong. He particularly stressed the
Church's influence with the farmers, with the
workers, and with the intellectuals who were now
viewing the Church "as a protector of national cultural values."[79]

Attesting to the strength of the Church in Poland was Edward Gierek who arrived at the Vatican
on December 1. He praised the policy of Ostpolitik
and announced that there was an "absence of conflict
between the Church and State" in Poland. The Pope,
in turn, commended the vitality of Catholicism in
Poland and declared that "the Catholic Church is not
asking for privileges for itself, but only for the
right to remain itself, and to be able to develop
freely its proper activities in accordance with its
substance and mission."[80] On December 4, in a pastoral letter, the Polish bishops decried the government's continuing "campaign of atheism and godless-
ness."[81]

At the beginning of the new year, Cardinal
Wyszynski criticized government censorship and called
for greater freedom of the press so that the Polish
nation "could have an authenic Catholic press."[82]
In March 1978, Polityka, a Warsaw weekly, praised

120

the Vatican's Ostpolitik and concluded that "the change in the Vatican doctrine has been prompted by the growing influence of communist and socialist ideas on the consciousness of the masses, both in the highly developed capitalist states and in the third world countries." Of course, though, the journal went on, "co-operation between Marxists and the Catholics cannot mean blurring ideological differences between the two outlooks."[83] Another Warsaw weekly, Kultura, praised the Vatican's policies but emphasized that where the philosophy of life is concerned, there is no possibility of concord and understanding between Catholics and Marxists.[84]

The Polish bishops in May released a document to the foreign press correspondents in Poland which denounced the government's limitation on the number of religious books published. According to the bishops, in 1977, only 300,000 copies of the catechism were published, one copy for twenty-six children.[85] In early May, Cardinal Wyszynski approved of the efforts to improve Church-State relations, but emphasized that "the cornerstone of a healthy normalization of relations must be the recognition of the public and legal character of the Church."[86] In June, the Cardinal declared that "the Church must enjoy full interior freedom." He particularly stressed that the Church must never allow the government to interfere in the choice and education of seminarians and in the assigning of priests to Church posts. The government tried to dictate to the Church, the Cardinal went on, but "little by little" it realized "that the Church will not give in."[87]

Poland is on the threshold of major change. The "vertigo of possibilities," to borrow from Kierkagaard, stems from the specter of Soviet intervention to the emergence of a "liberal conscience" that has united intellectuals, churchmen, and workers. The Catholic Church has never had more influence in Communist Poland than it has today, because its efforts and ideas are attuned to the interests of the Polish people.

Because of the Church's preeminence, it follows that the regime's interest in accommodation with the Vatican is greater than ever. It would dearly value any lever over the Polish Church. At the moment (1978), the Papacy's relations with the Polish regime have stabilized. Certainly the explosive events of 1976 urged upon the Vatican a cautious approach and possibly opened the eyes of Papal diplomats to

121

the real nature of Church-State relations in Poland.
At any rate, the stabilization diminishes the possibility of Papal Ostpolitik becoming a trojan horse
in Poland.

NOTES

1.   Radio Vatican, January 2, February 12, 13,
1971; Radio Warsaw, February 11, 1971; New York Times,
January 30, February 15, 1971.
2.   Elizabeth Valkenier, "The Catholic Church in
Communist Poland, 1945-1955," The Review of Politics
8 (July 1956): 305. Also see Edward D. Wynot, "The
Catholic Church and the Polish State, 1935-1939," The
Journal of Church and State 15 (1973): 223-40.
3.   For an excellent evaluation of the Party and
recent Polish history, see M.K. Dziewanowski, The
Communist Party of Poland  (Cambridge, Mass., 2nd ed:
1976).
4.   Ibid., pp. 306-7;   Edward Dolan, "Post-War
Poland and the Church," The American Slavic and East
European Review (1955); 84-85.
5.   For details on the Concordat, see Markiewicz,
Kościół, pp. 20-21.
6.   Valkenier, "Church in Poland," pp. 306-7;
Dolan, "Post-War Poland," pp. 84-85;   Markiewicz,
Kościół, pp. 22-28.
7.   Valkenier, "Church in Poland," pp. 307-8.
For a biography of Piasecki, see Lucian Blit, The
Eastern Pretender  (London, 1965);   Also see
Hansjakob Stehle, The Independent Satellite:  Society
and Politics in Poland Since 1945  (New York, 1965),
p. 108.  For the positions of the Pax Society, see
Boleslaw Piasecki, Zagadnienia istotne  (Warsaw,
1945), Patriotyzm polski  (Warsaw, 1958).
8.   Valkenier, "Church in Poland," pp. 314-15;
Frank Dinka, "Sources of Conflict Between Church and
State in Poland," The Review of Politics 28 (July
1966): 338.
9.   Stanislaw Staron, "State-Church Relations in
Poland," World Politics 21 (July 1969): 591;
Valkenier, "Church in Poland," pp. 322-23;   Stehle,
Independent Satellite, pp. 90-91.   In 1975 and 1976,
the bishops bitterly complained about government interference in the Church's higher educational system
and demanded accreditation for the non-university
Papal Theological faculties, especially in Cracow.
See Radio Vatican, May 2, April 29, 1975;   Radio
Vatican, October 11, 1976.
10.   Staron, "State-Church Relations," p. 593.
11.   Ibid., p. 591;   Cf. Stehle, Independent

<u>Satellite</u>, pp. 90-91.
12. Staron, "State-Church Relations," pp. 583-584; Adam Bromke, <u>Poland's Politics: Idealism vs. Realism</u> (Cambridge, Mass.: 1967), pp. 247-48. On the Church's reaction to <u>Znak</u> Group as well as the <u>Pax</u> Society, see Ludwik Dembinski, "The Catholics and Politics in Poland," <u>Canadian Slavonic Papers</u> 15 (1973): 176-83.
13. Staron, "State-Church Relations," p. 588.
14. Ibid., p. 591. Cf. Stanislaw Markiewicz, <u>Panstwo i Kościól w okresie dwudziestolecia Polski Ludowej</u> (Warsaw: 1965), p. 51.
15. Staron, "State-Church Relations," p. 588, 596-97.
16. Polish Press Agency, January 19, 1978, and April 20, 1976; Radio Vatican, December 14, 1976, March 21, 1978, April 17, 1978.
17. <u>New York Times</u>, April 30, 1963.
18. <u>The Observer</u>, May 5, 1963.
19. <u>Ibid.</u>, May 10, July 6, 8, August 9, 16, 27, September 15, October 26, November 3, 1973; <u>l'Osservatore Romano</u>, July 19, 1963; Radio Vatican, August 1, 1963.
20. <u>New York Times</u>, May 4, 1964.
21. <u>Ibid.</u>, August 27, 30, 1964.
22. Ibid., December 26, 1964.
23. Ibid., November 16, 1964.
24. Staron, "State-Church Relations," p. 595. Cf. M. Czerski and A. Walicki, eds., <u>Dialog episkopatow Polski i Niemiec</u> (London: 1966), pp. 5-7.
25. <u>Trybuna Ludu</u>, April 14, 1966; <u>The Times</u> (London), April 15, 1966. Henryk Korotynski, "Church and State in Poland," <u>New Times</u>, No. 36 (September 7, 1966), pp. 14-16.
26. <u>The Times</u> (London), April 15, 1966.
27. Staron, "State-Church Relations,: p. 595.
28. Walf, "The Vatican's Eastern Policy," p. 420; Jan Nowak, "New Thaw in Church-State Relations in Poland," <u>East Europe</u> (February 1969), p. 11.
29. <u>New York Times</u>, May 28, June 4, 1967.
30. <u>Ibid.</u>, December 26, 1967.
31. Ibid., February 2, November 5, 1968; <u>l'Osservatore Romano</u>, February 8, 1968.
32. <u>New York Times</u>, June 6, October 8, 1969; Walf, "The Vatican's Eastern Policy," p. 420.
33. <u>New York Times</u>, December 24, 1970.
34. <u>Ibid.</u>, December 26, 1970.
35. "Current Developments in Poland," <u>East Europe</u> 20 (February 1971): 45.
36. Radio Vatican, January 1, 4, 6, 8, 1971.

Cf. Slowo Powszechne, January 6, 1971; Zychie
Warszawy, February 2, 1971.
37. Radio Warsaw, January 20, 30, 1971; New
York Times, January 26, 1971. Commentary in Slowo
Powszechne, February 11, 1971. Also see Adam Bromke,
"Poland Under Gierek: A New Political Style,"
Problems of Communism (September-October 1972),
pp. 1-19.
38. Radio Vatican, January 2, 1971; Radio
Warsaw, February 11, 1971; New York Times, January
30, 1971.
39. Radio Vatican, February 12, 1977; New
York Times, February 15, 1971.
40. Radio Warsaw, February 25, March 13,
April 6, 1971.
41. Radio Warsaw, March 3, 5, 1971; New York
Times, March 4, 6, 1971. Commentary on general
problems in Kierunki, March 5, 1971; Slowo Powszechne,
February 2, 11, 1971; Gazeta Posnanska, September 24,
1971.
42. Radio Warsaw, April 10, 14, 28, 1971.
Cf. Slowo Powszechne, April 10, 1971.
43. Slowo Powszechne, April 28, 1971; Zycie
Warszawy, May 16, 1971; Radio Warsaw, April 27, 28,
May 3, 16, 1971; New York Times, May 3, 5, 1971.
44. Radio Warsaw, June 26, 29, 1971; New York
Times, June 24, 1971.
45. Radio Vatican, September 14, 1971; Radio
Warsaw, September 21, 24, 29, October 2, 4, 6, 1971;
Zycie Warszawy, October 2, 1971.
46. Radio Warsaw, September 24, 1971, October
13, 14, 1971; New York Times, November 11, 1971;
Slowo Powszechne, October 15, 1971.
47. Radio Warsaw, November 19, 1971; Radio
Belgrade, November 11, 1971; Radio Tirana, November
22, 1971; New York Times, November 11, 18, 21, 1971.
48. Radio Warsaw, February 8, 10, 12, 15,
March 4, 7, 30, 1972, June 5, 7, 16, 1972; Radio
Vatican, February 12, May 9, 1972. Cf. Slowo
Powszechne, March 4, 1972.
49. Radio Warsaw, June 28, July 7, 10, November
7, 1972; Radio Vatican, June 29, July 5, September
16, 1972; New York Times, June 29, 1972; Polityka,
July 8, 1972; Tygodnik Powszechny, July 9, 1972;
Markiewicz, Kościół, pp. 77-80; Maciej Wrzeszczm
"Ważny krok na drodze normalizaciji," Zycie i myśl
24 (Warsaw, 1974): 5.
50. Radio Vatican, November 7, 1972, December
29, 1972; Radio Warsaw, October 8, 12, November 9,
December 4-6, 1972; New York Times, September 8,
November 3, 8, 1972; Trevor Beeson, Discretion and

124

Valour (London: 1974), p. 137.
    51. Markiewicz, Kościół, p. 89.
    52. "Poland: Chilled Coexistence," Christian-
ity Today, September 20, 1973, pp. 54-55; Radio
Warsaw, January 4, February 2, 6, 8, April 3, 6,
June 30, July 31, October 15, 24, 1973; Radio Vati-
can, April 3, October 25, 1973.
    53. Christian Science Monitor, November 28,
1973; Radio Warsaw, December 7, 1973; Radio Vatican,
February 18, 1974.
    54. Zycie Warszawy, February 3, 1974; Radio
Warsaw, February 3, 1974; Radio Vatican, February 5,
1974.
    55. New York Times, May 4, 1974.
    56. Ibid.
    57. Adam Bromke, "A New Juncture in Poland,"
Problems of Communism (September-October 1976),
pp. 9-10.
    58. Ibid., pp. 10-11.
    59. Ibid., p. 11; Radio Vatican, March 31,
June 5, 1974.
    60. Bromke, "New Juncture," p. 11.
    61. Ibid., pp. 11-12.
    62. New York Times, July 7, 1974; Radio
Warsaw, September 24, 1974.
    63. The Tablet (London), June 21, 1975, p. 573.
    64. Markiewicz, Kościół, pp. 97-99; Polish
Press Agency, July 31, 1975.
    65. New York Times, June 9, 1975.
    66. Ibid., October 2, 1974.
    67. Bromke, "New Juncture," p. 12.
    68. Ibid., pp. 12-13.
    69. Ibid.; The Christian Science Monitor,
December 20, 1976.
    70. The Christian Science Monitor, December 20,
1976, and January 27, 1977; Radio Vatican, Septem-
ber 27, 1976, August 27, 1976, September 15, 1976.
    71. For a good chronology, see Rudolf Buchala,
"Wydarzenia zwiazane z polityka wschodnia Stolicy
Apostolskiej: Kalendarium za lata 1975-77,"
Chrześcijanin w świecje, No. 61 (Warsaw: January
1978), pp. 21-41.
    72. Radio Warsaw, February 9, 16, 1976; War-
saw T.V., April 30, 1076; Polish Press Agency,
May 18, 1976.
    73. Radio Vatican, Mau 1, 1976.
    74. Ibid., June 16, November 27, 1976.
    75. Polish Press Agency, February 23, 1977.
    76. Warsaw T.V., March 7, 1977.
    77. Radio Vatican, July 10, 12, 1977.
    78. Radio Warsaw, October 29, 1977; Radio

Vatican, November 7, 1977.
    79.  Radio Vatican, November 12, 1977.
    80.  Polish Press Agency, December 1, 1977;
Radio Warsaw, December 1, 1977, November 28, 30, 1977;
Radio Vatican, December 1, 1977.
    81.  Radio Vatican, December 4, 1977.
    82.  Ibid., January 7, 1978, February 5, 1978.
    83.  Polish Press Agency, March 27, 1978.
    84.  Ibid., April 23, 1978.
    85.  Radio Vatican, May 4, 1978.
    86.  Ibid., May 8, 1978.
    87.  Our Sunday Visitor (U.S.A.), July 2, 1978.

# 6. Hungary: Victim or Beneficiary of Ostpolitik?

The travails of Jozsef Cardinal Mindszenty, the late leader of Hungarian Catholicism, reflected in many ways the experience of the Hungarian Catholic Church and the Hungarian nation from the end of the Second World War to this day, so it is right to begin this chapter with an assessment of Mindszenty's role. Although the Roman Catholic Church numerically constituted only 68% of the population, Mindszenty became a symbol of the Hungarian people, a fountain of Hungarian nationalism. Additionally, he was a hero for millions of people in Western countries. He was viewed as a courageous and unbending opponent of Communism and Communist dictatorship, a man who unflinchingly defended Catholicism and Hungarian tradition against religious persecution and Soviet imperialism. He was lauded by the Vatican and heralded by Western intellectuals.[1] On May 6, 1975, Cardinal Mindszenty died in Vienna, a lonely old man, estranged from his archepiscopal see, deserted by the Vatican, and criticized by not a few Western commentators. Many obituaries and review articles were, although distantly sympathetic to his agonies, rather disapproving and critical. George Schöpflin, for example, writing a eulogistic review of Mindszenty's Memoirs, claimed that the Cardinal was a man of principle, of courage, and one who suffered hideously at the hands of the Communists but, "in the final analysis, he achieved nothing."[2] He was accused roundly of being out of step with the times. Hungary after the Second World War had changed and, so the argument went, the Cardinal had not--he was still attempting, even up to his death, to revive in Hungary a socio-political-economic order that was passé.

Though Cardinal Mindszenty is often represented by foreign commentators in the West as a defender of

the old regime, he was in fact a consistent defender
of human rights and liberties, both against the
Nazi and Communist tyrannies.  No doubt he would have
preferred recognition by the State of the Church,
established as it used to be, with control of education and mandatory religious instruction and extensive land ownership in order to fulfill the charitable
and social functions performed in most Western
countries by the civil authorities.[3]  Such conservative views were little regarded during the 1950s and
1960s because of his heroic stand at his trial and
in the Hungarian national rising.  After he had
been removed from Hungary on September 28, 1971, he
was no longer a David challenging Goliath and he was
suddenly found by enlightened writers to be an anachronism not only because of détente but because of
his traditional views.  Thus, in retrospect, he
could be dismissed as a "gallant but misguided
Cardinal,"[4] or as a myopic reactionary who "failed to
recognize that the great mass of the Hungarian people
supported radical changes in 1945 and that there
could be no return to the pre-1945 political order."[5]
     The implication of such summaries, intended or
not, is that the Communists were well guided, if not
gallant, and that they were in step with the great
majority of the Hungarian people.[6]  It is quite true
that the Communists, when they came to power, supported necessary land reform.  That was an improvement and a needed one.  On the other hand, the
Communists worked diligently to suppress the budding
seeds of democracy and establish a dictatorship.
That also was an alteration, but was it needed?
Change is not good in and of itself--it can be beneficial, harmful, or neutral.  The fact that the cardinal often opposed change is not enough to justify
the charge that he "achieved nothing" by opposing
the Communist government of Hungary, though some of
the cardinal's positions were certainly ill-founded.
Mindszenty took his stand on moral principle.  Leninist Communism may eventually evolve into something
different.  Or it may not.  If we do not know the
answer, still less could Mindszenty know it thirty
years ago.  It is true that Leninist Communists rule
in a number of countries and it is necessary for
statesmen in the West to come to terms with that
fact.  That is a valid argument for détente but that
was not the question before Mindszenty.  Was the
Communist philosophy and practice in the form presented in Hungary after the Second World War com-
patible with the moral values in which Mindszenty
believed?

Mindszenty held that a philosophy and a leadership which suppress dissent, political or religious,
as a core doctrine can never be reconciled--no matter
how many rationalizations are marshalled--with the
Western tradition of freedom. Mindszenty, in the
final analysis, was a man of the Western tradition.
He might have felt more comfortable--and this is not
that clear--with the Hapsburg tradition, but that was
not alien to Western civilization. Gregor Mendel
was a citizen of the Dual Monarchy and no one would
argue that he was outside the mainstream of Western
culture. Mindszenty was not an autocrat. He favored
a multi-party system and he felt that Catholic-
Christian parties had a vital role to play in Hungary's political life.[7] He did not oppose the idea
of land reform, but rather that it was imposed by the
Soviets and especially that it "removed the material
basis that supported many ecclesiastical institutions."[8] From the cardinal's point of view, Christianity was an inseparable part of the Hungarian
nation and could not be denied a role in Hungarian
society. The cardinal's point that Hungary was not
yet ready for radical change could have very well
been right in the same sense that Solzhenitsyn and
some of the Russian intelligentsia assert that the
Soviet Union is not prepared today for such dramatic changes as democratic government.[9] At any rate,
it was obvious to him and to any informed observer
that the Communists implemented reforms involving
the Church not because they were advocates of liber-
alism but because such measures served as a convenient
pretext to strangle the Church. Mindszenty believed
in the supremacy of the spirit over matter. He held
to the value and uniqueness of man. He was committed
totally to a unitary and integral world view that
embraced all aspects of life and death. He believed,
in short, in God. His personality often led him to
take adamant, politically naïve, and sometimes un-
reasonable stands--all of which could be and were
exploited by his opponents to discredit him. But his
motives were above reproach. George Schöpflin reasoned that Mindszenty must be weighed on the scale
of history and, then, from the vantage point of six
or seven months after his death, concluded that "ultimately, history dealt harshly with Cardinal Mindszenty, for he seemed too often to be the wrong
person at the wrong time, and his courage had few
tangible results."[10] It is premature, of course, to
make an historical evaluation. But, what can be said
is that history, like man, has a moral dimension.
Mindszenty took his stand, at times too rigidly and

without tact, but always with a sense of moral recti-
tude judged, by the light of history, to be protec-
tive of western mankind's heritage of freedom and of
the value of knowledge.

The heritage of Mindszenty hangs heavily upon
Hungary and upon the Vatican's policy of compromise
with Communist governments. It is against his experience that the contemporary position of Hungarian
Catholicism must be balanced and the Papacy's Ostpolitik, at least in the case of Hungary, must be
evaluated.

Before World War II, the Hungarian Catholic
Church was a potent political, economic, and social
force, as indeed, in its own way, was Hungarian Pro-
testantism. It was not as influential as the
Catholic Church in Poland, but it was the faith, at
least in name, of 68% of the population and it did
have national roots. Catholic bishops were not only
sheperds of souls but powerful public figures and,
by law, ex officio members of the Upper House. The
Church published an array of newspapers and journals
and owned or had a direct interest in several publishing houses. A number of political parties, trade
unions, and charitable associations also had a direct
affiliation with the Church. The Catholic Church
ran almost half of all the educational institutions
in Hungary while the other Christian churches controlled the rest with a few exceptions.[11] The Church
owned a good deal of land (including vineyards) and
many other tangible assets.[12] While, as indicated
earlier, it was a traditional backbone of the established order, the Church was not an opponent of in-
novation and, actually, in the 1930s, created the
gigantic Catholic Agrarian Youth League (KALOT) which
argued for a number of major reforms, including land
reform.[13]

The war did not diminish the Church's influence
in Hungary but, if anything, increased it as a protector of traditional values against the dehumani-
zing tendencies of both Nazism and Communism. During
the conflict, the Church stood against the Hungarian
government's extreme policies of the Right and when
the Germans set up the Arrow Cross government in
October 1944, the Church refused to cooperate and
patently instigated opposition. The Prince Primate,
Justinian Cardinal Seredi, actually endorsed the widespread underground Catholic resistance to Szalazi's
regime. Despite the fact that the Hungarian government joined the Nazi forces in the war, the Church
could not be compromised as pro-Nazi by the Communists and was, in fact, clearly one of the principal

130

institutions offering both moral and political defiance to Nazism.

With the conclusion of the war, the Communists initially avoided drastic measures to reduce the Church's status.[14] Land reform was undertaken early in 1945 and that was a severe economic blow for the Church, since it meant wholesale confiscation. But for the most part, the Communists were more preoccupied with fashioning a popular political base than with oppressing religion. In pursuit of that goal, the Soviets allowed, in a gross miscalculation of Communist support, free elections to be held in October 1945. The elections produced a republic and a coalition government under the leadership of the Small Farmers' Party and headed by Zoltan Tildy and Ferenc Nagy. The Communists, to their dismay and embarrassment, received only seven per cent of the vote. With the Red Army in occupation, there was little doubt who was the master in Hungary, but the electoral defeat and the confidence which allowed it explain, in part, why the Communist Party was not concentrating on the Catholic Church. Catholics were permitted, in 1945, to organize their own political party, the Christian Democratic People's Party led by Count Joszef Palffy.[15] Two small weekly Catholic newspapers also came out at the same time. The authorities did not interfere with religious worship, the duties of the clergy, or the publication of pastoral letters.[16] With the death of Cardinal Seredi in March 1945, there was no effort to impede the appointment of Jozsef Mindszenty as his successor or to curb the new Primate's extensive influence.[17]

The relationship between the Communists and the Church, however, was not without its strains. In March 1945, the Apostolic Nuncio was expelled, but that action had to be viewed in the context of the expulsion of all foreign delegates.[18] In addition, in 1945, the Communist authorities undertook major land reforms and decided, as described earlier, to include the property of the Catholic Church. The Church's efforts to prevent it proved futile.[19]

In 1946, recovering from their electoral faux pas, the Communists moved against their political opponents and the Church. Catholic associations were derided in the Communist press and accused of conspiracy against the Red Army and the "new democratic order."[20] By the end of the year, about 4,000 Catholic associations, including the large Catholic youth organization, were forcibly dissolved and the entire Catholic lay movement was destroyed.[21]

131

In the following year, after pressuring the Small
Farmers' Party out of power, the Communists took
control of the Church's huge charitable enterprise,
Kartasz (Caritas).[22] With the Communists firmly
entrenched in power by the end of 1947, the result
of the free election of 1946 was undone and the voice
of the Hungarian people stifled, not to be heard
again until the fateful days of October 1956. A
forbidding future awaited the Church.

Nationalization of Catholic schools overshadowed,
in 1948, all other issues in the Catholic-Communist
contest. In early spring, the government made clear
its intention to nationalize Catholic schools and precipitated strenuous opposition from Cardinal Mindszenty, lay Catholics, and the Vatican. Bloody
clashes between Catholics and the authorities en-
sued.[23] Nonetheless, on June 16, the Hungarian
Parliament ratified a bill nationalizing confessional
and private schools and all hostels and kindergartens
related to them. The Catholic Church lost all of
its 1,216 primary schools (six grades), 1,669 general schools (eight grades), eighty-six high schools,
forty-nine gymnasia, thirty-two teacher training
schools, and its other educational enterprises.[24]
Cardinal Mindszenty protested by having church bells
tolled throughout the country on June 18 and, then,
on July 3, excommunicated all Catholic deputies in
the Parliament who had supported the nationalization
program.[25] All Catholics who backed the plan were
also excommunicated. The Cardinal urged Catholic
instructors to demur from teaching and simultaneously
ordered parents to continue religious instruction at
home.[26] The government retaliated by arresting a
number of Catholic priests, including Rev. Edmund
Lenard, the Secretary of Catholic Action. They
were charged with involvement in an alleged Vatican-
United States plot against the government.[27] The
Secretary of the Hungarian Woman's Catholic Action,
Mercedes Sprenger, was also detained without an
explanation.[28] Other incarcerations followed, culminating in Mindszenty's arrest on December 27. The
Vatican denounced the detention and demanded that
the government publish its "evidence" of Cardinal
Mindszenty's alleged involvement in "high treason,
espionage, illegal dealings in foreign exchange, and
other crimes aimed at the overthrow of the Republic."[29] The Pope excommunicated all Catholics who
participated in the arrest of the cardinal. At the
same time, the Vatican initiated a wide-ranging
publicity campaign to disparage the police regime of
Hungary and to win support for the beleaguered

cardinal.[30]   The government accused the Pope of
attempting to overthrow the Hungarian regime.[31]
     On February 3, Mindszenty's trial began.   He was
found guilty of all the crimes mentioned above.   The
Cardinal later claimed that the charges and the trial
were complete travesties and that he was beaten and
tortured extensively during his imprisonment before
the trial.   He was sentenced to life imprisonment.[32]
The Vatican derided the trial as a farce and the
punishment as a miscarriage of justice.   It directed
the Hungarian people to remain steadfast in the face
of such adversity.[33]
     With the removal of Cardinal Mindszenty, the
regime moved quickly to make further inroads against
the Church.   Religious instruction in schools became
optional on September 3, 1949, and complicated administrative regulations and extensive pressure on
parents reduced the number of children receiving
religious instruction in school to only 11% by
1952.[34]   An accord was foisted on the Hungarian
bishops on August 29, 1950, by which they agreed to
the new political and educational status quo.   Eight
gymnasia were returned to the Catholic Church and,
up to the present, the administration of these
schools is the only legal function of the Catholic
orders in Hungary, though in January 1975, the
Kadar government allowed a certain amount of religious instruction in primary schools.[35]   Like the
Catholic schools, seminaries and theological academies were also dealt with harshly.   From thirteen
seminaries and nine theological academies of the
religious orders in 1948, there were only six seminaries left in 1965, and the number of students declined from 1,079 in 1948 to 303 in 1965.   Today
there is a severe shortage of priests.[36]
     In May 1951, a State Office for Church Affairs,
modeled after the Soviet Union's Council for Religious Affairs, was created with full powers over all
church institutions and personnel.   Priests and bishops were now virtually made employees of the state
and all received salaries.[37]   Archbishop Jozsef
Grosz, the leading bishop during the Primate's imprisonment and a man much more inclined to negotiate
with the Communists than Mindszenty, was arrested
and sentenced to fifteen years imprisonment in 1951.
He was released in 1956, and became chairman of the
Bench of Bishops until his death in 1961.   No matter
what attitude the Church adopted--Mindszenty's ob-
stinacy or Grosz's flexibility--, the Communists
would be content only with its obliteration as a
political, social, and cultural force.   Miklos Věto,

a keen observer of East European affairs, makes the
point that Communist religious policies in East
Europe were determined not by the attitude of ecclesiastical leaders but rather "by the particular needs
of the regime and the extent of the Church's influence among the masses."[38]  Beginning in 1951, the
main tool of subversion within the Church became the
"Peace Movement of the Clergy" which had been founded
by a number of priests who wanted to prove their
loyalty to the Communist regime and to encourage their
fellow clerics to do likewise.  The movement, needless to say, received the enthusiastic endorsement of
the authorities.[39]

From 1951 until the Revolution of 1956, the
Catholic Church remained repressed, bludgeoned into
subservience and silence.  Even during the de-Stalinization period, during the governments of Imre Nagy
(1953-55) and Matyas Rakosi (1955-56), when religious
persecution was eased in other parts of East Europe,
priests continued to be arrested in large numbers.[40]
Then came the national rising in October 1956.  Cardinal Mindszenty was freed from prison and the Catholic Church, along with the other Hungarian Churches,
attempted to regain their lost rights.  The Church,
however, played hardly any role in the uprising and
Mindszenty did not directly intervene in the political developments.  His two radio broadcasts were
singularly free of criticism of the socialist order.[41]

Soviet tanks soon crumbled into rubble the
Church's dream of regaining its freedom.  As the
rebellion was repressed, Cardinal Mindszenty sought
and received asylum in the American Legation in
Budapest, a fatal mistake in retrospect since it removed him from the mainstream of Hungarian society.
The Communists soon reasserted their control over
the churches.  The collaborationist priests and members of the Communist sponsored "Peace Movement of
the Clergy," who had been removed from positions of
authority by Cardinal Mindszenty during the revolution, were reconfirmed.  The State Office for Church
Affairs reclaimed its authority and stated that it
"would take under its protection those priests who
have been relieved of their duties because of their
progressive views."[42]  In March 1957, the Presiden-
tial Council decreed that all church appointments
made since October 1, 1956 were in effect voided and
ruled that all future appointments were contingent
upon state approval.  In subsequent months, scores
of clerics and ministers were detained and charged
with "counter-revolution" and many others were

expelled from their offices and replaced by the clerical fellow travelers, the "peace priests." Pius XII, in September 1957, ordered, under the threat of excommunication, all clerics to desist from political activity. The regime accused the Vatican of interference in its domestic affairs and not only demanded that three well known "Peace priests" take seats in Parliament, but accorded them high honors. The Papal excommunication was flouted by the government and the three priests persisted in saying Mass and dispensing the sacraments.[43]

With the campaign to reimpose government leverage over church administration and personnel, there commenced a determined propaganda campaign to replace religious beliefs with atheism. Registration for religious education, which had risen after the revolution to eighty and ninety per cent of the students in the elementary and high schools, was soon cut, through the intimidation of parents and pupils and administrative chicanery, to less than ten per cent. According to Professor Leslie Laszlo, "by 1960 the pre-revolutionary status quo was fully restored, the Churches were reduced once again to impotence and subservience vis-à-vis the Government."[44] The ecclesiastical policies of Janos Kadar, the new leader of the Hungarian Communist Party following the revolution, seemed identical to those of his predecessor, Matyas Rakosi.

However, while not amending the 1950 "agreement," which legalized the subservience of the Church in return for assurances of financial support and freedom for religious worship, Kadar began in 1961 to pursue moderate "centrist" policies. He was undoubtedly convinced that the regime had to obtain some popular support if it wished to avert another 1956. The Communist power in 1961 was secure but it was founded upon the Red Army. That condition had to be modified. Accordingly, a series of directives and policies which obviously courted popular acceptance, in both the ideological and economic realms, were implemented. "Whoever is not against us is with us" became the famous Kadar slogan reflecting the government's new pragmatism.

A major element in the novel approach was a determination to reach a modus vivendi with the Papacy. The motivation in this regard assuredly went well beyond that of a government attempting to gain popular support. The regime also certainly hoped that rapprochement with the Vatican would lead it to sanction, either de facto or de jure, the total subservience of the Church in Hungary, and to

135

remove Cardinal Mindszenty, the traditional leader of
Hungarian Catholicism, or at least treat him as a
reactionary and an anachronism, and, finally, would
give the Kadar regime legitimacy and respectability.
From this point of view, the ultimate aim of Kadar's
new flexibility toward the Vatican could be interpreted as a sophisticated tactic further to weaken
and control the Church.

The policy to find a new relationship with the
Vatican got under way simultaneously with Khrushchev's
démarche. The regime permitted two Hungarian bishops,
five priests and two lay Catholics to attend the
first session of the Second Vatican Council in
October 1962.[45] Shortly thereafter, Cardinal Koenig
and Monsignor Casaroli arrived in Budapest at the
government's invitation. Koenig's primary role
appeared to be an attempt to convince Cardinal Mindszenty that it was now time for him to leave Hungary.
If that was Koenig's purpose, the Hungarian Cardinal
was unresponsive. Casaroli conferred also with
Cardinal Mindszenty as well as with various government officials. It was clear that both the Vatican
and the Communist authorities agreed that antecedent
to good relations, something would have to be done
with Cardinal Mindszenty, and probably he would have
to be removed from Hungarian soil. The Vatican
may have decided that Hungary should be a test case
for its own new policy of Ostpolitik; it wanted
some agreement to break the ice and to demonstrate
to the regimes in the Soviet orbit that it no longer
anathemized them. If that was so, Hungary was an
unfortunate choice for the experiment. Already the
Church was totally under the regime's thumb and it
was transparent that the government would not alter
this fact. Thus, the Vatican a priori had not only
to accept but to approve, tacitly at least, the
enslavement of the Hungarian Catholic Church. Secondly, because the leadership of the Church was a
virtual tool of the government, the true opinion of
Hungary's Catholics could not be heard at the
negotiating table. The Vatican would have to strike
a bargain over the heads of Hungary's Catholics.
Mindszenty and everything he stood for would have
to be jettisoned. Mindszenty was a symbol, an em-
bodiment of Hungary's perservering spirit in the face
of religious and political persecution.

Be that as it may, on September 15, 1964,
Monsignor Casaroli and Jozsef Prantner, Chairman of
the State Office for Church Affairs, signed a partial
Church-State agreement which contained two major
documents.[46] Cardinal Mindszenty was bypassed

because he refused to leave his place of asylum unless the government declared him innocent of all crimes and restored full freedom of the Church.[47] The first document, called an act, listed the points of agreement and the other document, called a protocol, contained unsolved problems. The act had three points: (1) five bishops were named to administer a number of vacant dioceses but not all episcopal vacancies were filled (Hungary has three archdioceses and eight dioceses, one of the dioceses being Uniate); (2) the government's loyalty oath, imposed on both bishops and priests, was recognized as valid and binding in as much as the constitution and the laws were not contrary to Christian morals and faith; (3) the status of the Papal Hungarian Ecclesiastical Institute located on the second floor of the Hungarian Academy in Rome was settled. The Institute was run by Hungarian émigré priests for sixteen years under Papal protection. The Vatican now removed its protection and forced the émigrés to vacate the Institute, placing it under the jurisdiction of the Hungarian Bench of Bishops. The regime promised to keep the Institute and permit at least one priest from each Hungarian diocese to study there.[48]

The text of the protocol has not been published, but a list of outstanding problems between the Church and State in Hungary was publicized by leaders of the Catholic clergy engaged in pastoral work among Hungarians living in Western Europe. The major points were reported to be: (1) The future of Cardinal Mindszenty; (2) Freedom of communication between the Vatican and the bishops; (3) The future of the bishops exiled from their diocese. The bishops of Vác and Veszprém (and of course the archbishop of Esztergom, that is, Cardinal Mindszenty) were still not allowed to return to their dioceses despite the 1964 agreement. (4) Recognition of the Pope's right to appoint bishops. The regime persisted in blocking the consecration of Mgr. Gellért Bellon who was named bishop by Pius XII in 1959. (5) The right of the bishops to run their diocese without interference from the State Office for Church Affairs. The latter organization still controls the bishops' activities and has its representatives in every episcopal chancery. (6) The future of the "Peace Movement of the Clergy." It remained a dangerous threat, from the point of view of the Holy See, to church unity. (7) The freedom of religious instruction and the free exercise of religion. This has been the greatest grievance of the Church. In spite of the freedoms guaranteed in the

constitution of 1949 and subsequent legislation, religious instruction has been practically eliminated
from city schools and severely restricted in the
villages. Religious instruction outside the schools
even in the church or in the parish hall, is considered conspiracy against the State and the priest,
or whoever is in charge, is thrown into jail. People
who participate in religious services are discriminated against, e.g., denied admission to the universities, while large categories of employees, notably
certain classes of civil servants and practically
all educators, are expressly forbidden to attend
church (there is evidence of the relaxation of these
restrictions since the economic reforms of the 1960s).
(8) The fate of the religious orders and the fate of
their members. Over 10,000 monks and nuns were
evicted from their monasteries, convents, schools
and hospitals in 1950. In the agreement reached between the bishops and the government in 1950, eight
schools were restored to the Church and three male
and one female religious orders were allowed to re-
occupy two houses each and to provide the faculty
for two schools each. The membership of these four
orders is severely restricted and each one is allowed
to admit two candidates per year. The remainder of
the surviving religious orders, making up several
thousand priests, teachers, nurses, etc., are toiling
in government-controlled co-operatives, producing
gloves and various other textile articles for scanda-
lously low wages. (9) Lastly, there was no agreement on the Church's right to establish and maintain
schools, hospitals, and other charitable institutions; visit the sick in the hosptials, prisoners
in jails; and to organize religious associations;
to publish a free Catholic press.[49]

Casaroli recognized that the 1964 agreement left
much to be desired but he was cautiously optimistic.
At the signing of the agreement he declared that

> The Holy See wishes to see in this agreement
> not the goal achieved but the starting point
> to further negotiations. That does not mean
> that it does not appreciate the results
> obtained. However, the continuation of the
> work that has been started depends on whether
> the Government of the Hungarian People's
> Republic and the Holy See keep their assumed
> obligations. There is no lack of goodwill
> on the part of the Holy See. The sole con-
> cern of the Holy See is directed towards
> securing the rights and freedom of the Church,

138

as well as the interests and spiritual welfare of the Catholics in Hungary; and it does
this in the conviction that in this way it
will contribute in all spheres of life to
the development of the country.[50]

The government broadcast the following commentary on the agreement:

This agreement furthers the continuing improvement of relations between the State and
the Roman Catholic Church. . . . We note with
satisfaction that in regard to some questions
a more realistic appreciation of the development of the Hungarian People's Republic prevailed also in the Vatican, due to the growing
prestige of the socialist states it (the
Vatican) showed willingness to regulate relations. . . . In continuing this realistic
policy it will be possible to settle also
other questions in the relationship between
State and Church which still await solutions.[51]

If the Vatican expected the Hungarian Communists
to relent in their antireligious policies in the
wake of the 1964 agreement, it was disappointed.
At the Central Committee Plenum in March 1965, the
Party declared that cooperation with the churches is
welcome but that Communists must "continue to criticize the political stand and activity of ecclesias-
tics when these mirror strivings contrary to our
policies. . . ."[52] Two tactics eminated from the
new policy statement: greater stress on atheistic
education and, secondly, a return to administrative
measures against clerics and believers who, in the
spirit of the 1964 Agreement, practiced their faith
openly. In July 1965, seven priests were imprisoned
for alleged activities against the State.[53] That
was the beginning of a campaign of periodically
arresting priests and charging them with conspiracy.
Their trials have been usually held in camera, but
according to Professor Laszlo, "enough had tran-
spired to show that their true 'crime' consisted
of spreading religious views, distributing devo-
tional literature, and having given religious instruction for the young 'illegally,' although this was
often done at the explicit request and always with
the consent of the parents."[54]
It is typical of Communist tactics to keep up
measures of this kind, repugnant to their interlocutors, while negotiations are in progress, as they

139

were for the years after 1965 with the Holy See, as
a bargaining counter: it has happened time again in
dealings with the Western Powers over Berlin.  House
searches to harass priests, former nuns, monks, and
seminarians and other forms of petty persecution diminished progressively as progress toward the normalization of Church-State relations, according to
Kadar's desire to popularize his regime, seemed to
be near.  After the removal of Cardinal Mindszenty
in 1971, attacks by militant atheists on believers
were frowned upon by the government.

Cardinal Mindszenty finally left his place of
asylum in the American Embassy for Vienna on September 28, 1971.  The American government and the
Vatican both wished to jettison a man whom the
Hungarian regime claimed stood in the way of improved
relations.  The Vatican, of course, had been putting
pressure on the cardinal to leave Budapest for years,
but it was not until the American government informed Mindszenty that he was no longer a welcome
guest at the embassy that the Hungarian leader
acceded to the Papal request.[55]  He departed without
being cleared of his "alleged crimes," although the
Communists did grant him an unsolicited amnesty.
A few days after his departure, Jean Cardinal
Villot, Papal Secretary of State, amidst denials of
a quid pro quo for the amnesty, transferred to the
Hungarian bishops the right to absolve the excommunicated "peace priests," until then a power re-
served to the Pope.[56]

The Cardinal proceeded to complete and publish
in all the main languages of the world his out-
spoken and very moving memoirs, and a serious quarrel
developed with the Vatican over his forthright state-
ments about the religious situation in Hungary,
which could only be seen as disparaging the efforts
of the Holy See to pursue its negotiations with the
Kadar government.

On February 5, 1974, the Pope dismissed Cardinal
Mindszenty from his See of Esztergom and declared
the archdiocese vacant.  The Hungarian government
hailed this decision and Imre Miklos, the chairman
of the State Office for Church Affairs, declared
that Mindszenty's removal "made it perfectly clear
that even complicated questions can be resolved"
through "the process of détente."[57]  Cardinal Mindszenty made it clear that the move was the Vatican's
alone and justified his lack of endorsement by offering a summary of contemporary religious conditions
in Hungary:

1. Hungary and the Catholic Church of Hungary are not free.
2. The leadership of the Hungarian dioceses is in the hands of a church administration built and controlled by the communist regime.
3. Not a single archbishop or apostolic administrator is in a position to alter the composition or the functioning of the above-mentioned church administration.
4. The regime decided who is to occupy ecclesiastical positions and for how long. Furthermore, the regime also decides what persons the bishops will be allowed to ordain as priests.
5. The freedom of conscience and religion guaranteed by the Constitution is in practice suppressed. "Optional" religious instruction has been banned from the schools in the cities and the larger towns. At present the struggle for optional religious instruction in the schools is continuing in the smaller communities. Young people, contrary to the will of their parents, are being educated exclusively in an atheistic spirit. Believers are discriminated against in many areas of daily life. Religious teachers have only recently been confronted with the alternative of choosing between their professions and their religion.
6. The appointment of bishops or apostolic administrators without the elimination of the above-mentioned abuses does not solve the problems of the Hungarian Church. The installation of "peace priests" in important ecclesiastical posts has shaken the confidence of loyal priests and lay Catholics in the highest administration of the Church. In these grave circumstances Cardinal Mindszenty cannot abdicate.[58]

Despite Mindszenty's attitude, the Vatican and the Hungarian government reached agreement in 1974 and 1975 on the appointment of bishops, drawn mainly from the "Peace Priest Movement," for the many vacant dioceses in Hungary. The leadership of the Church was now acceptable to the Communist authorities. In January 1975, the government legalized the teaching of catechism in churches and other places of worship, but this proved to be a minor concession.

After Mindszenty's death in May 1975, the Vatican was ready to appoint a permanent bishop to his

diocese of Esztergom. From May 8th to July 12th,
1975, Archbishop Luigi Poggi, Apostolic Nuncio,
visited Hungary and met with Church and State officials. In late January 1976, he returned and continued the discussions.[59] Finally, in February, the
Pope appointed Bishop Dr. Laszlo Lekai, Apostolic
Administrator of Esztergom, to the position of Archbishop of Esztergom (which automatically elevated
him to the chairmanship of the Bench of Hungarian
Bishops), and at the same time, named Archbishop
Ijjas as Assistant to the Papal Throne.[60] After his
appointment, the successor of Cardinal Mindszenty declared that in a socialist society believers and non-
believers coexisted. He praised the Vatican for its
policies and efforts which were directed "at rein-
forcing good relationships between State and Church
in the socialist countries."[61] Two new bishops were
named in April 1976 to complete the Bench of Bishops.
These appointments, along with a visit by Archbishop
Lekai to the Vatican, according to the weekly
Katolikus Szo, closed a thirty year chapter in the
life of the Hungarian Catholic Church. The Church
was finally adjusting to reality.[62] In June, Archbishop Lekai was named a Cardinal.[63] As of the middle of 1976, according to the Hungarian Telegraph
Agency, the Catholic Church's eleven dioceses held
4,000 priests and 4,400 churches or chapels. However, there were only 288 students studying for the
priesthood.[64] In the middle of August, the Agency,
quoting an article in Nepszabadsag reported that
"relations between the State and the Churches have
never been so sound and undisturbed since the liberation as they are now."[65] In late November, Archbishop Poggi returned to Budapest for discussions
with Church and State officials.[66] At the end of the
year it was announced that over 90% of the clergy
belonged to the "Peace Priest Movement." The chief
dividing line in Hungary, according to the government, was "not between believers and Marxists, but
between the builders and opponents of a socialist
society."[67]

In January 1977, Imre Miklos declared that "since
realism has prevailed over a number of issues in
the Vatican, and the wish to settle questions of
mutual interest has strengthened, the possibilities
for conducting talks as between parties with equal
rights and for the normalization of links, have
opened."[68] In April, the Hungarian archbishops
and bishops went to Rome and were warmly received by
the Pope.[69] Cardinal Koenig visited the Roman Catholic Academy of Theology in Budapest at the end of

142

April.[70]
Janos Kadar arrived at the Vatican to meet with the Pope on June 9, 1977. In the meeting with Kadar, the Pope, according to a summary issued by Radio Vatican, discussed

the slow but uninterrupted process which during the course of the past 40 years has little by little drawn the Holy See and the Hungarian People's Republic closer together. The judgment of history after that of our conscience, the Pontiff said, will weigh on the initiative for this drawing together, which was desired by Pope John, and indeed on the results of this initiative. Paul VI also wished to emphasize that even in bold decisions such as these the Holy See is guided not by considerations of the advantage or the popularity of the moment but by the profound demands of its religious mission and by its vocation to be at the service of man. We believe, the Pontiff affirmed, that experience confirms the validity of the path undertaken; the path of dialogue on various matters attentive to the safeguarding of the rights and legitimate interests of the Church and of believers but at the same time open to an understanding of the preoccupations and action of the State in fields which lie within its proper competence. He added that the Holy See and the Church of Hungary are sincerely disposed to continue along the road with clarity and loyalty and with the wish that it be possible to proceed towards more advanced goals.[71]

The Pope and the Hungarian leader along with the Hungarian Foreign Minister, Mr. Frigyes Puja, and Monsignor Casaroli also met privately and discussed at length efforts to maintain peace and to implement the provisions of the Helsinki Conference. The Pope insisted that all of the agreements in the Final Act be implemented.[72] In the fall of 1977, Cardinal Lekai attended the Synod of Bishops in Rome. In an address to the Synod, he praised the development of religious education in Hungary. On Radio Vatican, as reported by the Hungarian Telegraph Agency, he announced that "the State never wished to control the subject-matter of theological lessons in churches, their structure or those attending them. But in its view, it has the right to see that really theological lessons are delivered during the hours announced for the teaching."[73]  In late December, Monsignor Poggi returned to Budapest for talks with Church and State leaders.[74]

In March 1978, the international Catholic Pax Christi peace organization and the Christian Peace Conference met in Budapest to discuss the part that the churches were playing in support of détente and disarmament.[75]  Later that month, the two Ecclesiastical Courts of Appeal, suspended since 1949, resumed operation.[76]

What conclusion can be drawn from the existence of fourteen years' negotiations between the Holy See and the Communist Hungarian government?  The force and sincerity of Cardinal Mindszenty's denunciation of the Church's bondage to the State are difficult to fault, even if there has been some real improvement in the discrimination against believers which he records.  The admiration for his championship of faith and freedom which has inspired this chapter is shared by a multitude of Christians, who cannot believe that the Church's compromise with Leninist Communism is possible without sacrifice of essential principles.

But there is another side to the picture which must be recorded.  Every diocese in Hungary now has a bishop, which means that the essential mechanism of the Catholic Church can work normally.  A group of new bishops, acceptable to the government, were appointed in 1974 and the remainder in 1975 and 1976. The Pope, receiving all the Hungarian archbishops and bishops in April 1977, declared his belief that the position of the Church was clearly hopeful and his joy at seeing clear signs that the religious situation in Hungary had improved.  In other words, from the Vatican's point of view, the prolonged pursuit of Ostpolitik had been at least a qualified success.  The Pope recognized that there remained problems to be overcome, such as hindrances to religious vocations and limitations placed upon religious education.  This he, no doubt, took up with Kadar in a long conversation at the Vatican on June 9, 1977, and as mentioned, he is known on that occasion to have insisted on the respect for religious liberty stipulated in the Final Act of the Helsinki Conference.  Cardinal Lekai, the new Archbishop of Esztergom, has been eloquent in describing to the rest of the world on Radio Vatican and elsewhere the many signs of religious revival in Hungary—50,000 Catholics at a pilgrimage, for instance.  In the country itself, he and the bishops as a whole

144

have thrown their weight behind the new movement for cooperation in public life between believers and atheists, and he himself spoke at the Sixth National Congress of the Patriotic National Front. The question at issue is how far bishops, paid and politically approved by an atheistic, Communist government, can give the spiritual leadership and the disinterested pastoral care which the faithful need. The "Peace Movement Priests," from which most of them were chosen, was condemned by the Church until a few years ago, like the adherents of similar movements in Poland and Czechoslovakia, not indeed from any aversion to true peace, but because the movement was an integral part of the Communist propaganda campaign (directed chiefly against the United States) and was used as a means of subordinating the Catholic clergy to the Communist Party. The fact that they are now pardoned and promoted is a sign of the price which the Holy See has had to pay for the restoration of the Church's spiritual establishment in Hungary. In addition, the Roman Catholic organization has markedly shrunk since the late 1940s.[77] More serious is the official teaching of atheism in this and in all the countries of the Soviet bloc and, while there is evidently an expansion of the limited opportunities for Christian education, at least in the countryside, one must ask how far concessions are made in that education to socialist dogma, as, for instance, the class war. The rather sibylline contribution to the discussion of catechesis made by Cardinal Lekai in the World Synod of Bishops in October 1977, indicated an unwillingness to teach children anything uncongenial to that dogma.

Although the episcopal structure is intact, Hungarian Catholicism is not in good straits. There is a severe shortage of priests and two-thirds of the clergy are over fifty. Priests are isolated, and disheartened. The faithful are apathetic. The gnawing question of whether Hungary is a victim or beneficiary of Ostpolitik has not yet been resolved.

NOTES

1. Even Jean Paul Sartre, who cannot be charged with pro-Catholic bias, hailed the Cardinal in his struggle against Stalinism. See Miklos Vetö, "The Catholic Church," Survey (January 1962), p. 134, n. 2. Cf. Temp Modernes, (November-December 1957), pp. 620-21.

2. George Schöpflin, Religion in Communist Lands, Vol. 3, No. 6 (November-December 1975), p. 25.

3.  Simon, "Catholic Church and Communist State," pp. 198-99.
4.  Catholic Herald, April 11, 1975, p. 4.
5.  Schöpflin, p. 25.
6.  One Soviet author claimed that Mindszenty not only tried and failed to stop socialism in Hungary, but that he was also an embarrassment to the Pope. See Koval'skii, Religioznye, pp. 39-40.
7.  Cardinal Mindszenty, Memoirs. (London, 1974), p. 31.
8.  Ibid., pp. 31. 41.
9.  George Feiffer, "No Protest: The Case of the Passive Minority," in Rudolf L. Tökes, ed., Dissent in the USSR: Politics, Ideology and People (Baltimore, 1975), p. 422.
10.  Schöpflin, p. 25.
11.  George N. Shuster, In Silence I Speak (New York, 1956), p. 8; Albert Galter, The Red Book of the Persecuted Church (Westminster, Md., 1957), pp. 196-97. For a roster of bishops and dioceses, see Emmerich András and Julius Morel Bilanz des Ungarischen Katolizismus (Munich, 1969).
12.  Robert Tobias, Communist-Christian Encounter in East Europe (Indianapolis, Ind., 1956), p. 24; G.W. Schuster, Religion Behind the Iron Curtain (New York, 1954), pp. 166-68, 173-74; Free Europe Committee, The Red and the Black (New York, 1953), pp. 51, 73-74.
13.  For a good survey of the history of Hungarian Churches between 1919 and 1945, see Leslie Laszlo, "Church and State in Hungary, 1919-1945," (Ph.D. Dissertation, Columbia University, 1973).
14.  Dunn, Catholic Church and the Soviet Government, 1939-1949, pp. 155-56.
15.  Ibid.
16.  Ibid.; Stephen Kertesz, "Church and State in Hungary," Review of Politics 11 (April 1949): 209-10.
17.  Shuster, In Silence, p. 8; Galter, Red Book, pp. 196, 212; Gary MacEoin, The Communist War on Religion (New York, 1951), pp. 113-14.
18.  Galter, Red Book, pp. 200-201; MacEoin, Communist War, p. 118; Mourin, Le Vatican, p. 167; Camille Cianfarra, The Vatican and the Kremlin (New York, 1950), p. 152.
19.  New York Times, February 18, 1946; Galter, Red Book, p. 201; Schuster, Religion Behind, pp. 166-68; Shuster, In Silence, p. 18; Cianfarra, Vatican and Kremlin, p. 154; Hugh Seton-Watson, The East European Revolution (New York, 7th printing,

1971), p. 192;  Kertesz, "Catholic Church," p. 214.

20.  Simon, "Catholic Church and Communist State," p. 200.

21.  Seton-Watson, East European, p. 196; Kertesz, "Catholic Church," p. 215;  Simon, "Catholic Church and Communist State," p. 200.

22.  Galter, Red Book, pp. 200-1.

23.  Simon, "Catholic Church and Communist State," p. 198;  Mindszenty, Memoirs, pp. 78-83, passim.

24.  Simon, "Catholic Church and Communist State," p. 198.

25.  Tablet (London), June 19, 1948, p. 388; New York Times, June 25, 1948;  Kertesz, "Catholic Church," p. 216.

26.  Radio Vatican, August 28, September 7, 1948; J.B. Barron and H.M. Waddams, eds., Communism and the Churches:  A Documentary (London, 1950), p. 66.

27.  Radio Vatican, July 16, 1948;  Radio Budapest, July 2, 1948;  New York Times, July 3, 1948.

28.  Radio Vatican, July 17, 1948.

29.  Radio Vatican, January 5, 1949, January 17, 1949;  l'Osservatore Romano, January 16, 1949; Radio Budapest, December 27, 1949, December 28, December 30, 1948;  (Hungarian Government), Documents on the Mindszenty Case (Budapest, 1949), p. 3; Joszef Cardinal Mindszenty, Four Years' Struggle of the Church in Hungary (London, 1949), p. 188.

30.  Radio Vatican, December 28, December 30, 1948;  January 5, January 17, 1949.

31.  Radio Budapest, January 24, 1949.

32.  For details, see Mindszenty, Memoirs, pp. 92-138, passim.

33.  Radio Vatican, February 10, 14, 15, 1949.

34.  Simon, "Catholic Church and Communist State," p. 199.

35.  Ibid., p. 198;  András and Morel, Bilanz, pp. 83-85.

36.  Simon, "Catholic Church and Communist State," p. 200.

37.  Ibid., p. 197;  Leslie Laszlo, "Towards Normalisation of Church-State Relations in Hungary," in Bociurkiw and Strong, Religion and Atheism, p. 292.

38.  Miklos Vetö, "The Catholic Church," Survey (January 1962), p. 134.

39.  Laszlo, "Towards Normalisation," p. 292; Beeson, Discretion, p. 240.

40.  Vetö, "Catholic Church," p. 134.

41.  Ibid.

42.  Laszlo, "Towards Normalisation," p. 292.

147

43. Ibid., pp. 292-93; Vetö, "Catholic Church," p. 135.

44. Laszlo, "Towards Normalisation," p. 293.

45. Ibid., p. 295.

46. Markiewicz, Kościół, pp. 201-202.

47. Laszlo, "Towards Normalisation," p. 296.

48. Ibid., pp. 296-96; l'Osservatore Romano, September 16, 1964. Also see RE/Hungarian Unit, "The Hungarian Vatican Accord," Hungarian Background Report, Radio Free Europe Research, September 18, 1964; and "The Partial Agreement Between Budapest and the Holy See: Ten Years After," October 10, 1974.

49. Laszlo, "Towards Normalisation," pp. 297-299. Also see Vetö, "Catholic Church," pp. 136-39; András and Morel, Bilanz, pp. 92-93.

50. l'Osservatore Romano, September 19, 1964; Cf. Laszlo, "Towards Normalisation," p. 300.

51. Laszlo, "Towards Normalisation," p. 300.

52. Ibid., p. 303.

53. New York Times, July 9, 1965; l'Osservatore Romano, July 17, 1965.

54. Laszlo, "Towards Normalisation," p. 303.

55. Mindszenty, Memoirs, pp. 232-37.

56. Ibid., pp. 305-6.

57. RE/Hungarian Unit, "Hungarian Press Survey," Radio Free Europe Research, March 22, 1974.

58. Mindszenty, Memoirs, pp. 246-47.

59. Radio Vatican, July 15, 1975; Hungarian Telegraph Agency, July 13, 1975, January 24, 1976.

60. Radio Budapest, February 12, 1976.

61. Hungarian Telegraph Agency, February 14, 20, 1976; Radio Budapest, February 24, 1976.

62. Hungarian Telegraph Agency, April 21, 29, 1976.

63. Ibid., June 26, May 21, 1976.

64. Ibid., June 3, 1976.

65. Ibid., August 18, 1976.

66. Radio Vatican, November 26, 1976.

67. Hungarian Telegraph Agency, December 3, 1976.

68. Ibid., January 17, 1977.

69. Radio Budapest, April 11, 1977.

70. Hungarian Telegraph Agency, April 28, 1977.

71. Radio Vatican, June 9, 1977.

72. Ibid.

73. Hungarian Telegraph Agency, September 29, October 8, 12, 1977.

74. Radio Vatican, December 19, 1977.

75. Hungarian Telegraph Agency, March 13, 1978.

76. Ibid., March 25, 1978.

148

77. For statistical information, see András and Morel, *Bilanz*, *passim*.

# 7. Czechoslovakia: A Religious Winter

Czechoslovakia was liberated from Nazi rule in May 1945 by the Soviet Army, the advancing American force under General Patton having been pulled back by General Eisenhower, in accordance with the division of occupied territory agreed by President Roosevelt and Winston Churchill with Stalin at the Teheran Conference. The Red Army was popular and well-behaved and withdrew before the end of the year. Almost the whole of the German minority was expelled, the Sudetenland being returned to Czechoslovakia; but for the bulk of the Czech and Slovak peoples, the end of the war meant freedom. Nor was the democratic atmosphere, it seemed, adulterated by the first parliamentary elections held in May 1946 at which the Communists won one-fourth out of 300 seats in the national assembly (38% of the vote in Bohemia and Moravia; 30% in Slovakia). No party having a clear majority, Eduard Beneš, the last pre-war President, having resumed the presidency, invited Klement Gottwald, leader of the largest party, the Communists, to form a coalition government. This he did with twenty-six ministers, of whom nine were Communists. But, of the latter, two held key ministries--the information and the interior--which gave them control of the radio and the police. These advantages served to prepare the seizure of power which brought Czechoslovakia'a short democratic honeymoon to an end in February 1948.

Beneš knew that Eastern Europe, including Czechoslovakia, was bound to fall within the Soviet sphere of influence. Accordingly, in December 1943, immediately after the Teheran meeting and to the great chagrin of Winston Churchill, he signed a treaty of alliance and friendship with the Soviet Union. As part of the agreement, the Soviets requested and received "rectifications," which were satisfied in 1945 when the Soviet Union annexed the Carpatho-Ukraine (Ruthenia).

Beneš undoubtedly believed that his show of friendship in 1943 and his agreement to the loss of Czechoslovakia's northeastern province to the USSR were guarantees for the re-establishment of Czech democracy and independence. He and the Czech people thought they had no reason to mistrust the Soviets and, in fact, they shared a longstanding Russophile tradition. The Soviet Union and, accordingly, the Communist Party, were quite popular in Czechoslovakia because of their struggle against the Nazis and because, in contrast to the Western countries, the USSR appeared in 1938 to be the only state ready to protect Czechoslovakia against German aggression.

The hopes of Beneš and the Czech people, however, were dashed by the Communist coup d'etat of 1948. The occasion for it was provided by the justifiable, but imprudent resignation from the government of the National-Socialist People's and Slovak Democratic ministers in protest at the Minister of the Interior packing the police force with Communists. The Communists immediately opened a barrage of propaganda in the media, brought the workers' militia out into the streets and seized the public buildings -- tactics which were to be almost exactly reproduced in Lisbon in April 1975, but fortunately with less success. Beneš capitulated and asked Gottwald to remain in office and fill the vacant ministries with people of his choice, who were, inevitably, Communist stooges and "yes men." With the entire mechanism of government in Communist hands, a general election was held in May to provide the mask of legitimacy with only one list of Communist and Social Democrat candidates presented to the voters. In consequence, Gottwald won 90% of the Czech vote and 86% of the Slovak. Beneš resigned and died three months later. The full Stalinist regime was promptly instituted and for the next twenty years repressive and authoritarian policies were the order of the day. "Reactionary" elements were purged from the universities, schools, army, and civil service, and the full force of this repression fell upon the Catholic Church, the religion of the majority of the population. The successive Communist Party leaders up to the day when Alexander Dubček was elected to that post in January 1968, were committed Stalinists who even balked at the minor changes associated with Khrushchev's de-Stalinization campaign. It is an ironical tragedy that the country in Eastern Europe which had the strongest democratic institutions should have looked

151

to the Soviet Union for protection and, then, once under the Communist wing, should have been degraded to that condition of servitude.  But the intensity of the repression by the governments of Gottwald, and of Zapotocky, and Novotny who succeeded him, showed that only unrelenting force could shackle the Czechoslovak traditions of freedom and democracy. Any relaxation, such as that which began in the three years previous to the attempted liberalization of socialism in what has been called the "Prague Spring," would lead, almost inevitably, to the re-surfacing of those traditions.  The Soviets understood clearly the infectiousness of the freedom achieved throughout Czechoslovakia by Dubček's reforms and, in August 1968, used their Warsaw Pact armies to crush it and re-establish the orthodox Muscovite regime under Gustav Husak.

The major developments in the history of the Catholic Church in Czechoslovakia since the end of the Second World War to the present parallel the state's political history.  In general, up to 1948, the Church, recovering from the Nazis' ill-treatment, was free of persecution; from 1948 to 1968, it was systematically repressed; during the months of the Dubček reforms, it gained a measure of freedom, only to be attacked again with the return of the Muscovite Communists.

The Catholic-Communist encounter in Czechoslovakia, however, was not simply a case of a religious institution having the misfortune of living under a belligerently atheistic regime.  The Communists, whose objective was total power, had an additional motive for pressure upon the Church, namely, to force it--since it could not be destroyed--to serve the state.  The Communists in their drive against Catholicism exploited certain characteristic weaknesses of the Church in Czechoslovakia.  On the one hand, it claimed the allegience of almost 78% of the total population.  It also had many priests and bishops, including Archbishop Joseph Beran of Prague, who were identified with the anti-Nazi struggle.  Quite a few, in fact, were war heroes.

On the other hand, the Catholic Church, like the state, was divided along lines of Czech and Slovak nationalism.  In Slovakia a Catholic priest, Monsignor Joseph Tiso, had set up a pro-Nazi puppet government during the war which was supported by the Roman Catholic Church in Slovakia.  His action was bitterly resented by the Czechs and, immediately after the war, he was tried for treason and executed, much to the discontent of the Slovaks.  Furthermore,

the Czechs, who lived mainly in the provinces of
Bohemia and Moravia and outnumbered the Slovaks two
to one, were more secularized than the latter and included an element of anticlericalism. This was, in
part, the result of the process of modernization
and, in part, a reaction against the Catholic Church's
historical identification with the Hapsburg empire.
   This ambivalence, needless to say, eased the
Communist onset against Catholicism. Following the
Communist purge of democratic politicians in 1948,
a major drive to reduce the Catholic Church's economic and social position was undertaken. A Catholic
priest, Father Joseph Plojhar, was appointed Minister
of Health and soon became a threat to clerical unity
in the face of government persecution; he also got
a name for himself for his abuse of the Vatican.[1]
He was soon suspended from the priesthood and later
excommunicated. More significantly, the Communists
passed two laws in 1948 which acutely damaged the
Church. The Law Concerning Agrarian Reform precipitated the confiscation of nearly all church lands,
some 320,000 hectares, which belonged to the Church
for centuries and provided basic sustenance. The
government did step in to continue the salaries of
the clergy but this was hardly fair compensation
and, soon, the financial support became a tool used
to regulate Church affairs.[2] The Law Concerning
Education was even more of a blow, since it nationalized all Catholic schools and prohibited religious
teaching in the schools.[3] The reforms of the Dubček
Administration in 1968 introduced some relaxation
of the latter prohibition and today some religious
instruction is permitted in certain schools, but it
is highly controlled and offered only outside of the
curriculum.[4] Pressure on parents to forego religious
instruction for their children continues.[5]
   It was also in 1948 that nearly all Catholic
publications were suppressed by a decree from the
Ministry of Information.[6] Furthermore, Catholic
Action associations were outlawed by the end of the
year and most Catholic charitable organizations,
including Caritas, and Catholic hospitals were transferred to the government.[7]
   The next year saw an acceleration in the campaign against the Church. A major set of directives
was given to local Communist groups with the following aims:

1. Separating the bishops and the priests by the
   suppression of the Acta Curiae (official
   diocesan bulletin); to weaken the religious

spirit of the priests by the prohibition
of all meetings, retreats, clerical con-
gresses, etc.
2.  Separating the priests from the laity who
might help them.
3.  Limiting religious activity to the inside
of Church buildings and to control it even
there.
4.  Liquidating whatever remained of Church
property and thus to deprive the clergy of
all economic independence.[8]

The bishops, in January 1949, criticized the
antireligious campaign and in May, issued a major
pastoral letter which protested against the closure
of Catholic schools, censorship, and a new law which
prohibited the Church from collecting money for charitable purposes.[9]

The government, however, did not relent and soon
it aided in the organization of a schismatic Catholic Action association whose function was to elicit
Catholic support for the government.  The new group
was allowed to publish a journal, Katolicke Noviny
(Catholic News).[10]  At the first meeting of the
leaders of the new "Catholic Action" group, a note
of warning was issued to the Czech hierarchy and the
Vatican:

We hope that our bishops will regard our
action with understanding.  However we exhort
those who might dare to penalize in any way
our priests or the Catholic people because
of their attitude to the State to note well
that we have with us the overwhelming majority
of the faithful. . . .  We cannot accept any
order of a political nature from outside the
country.[11]

The Secretary of the authentic Catholic Action, Dr.
Antonin Mandl, was arrested simultaneously with the
founding of the regime's Catholic Action organization.  The Catholic bishops responded with a pastoral
letter that denounced the pseudo-Catholic action
movement and demanded that the government respect the
rights of the Pope and the bishops in ecclesiastical
affairs.  The Vatican also remonstrated against the
government-sponsored Catholic Action group.[12]

On June 15, police broke into Archbishop Beran's
chancery and stole his official seal.  Shortly thereafter the government began issuing pastoral letters
to the clergy bearing the official seal of the

archbishop. The Vatican was at the same time casti-
gated for interfering in Czechoslovak affairs.[13]
During a sermon in which he criticized the Communists
on June 19, the archbishop was shouted down and then
placed under house arrest by police.[14] In response,
the Czechoslovak bishops protested against what they
called "a systematic persecution of the Catholic
Church in Czechoslovakia, well prepared and methodi-
cally executed." The Vatican also denounced the
regime's campaign.[15] The government, in turn, criticized the Holy See for involvement in Czech affairs
and disparaged Beran as a pawn of the Vatican.[16]

At the Jan Hus Memorial Day services in early
June, an array of government leaders attempted to
evoke, in support of their anti-Catholic campaign,
the memory of the national rising which he inspired
in Bohemia against the Papacy and the Emperor in the
fifteenth century. Deputy Premier Fierlinger declared in Husince that "Hus fought not only against
the immorality of the Catholic Church but also
against the increasing German influence in Bohemia
which was backed by the corrupt Catholic hierarchy
and the Pope. Now the battle between Czechoslovakia
and Rome is renewed."[17] Premier Zapotocky, in Devin,
stated that the "Catholic clergy are traitors and
are in the pay of foreign capitalists."[18] At
Sazala, Education Minister Nejedly declared that
"the Catholic Church is an enemy of socialism and of
the Slav people. The State will deal with those
bishops who are in the service of a foreign power
as traitors. The clergy should not follow their
bishops."[19]

A Communist Party directive in early July made
it clear that, from the government's point of view,
the Catholic Church was an unrelenting opponent of
the Czech and Slovakian peoples and emphasized that
all ties between Rome and the Czechoslovak bishops
had to be severed. The directive added that the
Papacy's influence could be undermined by isolating
the bishops, turning Catholics against Beran, and
having the Communist-backed Catholic Action group
accepted by Catholics. The circular stressed the
need to gain support for the new Catholic Action
movement in rural areas and among the peasants.[20]
In October 1949, the authorities created a state
office for Ecclesiastical Affairs, a parallel to
the Soviet department of religious affairs.[21] Government officials were now made responsible for
religious affairs. By this new arrangement, all
clergy received a state salary but their appointments had to be approved by the regime and they had

155

to swear an oath of loyalty to the State. All
religious organizations also had to have their budgets checked by the government and henceforth the
State assumed responsibility for the seminaries. The
oath of loyalty read as follows:

> I promise on my honor and conscience that
> I shall be loyal to the Czechoslovak Republic
> and its People's Democracy and that I shall
> do nothing that is detrimental to its interests,
> its security and its integrity. As a citi-
> zen of the People's Democracy I shall honestly
> and sincerely carry out all duties which are
> incumbent upon me in the position which I
> occupy, and I shall support with all my
> strength the efforts towards reconstruction
> which are being made for the welfare of the
> people.[22]

The bishops balked at taking the oath but they
allowed their priests to take it with the proviso
that the government would not order anything "that
is in contradiction to the law of God and to human
rights."[23] At the same time, state officials were
named to every diocese and, for all practical purposes, assumed the task of episcopal administration.
Not only church appointments but such minor events
as clerical meetings now required government approval. All ecclesiastical communications, including
pastoral letters, were subject to censorship. The
Church was also forbidden to punish any Catholic who
backed the regime.[24] By the end of the year, all
Catholic libraries and publishing enterprises were
confiscated by the government.[25]
      The government's assault against the Church per-
sisted into the 1950s. The remaining monasteries
and convents were closed down on April 14-15, 1950;
some of the religious were deported and several of
the former religious houses were turned into concentration camps.[26] The official Czechoslovak news
agency, C.T.K., reported the obliteration of the
religious orders on April 18, explaining that they
were "the tools of the foreign foes of the Republic
. . . being used to shelter hostile agents, spies
and even murderers. . . and many monasteries served
as bases for espionage and disruptive activities."[27]
Gerhard Simon, commenting on the explanation, stated
that "a better example of Stalinist language and
policy will hardly be found."[28] One year later,
the Vatican estimated that some two thousand out of
seven thousand secular and regular clerics had either

been deported, imprisoned, or subjected to forced labor.[28]  Seminaries were reduced from seven to two and affiliated with the theological departments in Litoměřice and Bratislava.  During the amnesty of 1960 about 800 priests were released, but only a few were permitted to practice their ministry.[30]  Today, as in Hungary, there is a severe shortage of priests.[31]

Between 1950 and 1955, the regime moved against the heart of the Catholic Church's resistance, namely the bishops.  Czechoslovakia had thirteen Latin rite dioceses and one Uniate rite diocese.  By 1955, thirteen bishops had been removed from their sees, five sentenced to imprisonment and the rest held in confinement.[32]  Archbishop Beran was forced out of his post in March 1951 and later transferred to Rozelov Castle and eventually to the so-called "concentration monasteries" in a remote part of southern Moravia-Bohemia.[33]  Thus all the bishops who were determined not to submit to the Communists were removed.  Through various machinations the regime managed to keep the dioceses without bishops and under the administration of collaborationist clergy.[34]

Another debilitating blow was delivered to the Church in September 1951, when the "Peace Movement" of Catholic clergy (MHKD) was organized under the leadership of Joseph Plojhar, the excommunicated priest who was the Minister of Health.  Its self-described function was to promote peace and toward that end the members were obliged in their pronouncements on that subject to endorse the Soviet line on world affairs, including denunciation of the supposed threat to  peace of the United States and its allies, to support "wars of liberation," and to back unhesitatingly the Czechoslovak government's policies of collectivization and socialization.[35]  The MHKD also published literature purporting to show that the Catholic Church was flourishing under the Communists. It became an important and pliable weapon for the regime in its struggle against Catholic unity.[36] This use of the traditional Christian devotion to peace as a means of securing the submission of the clergy to the slogans and directives of the Communists' international policies and, making that submission a condition of freedom and preferment, has become a feature of government characteristic of all European Communist countries.  In the Soviet Union, the Russian Orthodox hierarchy is entirely subject to this regime, most of all in its activities abroad in bodies such as the World Council of Churches.  In Poland, it has had the least success owing to the

157

struggle and solidarity of the Catholic body.  In
Czechoslovakia and Hungary, particularly after the
intensive pressure upon priests to join the Pacem
in Terris organization, named after Pope John XXIII's
encyclical of 1963 which was scrupulously exploited
for Communist propaganda, it has brought into being
a corps of clerics, from which, despite prolonged
opposition, the Holy See was obliged to chose the
majority of such bishops as the governments have permitted it to appoint to vacant dioceses.

The Greek Catholics, numbering some 356,000, in
the Ukrainian-speaking Prešov area of Slovakia, experienced not only persecution through the late
1940s, but eventually, institutional suppression.
The methods chosen by the Communists in Czechoslovakia for extinguishing the legal life of the
Ukrainian Uniate Church imitated the Soviet methods
employed for the liquidation of the main organization of the Uniates in Galicia and Carpatho-Ukraine,
and in the Soviet Union itself.  The principal measure was a forced "reunion" of the Uniate Church
with the local Orthodox Church.  The latter, with
government assistance, organized an elaborate program featuring "re-education" courses taught by the
police, the establishment of "committees" for "reunion," and the internment of "recalcitrant" clergy,
including Bishop Pavlo Goidych.  (The bishop died in
Leopoldovo prison on July 19, 1960.)  The farce eventually came to a head on April 28, 1950, with a lay-
controlled "Conference" in Prešov, which described
itself as a "Greek Catholic Sobor" and petitioned
"unanimously" for acceptance into the Orthodox Church.
The government, within a few weeks, ratified the
action of the "Sobor" and announced that the Greek
Catholic Church was no longer a legal entity in
Czechoslovakia.  The Auxiliary Bishop of Prešov,
Vasyl Hopko, was arrested in 1951 for opposing the
"reunion," and remained in jail until 1963.[37]

An impressive summary of the Church's tribulations was recorded in a petition which 22,317 Catholics signed and sent to Alexander Dubček on March 17,
1968.  It declared:

> After a number of unsuccessful negotiations
> between Church and State, an attack was mounted
> in the 1950s against the Catholic Church in
> the CSSR by the public authorities then in
> power.  This upset both the life of the
> Church itself and good mutual relations (with
> the State):

1. The dioceses were robbed of their bishops, who were interned or imprisoned.
2. The legal authority of those bishops who remained was reduced to a minimum.
3. Hundreds of priests were imprisoned--simply because they fulfilled their duties conscientiously.
4. Religious and ecclesiastical superiors were involved in show trials for which force was used to extort confessions of guilt referring to alleged facts that had no basis in reality.
5. In the course of the single night of 13-14 April, 1950, all the religious orders and congregations in the entire republic were dissolved in a manner in which no parallel can be found in the history of European civilization.
6. Relations with the Holy See were broken off.
7. 'Church secretaries' were established to whom in effect was transferred all episcopal authority in the administration of church affairs.
8. For this office people were chosen who made no secret of their attitude of hostility towards the Church.
9. Under the pressure of threats and discrimination religious instruction has until recently been almost completely abolished in the schools. Even today, though religious instruction is given here and there, in many places the same methods of intimidation are applied as in former years.
10. Many priests affected by measures described above, such as imprisonment, were not given the opportunity of returning to pastoral work, although the number of priestless parishes has been increasing.
11. For years incredible difficulties have been put in the way of young men wishing to devote themselves to the priestly vocation and to enter the seminary.
12. At the present time these restrictions remain for the most part in force. This gives rise to the remarkable situation that the condition of the Catholic Church in the CSSR probably represents the last enclave, in which to an undiminished extent those measures of coercion are still most strongly applied, which at one time were applied to citizens in general during the

period of the so-called cult of personality.
Five dioceses in Bohemia and Moravia and
five dioceses in Slovakia have been without
a bishop for several years. It is difficult to understand that such a state of
affairs is possible in the heart of Europe,
among peoples with a highly developed civilization.[38]

This distressing picture drawn by Czechoslovak
Catholics in 1968 provides striking evidence that
the Vatican's Ostpolitik, initiated as a general policy at the beginning of the 1960s, had not, by that
date, improved relations between Church and State in
Czechoslovakia. In general the efforts of the Holy
See to find some accommodation with the Czechoslovak
government were frustrated by the unrelenting persecution of the Communists, especially their imprisonment and restriction of bishops and priests, and
support for "peace priests."

The Vatican's Ostpolitik vis-à-vis Czechoslovakia began formally with the visit of Cardinal
Koenig, in July 1963, to Prague. Evidently his intervention, at a time when Khrushchev's policy of
de-Stalinization was in vogue, led to the government's decision to free, in July, three incarcerated
bishops and, then, in October, five more, including
the primate of Czechoslovakia, Archbishop Beran.
But none of the bishops were allowed to resume their
posts and Archbishop Beran was exiled to Rome where
he was named a Cardinal in 1969.[39] Novotny's release of the bishops proved to be of no value to the
Catholic population, although it certainly was, as
far as the individuals were concerned, an improvement over prison. With Beran's removal (he died in
Rome on May 17, 1969), the regime allowed Bishop
Frantisek Tomasek to become Apostolic Administrator
for the diocese of Prague.[40] The concession was important for it moved to a position of prominence a
bishop respected by Catholics. His influence on
decision-making, though, like all other bishops was
minimal, since he did not have the full powers of a
resident ordinary and since government-appointed
"Church secretaries" continued virtually to run the
diocese.

Nonetheless, once contact was made, discussions
between the Prague regime and the Vatican continued.
The principal topic up to the loosening of the
nation's fetters in 1968 was the filling of vacant
dioceses, but this remained unresolved since the
Vatican refused to name some "peace priests" to the

160

empty posts.[41]

With the coming to power of Alexander Dubček, in January 1968, the tribulations of the Catholic Church in Czechoslovakia suddenly lessened and, momentarily, in the animating atmosphere of general liberalization, hope flourished for a genuine amelioration in Church-State relations. The Communist system of authoritarianism gave way under the pressure of the country's democratic tradition, immense economic difficulties, and Slovak demands for equality within the Czech dominated state.

In the religious sphere, Erika Kadlecova replaced Karel Hruza as chairman of the Secretariat for Religious Affairs in March 1968. Hruza was identified with the repressive Novotny regime whereas Kadlecova characterized the tone of her tenure by writing in Rude pravo that "our society cannot be infringed upon by a consistent observance of religious liberty but rather by its restriction."[42]

The ensuing changes were dramatic. Imprisoned clergy and lay people were released. The strict numerus clausus for the seminaries was dropped and followed by a marked growth in the number of students. Women's religious orders were again permitted to operate openly and censorship of the church press was relaxed. A serious Christian-Marxist dialogue was initiated. The Uniate Church was again vested with legal life and nearly all of the Uniates, some 356,000 of whom had been coerced into "reunion" with Orthodoxy, returned to their Catholic status.[43] The "Peace Movement of Catholic Clergy" fell apart and was replaced by the Movement for Conciliar Renewal (DKO) which aimed at understanding and implementing the decrees of the Second Vatican Council. The government also disencumbered religious instruction, and opened negotiations for the return of Cardinal Beran and for the filling of diocesan vacancies with resident bishops.[44] The Catholic Church, as well as the other Christian Churches, was fully behind the government's new policies. Bishop Tomasek, in June, sent a telegram to Dubček to confirm that the Catholic Church supported the government in its liberalizing policies.

The Soviet-Warsaw Pact invasion in late August 1968 marked the ending of this interlude of freedom and the return of oppressive conditions for both the churches and Czechoslovak society. The change was not, however, immediate nor has the subsequent Communist regime, faithful as it is to Soviet doctrine and direction, ever been quite as rigid and obtuse as it had been in the days of Novotny. Dubček did not resign as First Secretary of the Communist Party, preferring Gustav Husak as his successor, till April 1969. Until then, universities, theatre, cinema, and press, censorship notwithstanding, were relatively free. It was the visit of Marshal Grechko, the Soviet defense minister to Prague in March 1969 which caused a tightening of the screw, after the defiant anti-Soviet demonstrations which followed the Czechoslovak ice-hockey victory over the Soviet Union at Stockholm. Husak promised that there would be no political trials, but the promise was broken in the summer of 1972 when about fifty journalists and others were tried and sent to prison for distributing leaflets. Since then, it is chiefly groups of intellectuals identified with the liberal episode of 1968 who have been the victims of police interrogations and obstruction in pursuing their professions. Since the Helsinki Conference on European Security and Cooperation, it is particularly those who have united in their demand for the human rights promised in the Final Act of the Conference that have acted as the gadflies of the Husak government, with much public support from other countries including Western Communist Parties. There have been many prominent Catholic names among the signatories of "Charter 77." It is in this setting that the lot of the Catholic Church in the last ten years has been cast. It has been a mixture of partial progress at the official level with the intermittent harassment of individuals and interference with pastoral functions at every level. Karel Hruza, the former head of the State Office for Church affairs took over from Mme. Kadlecova and resumed his previous duties.

The Vatican spoke critically of the Soviet invasion but did not categorically denounce the suppression of liberties to which it led.[45] On September 20, Cardinal Koenig called for a "dialogue" between Christians and non-believers, including Communists, and announced rather puzzlingly, that the Church enjoyed the same liberty in Czechoslovakia as before the Soviet invasion.[46] The cardinal's comment, made in September, was literally true, but the potential for improvement was not the same and by 1970 the comment seemed absurd. It may have been a tactic, admittedly far-fetched, to dissuade the Communists from reintroducing hard-line policies. But Ostpolitik being the order of the day, the diplomats of the Holy See might very well have determined that an uncompromising and pointed denunciation of the invasion of Czechoslovakia would have jeopardized the whole attempt at <u>rapprochement</u> with the Soviet Union and Warsaw Pact powers. It is revealing to contrast Pius XII's outright censure of the Communist coup in Czechoslovakia in 1948 and the reaction of Paul VI to the suffocation of the liberties restored in 1968. <u>Ostpolitik</u> has clearly effected a degree of self-censorship in the Vatican vis-à-vis Communist activities. The degree of Papal criticism of Communist tyranny is in inverse proportion to the growth of "détente." That development, of course, is not restricted to Rome. Robert Byrnes, one of America's leading historians of Russia, recently commented that American scholars, involved in exchange programs with the Soviet Union, no longer apply to study subjects which the Soviets have vetoed previously and, thus, do the job of the Soviet censors themselves.[47] And, of course, the desire not to jeopardize "détente" has evidently governed the policy of the United States in refraining from any effective opposition to the Soviet-Cuban intervention in Africa, just as it explained the unwillingness of President Ford to meet with Solzhenitzyn. But it was not unnatural to expect from the moral leadership of the Papacy something bolder than appeasement and self-censorship in view of the renewed suppression of human rights and liberties in Czechoslovakia.

The government of Husak slowly but surely over the course of 1969 and 1970 whittled away the gains of organized religion. By October-November 1969, a policy was outlined towards the Catholic Church:

1. The Church is to be strictly restricted in its activities to the ecclesiastical sphere.
2. A new movement for the clergy is to be founded to continue the work of the "Peace Priests."
3. Priests are to be restricted to particular geographical areas for pastoral work.
4. A reduction and tighter control of the publishing house of St. Adalbert.
5. The limitation of all lay apostolate.
6. The restriction of retreats, conferences and training courses to priests, monks and nuns.
7. New political chiefs to be selected for <u>Caritas</u> who are sympathetic to the Party.
8. Very close supervision of the Faculties of Theology and the purging of all staff members identified with the Movement for Conciliar Renewal.
9. Limitation of the activities of religious

163

orders; social work of nuns to be restricted to the care of the elderly and mentally
deficient; no re-grouping of men's orders;
only pastoral work to be allowed--no evan-
gelism.
10.  Tighter control by the State of religious
instruction.
11.  Research into the position of the Uniate
Church.[48]

Practically all of these directives had been
enforced by 1974.  Pressure on parents noticeably
reduced the number of children receiving religious
instruction.  A severe numerus clausus for seminary
training was re-introduced and the average age of
those completing their priestly training rose significantly.  Priests trained for the Uniate diocese
of Prešov were not given assignments and the government actively interferes with recruitment.  The Uniate Church today operates under increasing government pressure.[49]  The "Peace Priest" movement was revived in November 1971 under the title of Pacem in
Terris.  It has backed the regime's repressive measures and today its members hold the key posts in
the publishing, educational, and pastoral work of the
Church.  Propaganda against the Catholic Church again
became rife.  Priests again faced arrest and arbitrary government interference in their affairs.[50]
The Vatican did not escape criticism.  It was
denounced for attempting "ideological subversion"
of Eastern Europe and, in August 1970, for supporting
the Velehard Center, an organization of exiled Roman
Catholic Czechoslovak clerics in Rome.[51]  Nonetheless, discussions between the Vatican diplomats and
the Husak regime opened up in 1971 and continued into
1976, the major topic on the agenda being the vacant
dioceses.[52]  By the middle of 1972, due to deaths
and government interference, only one of Czechoslovakia's thirteen Catholic dioceses (including one
Uniate diocese) had a resident bishop with full
power.[53]  In April 1974, Cardinal Stefan Trochta,
bishop of Litoměřice in Bohemia, died of a heart
attack as the consequence of an hour-long interroga-
tion by a Communist official.
In early 1973, Mgr. Casaroli and the Czechoslovak regime finally reached agreement on the appointment of four new bishops: Jozef Feranec, Jan Pasztor,
Julius Gabris, and Jozef Vrana.  The first three
were assigned to the Slovak dioceses of Banska
Bystrica, Nitra, and Trnava respectively and the last
to the Czech diocese of Olomouc.  All four new bishops

were associated with the "peace movement" and Vrana was actually, up to his consecration, president of Pacem in Terris. The episcopal ordinations were performed by Mgr. Casaroli who, during the ordination of the first three bishops (Vrana was consecrated one day later), declared that "this is a great day for the Catholic Church in Slovakia and for the country as a whole."[54] In retrospect, the archbishop's declaration proved to be more of a hope than a fact. Vrana, although no longer the head of Pacem in Terris, has retained his membership in the Central Committee of the group's Czech branch and Pasztor, Gabris, and Feranec continue as members of the group.[55] In September 1974, Vatican and Czech officials, including Casaroli and Karel Hruza, held more talks on episcopal vacancies, religious instruction, and the status of religious orders and seminaries.[56] They proved not only ineffective but were conducted against a growing antireligious campaign in Czechoslovakia, including attacks upon the Vatican.[57] There can be no doubt that the Holy See made a major concession to the regime in allowing "peace priests" to be consecrated bishops in 1973 and that it hoped that its appeasement would elicit adjustments from the Communists.[58] The Czechoslovak government, however, did not reciprocate and probably viewed the Papal compromise as a sign of pusilanimity.

Casaroli returned to Prague at the end of February 1975, to discuss with Foriegn Minister Chnoupek the reduction of international tensions and the preservation of peace and security in Europe and the world.[59] Despite the non-religious nature of the talks, the Vatican obviously felt it important to keep in contact with the Czechoslovak regime. On his return to Rome, the archbishop stated that the talks were not direct nor complete negotiations but "contacts of a general nature at a highly responsible level on matters of bilateral interest." He went on to say that a highly positive assessment of the discussions was justified.[60] Yet, on January 1, 1977, "Charter 77," a manifesto drawn up by a group of intellectuals and supporters of Alexander Dubček decried, inter alia, the continuing discrimination against religion:

> Freedom of religious confession, emphatically guaranteed by Article 18 of the first Covenant (the International Covenant on Civil and Political Rights signed on behalf of Czechoslovakia in 1968 and reiterated at Helsinki

in 1975), is continually curtailed by arbitrary official action; by interference with
the activity of churchmen, who are constantly
threatened by the refusal of the state to permit them the exercise of their functions, or
by the withdrawal of such permission; by financial or other sanctions against those who
express their religious faith in word or action;
by constraints on religious training and
so forth.[61]

Despite these signs of the Communists' unaltered
hostility to religion and to the Catholic Church in
particular, the government evidently believed that,
in view of the Papacy's apparent support of the
"peaceful coexistence" policy of the USSR identified
with the Helsinki resolution, some concession to
Catholic opinion at home would be advantageous.   In
these circumstances, the diplomacy of Mgr. Casaroli
achieved an important success in securing official
consent to the installation of Cardinal Frantisek
Tomasek as Archbishop of Prague.  His enthronement
in the Cathedral on Easter Day, 1978, was an immensely popular event.[62]  Unlike the other four bishops
recently appointed to dioceses, he is not a member
of the political peace movement.  This event was
quite inaccurately reported in the international press
as evidence of the definite reconciliation of the
Church and State in Czechoslovakia.  All that can
reasonably be claimed for it, is that it is evidence
of the only tangible success of the Papal Ostpolitik
in Eastern Europe, which is the gradual restoration
of the episcopal hierarchy, even if the majority of
the bishops installed are no less subservient to the
secular powers than were many of those in the days
of the old regime of the Hapsburgs: but today the
secular power is one which denies the existence of
God.  Nine of the Catholic dioceses in Czechoslovakia
were still without resident bishops in the spring of
1978.  Archbishop Poggi was in Prague in April 1978
for discussions with Karel Hruza, head of the Secretariat for Church Affairs.[63]

NOTES

1.  Ludvik Nemec, Church and State in Czechoslovakia  (New York: 1955), pp. 247-55, 388.  Also see
Ludvik Nemec, "The Communist Ecclesiology During the
Church-State Relationship in Czechoslovakia," Proceedings of the American Philosophical Society
112 (August 1968): 256.

2. Beeson, Discretion and Valour, p. 201; Simon, "Catholic Church," p. 196; Cf. Nemec, Church and State, p. 156.

3. Beeson, Discretion and Valour, p. 210; Nemec, Church and State, pp. 257-58.

4. Simon, "Catholic Church,: p. 199.

5. Beeson, Discretion and Valour, p. 201.

6. Radio Vatican, December 31, 1948; January 10, 1949; Nemec, Church and State, p. 257; Galter, Red Book, pp. 349ff; Free Europe Committee, Red and Black, pp. 21-24.

7. Free Europe Committee, Red and Black, pp. 21-24.

8. Galter, Red Book, pp. 359-60.

9. Beeson, Discretion and Valour, p. 202; Nemec, Church and State, pp. 259-272.

10. Nemec, Church and State, p. 279; Beeson, Discretion and Valour, pp. 201-2.

11. Galter, Red Book, p. 364.

12. Radio Vatican, June 14, 1949; Nemec, Church and State, pp. 279-80; Barron and Waddams, Communism and Churches, p. 54; Free Europe Committee, Red and Black, pp. 21-24; The Tablet (London), June 11, 1949.

13. Radio Prague, June 20, 1949; Galter, Red Book, pp. 365-66; New York Times, June 17, 1949.

14. Galter, Red Book, pp. 366-68; Nemec, Church and State, pp. 281-82; New York Times, June 20, July, 11, 1949; The Tablet (London), August 27, 1949.

15. Suprema Sacra Congregatio Sancti Offici, "Decretum: Schismatica 'Action Catholica' in Cecoslovachia damnatur," Acta Apostolicae Sedis, XLI (1949), 33; l'Osservatore Romano, June 20, 1949; Nemec, Church and State, pp. 281-86.

16. Radio Prague, June 27, 1949.

17. MacEoin, Communist War, p. 40.

18. Ibid.

19. Ibid.

20. Ibid., p. 41; Nemec, pp. 306-7; New York Times, July 12, 1949.

21. Nemec, Church and State, pp. 335-41; Simon, "Catholic Church," p. 197.

22. Beeson, Discretion and Valour, p. 205.

23. Ibid.

24. Ibid., pp. 201-2; Simon, "Catholic Church," p. 197.

25. Simon, "Catholic Church," p. 201.

26. Ibid., p. 202; New York Times, April 18-20, 1950; A Michel, Religious Problems in a Country Under Communist Rule (Rome, 1954), pp. 24, 52.

27. Simon, "Catholic Church," p. 202.

28. Ibid.
29. New York Times, December 20, 1950.
30. Simon, "Catholic Church," p. 208.
31. Ibid., p. 200.
32. Ibid., p. 207.
33. Beeson, Discretion and Valour, p. 204.
34. Ibid., p. 206.
35. Ibid., pp. 207-8.
36. Ibid., p. 208.
37. Bociurkiw, "The Uniate Church," p. 111;
First Victims of Communism: White Book on Religious
Persecution in the Ukraine (Rome, 1953), pp. 58-59;
Svetlo Pravoslavia, No. 1-2 (1950), pp. 1-27;
Zh.M.P., No. 7 (1950), pp. 40-53.
38. Beeson, Discretion and Valour, pp. 199-200.
39. l'Osservatore Romano, October 3, 1963;
New York Times, July 21, October 4, 1963.
40. New York Times, February 19, 1965.
41. Peter A. Toma and Milan J. Reban, "Church-
State Schism in Czechoslovakia," in Bociurkiw and
Strong, Religion and Atheism, pp. 281-82.
42. Rude pravo, May 18, 1968.
43. For details on this event, and its history
after the Prague Spring, see: Michael Lacko, S.J.,
"The Re-Establishment of the Greek-Catholic Church in
Czechoslovakia," Slovak Studies, Vol. XI (Cleveland-
Rome, 1971), pp. 159-89; Athanasius B. Pekar, OSBM,
"Restoration of the Greek Catholic Church in Czechoslovakia," The Ukrainian Quarterly 29 (1973):
283-96; Theodore Novak, "L'Ostpolitik' du vatican et l'eglise catholique ukrainianenne," L'Est
Europeen, No. 124 (janvier 1973), pp. 12-25, No. 125
(fevrier-mars 1973), pp. 21-26.
44. New York Times, April 8, 15, 17, 20, 1968;
Beeson, Discretion and Valour, pp. 216-17.
45. New York Times, August 20, 22, 26, 29,
September 2, 3, 1968.
46. New York Times, September 22, 1968.
47. George Urban, "A Discussion with Robert F.
Byrnes," Survey (Autumn 1974), pp. 41-66. The
World Council of Churches also reacted mildly to the
Soviet incursion in Czechoslovakia. See: "Refining
Czech Communism," Christianity Today, September 13,
1968, pp. 33-35.
48. Beeson, Discretion and Valour, p. 218.
49. Ibid., p. 219; Michael Bourdeaux, "The
Uniate Churches in Czechoslovakia," Religion in
Communist Lands, Vol. 2, No. 2 (March-April 1974),
pp. 4-6.
50. Beeson, Discretion and Valour, p. 219;
Tablet (London), January 5, 1974, pp. 20-21;

Catholic Herald, September 27, 1974, March 3, 1975; Also see "Pressure on the Churches in Czechoslovakia," Religion in Communist Lands, Vol. 2, No. 2 (March-April 1974), pp. 7-9; "Catholic Church in Prague Subjected to New Attack," Central Europe Journal 18 (December 1970): 477.

51. Rude pravo, August 29, 1970.
52. Radio Free Europe Research, "Situation Report,: Czechoslovakia/36, October 2, 1974.
53. Radio Free Europe Research, "Regime Policy and the Present State of the Catholic Church in the CSSR," July 7, 1972--Czechoslovakia/17.
54. Beeson, Discretion and Valour, p. 224; Radio Free Europe Research, March 13, 1973; and Lidova Demokracie, April 27, 1973.
55. RFER, "Situation Report," October 2, 1974--Czechoslovakia/36.
56. Ibid.
57. Ibid., Radio Prague, December 7, 1974.
58. Radio Free Europe Research, "Czechoslovak Situation Report," March 5, 1975.
59. Radio Prague, February 24, 1975.
60. Radio Free Europe Research, "Czechoslovak Situation Report," March 5, 1975. Further talks were held in Rome between December 10 and 13, 1975. See Czechoslovak Press Agency, December 16, 1975; Radio Vatican, December 16, 1975.
61. Keston News Service, No. 34, February 3, 1977.
62. Radio Prague, March 6, 1978.
63. Ibid., April 29, 1978.

# 8. East Germany (GDR), Romania, Bulgaria, Albania

The Catholic Church in East Germany (GDR) enjoys relative freedom in comparison with the Church in the USSR and every other East European Communist country except Yugoslavia and Poland. The Church is not big, but it is a significant minority, representing approximately 1.3 million people or about 8% of the total population. Gerhard Simon calls it "primarily a diaspora-Church" because it depends in a large number of parishes "on co-operation with the Protestant Landeskirche."[1]

There is, to be sure, persecution of religion in East Germany. The Communist regime remains steadfast in its promotion of Marxism-Leninism. Believers are discriminated against, not in law, but in fact, in the competition for good jobs and higher education. The crucial contest for educating and influencing children and young people remains a major source of tension. The government wants support from the churches for its internal and external policies, and does not take criticism lightly. It also closely supervises the publications of the various churches and censures articles which do not agree with its political and/or social positions. The regime also sponsors, as mentioned earlier, the Berlin Conference (BK) of Catholic Christians from European States which Catholic laymen control and whose primary purpose is to garner support for Soviet foreign policy aims. The chairman of the BK is also the editor of the left Catholic journal Begegnung, published in East Berlin, which closely follows the developments in Papal Ostpolitik and editorially supports détente. The Catholic Church, though, has shunned the Berlin Conference and, thus far, no priests belong to it.[2] Hans Seigewasser, State Secretary for Church Affairs,

Herman Kalb, Deputy Secretary for Church Affairs,
and Rudi Bellman, Head of the Socialist Unity Party's
(SED) Central Committee's Working Group for Church
Questions are the government's central figures
dealing with the churches.

All in all, though, the Catholic Church in East
Germany has not fared too badly.  That is also true
of the Protestant religions, especially the main
faith, Lutheranism.  In 1952, the Catholic Church was
permitted to establish a seminary at Erfurt.  With
financial backing from West Germany, the Church also
built 325 churches, remodeled 302 churches, and re-
constructed twenty-five churches.[3]  There are over
1,400 priests and about 2,700 nuns.  The Church
carries on a rather substantial charitable work and
also publishes two weeklies.[4]  Cardinal Alfred
Bengsch of Berlin stirs the Church along a path which
keeps it politically and socially uninvolved.[5]  The
government also pays the churches over twelve
million marks annually for administration and clerical salaries.[6]

Even during the high tide of Stalinism, the
East German authorities never sought to make religion
a battle ground.  One reason for this is that secularization, supported by growing industrialization
and government-supported atheistic propaganda, took
root in East Germany and, from the government's
point of view, was a much more palatable and easy
way to undermine religion than through draconian
measures.  More important, though, was East Germany's
international position and specifically its delicate
relationship with the West, West Germany, and the
Soviet Union.  Immediately after World War II, political and economic issues overshadowed religion.  It
was a time of apprehension and uncertainty and the
East German Communists knew their position in the
Soviet-occupied part of Germany was dependent solely
upon the Red Army.  A state structure had not even
been created.  Confronting Western armies in West
Germany and West Berlin, it was hardly a time to
persecute violently religion.

After 1949, with the formal establishment of the
GDR, the Communists were particularly interested in
obtaining Western recognition and in making good
their claim to be a sovereign state, independent and
separate from the Federal Republic of Germany.  The
main religions all had strong ties in the West and
persecution would have led to immediate protests and
complications.  Four of the seven administrative
units of the Catholic Church were parts of West
German dioceses and the bishopric of Berlin included

West and East Berlin. Until 1952, priests could go
back and forth from East to West and vice versa.
West German bishops could visit the East German parts
of their dioceses up to 1958. The Evangelical
Church remained united in East and West Germany until
1969.[7] To attack the churches would have been need-
lessly provocative and foolhardy.

The East German Communists simply had no desire
to make religion a major complication in their relations with the West. In fact, by the 1960s, the
East Germans were looking to improve their relations
with the Vatican. Specifically, the Germans wanted
the Holy See to create East German dioceses separate
from West German administration, with a long range
goal of possible diplomatic recognition. In 1968,
Walter Ulbricht, the head of the SED and chairman of
the GDR State Council, declared that if the Holy See
wanted to establish diplomatic relations, his government would always be ready to do so.[8] Another major
objective was to persuade the Vatican and other
Catholics to support Soviet foreign policy initia-
tives, especially the over-all strategy of "peaceful
coexistence." A principal tool in carrying out this
policy was the previously mentioned Berlin Conference
(BK) of Catholic Christians from European States.
In 1971, Otto Harmut Fuchs, the head of the BK,
visited Rome and discussed "the service of Catholics
to peace" with the Secretary-General of the Papal
Commission Iustitia et Pax, Mgr. Joseph Gremillon.
Fuchs also, in his words, "continued at a higher
level the exchange of views" started with Vatican
officials two years ago.[9]

Cardinal Bengsch met with Premier Willi Stoph
in August 1972 to discuss "questions of common interest resulting from developments in Europe with special regard to the provisions under international law
in the Treaties between the USSR and FRG and between
the People's Republic of Poland and the FRG, as well
as other treaties and agreements."[10] According to
the East German News Agency, "the conversation took
place in a business-like atmosphere."[11] In January
1973, Pope Paul and Walter Ulbricht exchanged New
Year messages.[12] This development was indicative
of slowly improving relations. In the same month,
Archbishop Casaroli met with Werner Lamberg, a member of the SED politburo, in Rome.[13] In July 1973,
the Holy See, in a significant concession, reorgan-
ized the ecclesiastical units which had been under
the jurisdiction of West German bishops into three
new dioceses-- Erfurt, Meiningen, and Magdeburg-
Schwerin--and named three East German Apostolic

Administrators to run them.[14]  The East German News
Agency criticized the Vatican for not naming full
bishops to the dioceses and for its reluctance to extend de jure recognition to the GDR.[15]  In late 1974
the East Germans accused West Germany of interfering
in Vatican-GDR relations.[16]

The highlight of Papal Ostpolitik in East Germany to date was the visit of Archbishop Casaroli
to East Berlin in June 1975.  While there he had extensive discussions on issues relating to Church-
State relations with both government and Church
officials.[17]  Casaroli viewed the exercise as "positive" and declared "the openness of the discussions
and the atmosphere by which they were characterized
appear to me to be ground for hope."[18]  In August
1975, when the Holy See named a new Nuncio to West
Germany, it changed his title from "Nuncio to Germany" to the Papal Nuncio in the Federal Republic
of Germany.  The Polish Press Agency commended the
Vatican for taking a course "towards recognizing the
GDR."[19]  Discussions between the Church and State
continued when, in August 1977, Cardinal Bengsch and
Hans Seigewasser met and talked about "questions of
mutual interest."[20]  In September 1977, the Cardinal
and two other East German bishops visited the Vatican.[21]

## ROMANIA

After the Communists assumed power at the end
of World War II, the Catholic Church in Romania, like
other churches, experienced persecution.  The Romanian Communist government was rigid and narrowly
Marxist-Leninist, a dedicated opponent of organized
religion.  At the same time, though, the government's attitude in persecuting religion was and continues to be influenced by a strong desire to promote Romanian nationalism and to celebrate the past
glories and heroes of Romanian history.  Such a pro-
clivity led inevitably to positions which occasionally favored the Romanian Orthodox Church, the
national religion of Romania and the faith which was
identified in the past as the protector of Romanian
identity against Western Catholics in Austria and
Hungary and against Muslim Turks.  Interest in the
distant past (before the Nineteenth Century) has
been especially acute since Romania in the 1960s
managed to follow a somewhat independent line from
Moscow.

The fact that considerations of nationalism have
favored the Romanian Orthodox Church, however, did

not reduce the regime's animosity toward the Catholic
Church in Romania.  In fact, if anything, it reinforced it.  In 1948, the government forcibly merged
the 1½ million Uniate Church with the Romanian Orthodox Church.  Uniate monasteries and seminaries were
closed and the churches were turned over to the
Orthodox Church.  All six bishops were arrested
(four died in prison before 1960) and the clergy have
been decimated:  over fifty priests have been killed,
200 have been imprisoned, 200 have vanished, and
another 200 have been sentenced to forced labor
camps.[22]  Since then there have been continuing reports of underground Uniate activities and ruthless
government suppression.[23]  In 1951, the government
attempted to organize a national Catholic Church,
independent of Rome, but met with little success.[24]
    The Uniate Catholic Church was particularly re-
sented since it was viewed as a sophisticated Trojan
Horse, a dissimulation to persuade Orthodox Christians to accept Papal leadership.  The Latin Catholic
Church did not fit into that category, although it
was also viewed with suspicion and restrained dis-
like.  But at least the Latin Catholic Church was not
institutionally destroyed.  While it is greatly hampered by government restrictions on its activities
and especially by the government's refusal to allow
the appointment of bishops to all six dioceses, it
continues to function.  There are about 1½ million
Roman Catholics or close to 8% of the total population, mainly of Hungarian and German extraction and
mostly located in Transylvania.[25]  In 1949-50, monasteries and convents in Romania, like in Hungary
and Czechoslovakia, were closed down and a few were
transformed into concentration camps.  All Catholic
welfare organizations, including hospitals, were
nationalized or closed by 1950.  Contact with the
Vatican is only allowed through the Ministry of
Foreign Affairs.  The government controls the fi-
nances of the churches and provides a subsidy for
their support.  It censures all publications of the
churches, including pastoral letters.[26]
    Contacts between the Vatican and the Romanian
state began slowly, complicated by the problem of the
suppressed Uniate Church and the traditional rivalry
between Orthodoxy and Catholicism.  As early as 1965
Cardinal Franz Koenig visited Bucharest, and Cardinal Jan Willebrands travelled there shortly after.
In December 1965, the authorities decided to recognize the appointment of Petru Plesca as titular
bishop of Fico--for Iasi but without recognizing him
as titular bishop of Iasi.[27]  In November 1967,

Cardinal Koenig returned to Romania and met Patri-
arch Justinian of the Romanian Orthodox Church,
Bishop Plesca, and the general secretary of the
State Office for Church Affairs. He also met Bishop
Aaron Marton of Alba Julia, who was arrested in 1949
and had been living under house-arrest since 1955.
The cardinal was informed that henceforth Bishop
Marton was free to move about as he wished.[28]  In
January 1968, Prime Minister Ion Gheorghe Maurer and
Foreign Minister Corneliu Manescu called on the Pope
at the Vatican.  In February Ceausescu received
Bishop Plesca.[29]  In October 1970, Patriarch Justinian visited Cardinal Julius Doepfner of Munich and
Freising and Cardinal Doepfner visited Romania on
November 11-12, 1971, and the Roman Catholic bishop
of Regensburg, Dr. Rudolf Grabner, was in Romania
in April 1970.[30]  In 1971 the Holy See was given
permission to appoint Bishop Anton Jakab coadjutor
with right of succession to the aging Bishop Marton.[31]
     Romanian churchmen and political leaders soon
began a steady stream of visits to Rome.  In March
1972, Orthodox Bishop Antonie Ploiesteanu was received by the Pope.  The Pope said the visit was the
beginning of a new relationship between the Catholic
and Romanian Orthodox Churches.[32]  In May 1973,
Ceausescu and his wife were received in the Vatican
by the Pope.  They discussed, according to the New
York Times, the status of both Roman and Uniate
Catholics in Romania.[33]  One year later, the Romanian
Foreign Minister, George Macovescu, met at the Vatican with Cardinal Villot, Archbishop Casaroli, and
Archbishop Poggi, and reportedly discussed problems
relating to the Conference on Security and Cooperation in Europe and the Middle East.[34]  At the same
time, in an interview with the Italian journalist
Franco Piccinini, Ceausescu declared that "although
we do not maintain diplomatic relations I would say
that the relations between Romania and the Vatican
are good."  He added that "we believe that in the
light of the efforts to achieve European security and
a better, more equitable world, there are prospects
for the expansion and development of co-operation
between Romania and the Vatican."[35]  In January 1975,
Archbishop Poggi visited Bucharest to continue the
dialogue.[36]  In October 1976, the Archbishop was back
for more discussions with government officials.[37]
At the funeral of Patriarch Justinian in March 1977,
the Vatican was represented by Bishop Ramon Torella,
Vice-President of the Secretariat for Christian
Unity.[38]  Bishop Petru Plesca also died in March 1977
and one year later the government permitted the

Vatican to appoint Monsignor Petru Gherghel as the "ordinary ad nutum sanctae sedis" (at the disposal of the Holy See) for the administration of the diocese of Iasi. Monsignor Gherghel was not, however, made a bishop.[39] In May 1978, Archbishop Poggi was back in Romania for talks with government and religious leaders.[40]

## BULGARIA

Bulgaria, one of the Soviet Union's most faithful allies, has a small Roman Catholic population of about 50,000. In 1960 there were reportedly thirty churches, one bishop, and forty-six priests. The number of priests had climbed to forty-eight by 1969. There are also about 10,000 Uniate Catholics in Bulgaria with one bishop and twenty-one priests.[41] In contrast to Romania and the Soviet Union, the Uniates were not forcibly merged with the Bulgarian Orthodox Church.

Once the Communists took power, they showed themselves to be interested primarily, when it came to religious affairs, in reducing the influence of religion in the social and political life of Bulgaria. Religious instruction was removed from the schools and atheism was pushed.[42] From 1948 to the end of 1952, the regime launched a harsh campaign against the churches. Relations between the Holy See and Bulgaria were broken in 1949.[43] In 1952, the Roman Catholic bishop of Nikopolis, Mgr. Eugene Bossilkov, was arrested and reportedly executed.[44]

After Stalin's death the religious situation improved in Bulgaria, particularly for the Orthodox. Latin and Uniate Catholic delegates were allowed to attend the sessions of the Vatican Council, but neither rite was permitted a seminary.[45]

Relations between the Vatican and Bulgaria began to improve with the visit of Todor Zhivkov, the Prime Minister and Party leader, to the Vatican in June 1975. A brief communiqué, following a private meeting between Zhivkov and the Pope, mentioned that, inter alia, "both the Latin and Byzantine-Slavic rites" in Bulgaria had been discussed along with general, international problems, including the Middle East, peace and disarmament, Cyprus, security of Europe, etc. The Pope was said to have "expressed the hope that Catholics would continue to be permitted religious freedom in Bulgaria, which is in any case guaranteed by [its] constitution" and additionally that "although few in number, they would contribute to meeting the needs of Bulgarian society."[46]

In November 1976, Archbishop Casaroli went to
Bulgaria and held extensive discussions with Zhikov
and Petur Mladenov, the Bulgarian Foreign Minister.
The major topics discussed included bilateral relations, peace and security in Europe, and the implementation of the Helsinki Final Act.[47] At a dinner
given in Casaroli's honor, Mladenov declared that
"during the talks, we dwelt on the co-operation between Bulgaria and the Vatican in the future. With
our stands clarified, we went on to discover additional opportunities for further useful and mutually
advantageous activities." Casaroli responded that it
was beneficial to exchange views and exphasized that
the Holy See and Bulgaria understood the supreme
meaning of the fact that Europe was bound together
by common and vital interests.[48] In October 1977,
the Vatican sent five delegates to Sofia to attend
a conference of European Churches on ecumenism.[49]

ALBANIA

From the point of view of Communist-Papal
rapprochement, Albania stands in sharp contrast to
the other European Communist states. It has shown
no desire to improve relations with the Vatican and,
in fact, continues to denigrate the Holy See and,
at the same time, bitterly assails the other Communist states, including the Soviet Union, for their
attempts to reach a modus vivendi with Rome. Now
that China has broken with Tirana, it is difficult
to see how Albania, a small, backward country of two
million people, can maintain its isolation from
Europe. It stands as an inscrutable replica of
Stalinism, an authoritarian regime blindly dedicated
to atheism and the bankrupt theories of Marxism-
Leninism.
It is extremely difficult to obtain current
statistical information on the Catholic Church and
other religions in Albania. After the war, though,
the Church had the allegiance of about 10% of the
population. But since then, Catholicism has been
relentlessly attacked and pummeled. Radio Vatican
reported in April 1973 that "only vague and rare
traces of the Catholic Church remain."[50] In that
same month, l'Osservatore Romano announced, in the
wake of the execution of a Catholic priest, Father
Shtjeten Kurti, that

Places of worship either no longer exist or
have been transformed into dance halls,
gymnasia or offices of various kinds.

177

Scutari cathedral has become the "Sports
Palace;" a swimming pool with showers has
been constructed in place of the presbytery
and sacristy; the artistic bell-tower that
soared above it has been razed to the ground.
The ancient canonry chapel at Scutari, used
as a baptistry, among other things, has become a warehouse for tires.  The church of
St. Nicholas in the Catholic district of Rusi
has been transformed into flats for factory
workers.  The church of the Stigmatine Sisters
has become a lecture hall, the one of the
Institute of the Sisters of St. Elizabeth is
used as the headquarters of the political
police.  The national sanctuary of Our Lady
of Scutari, "Protectress of Albania," has
been pulled down.  On its ruins there now
rises a column surmounted by the red star.[51]

The drive against the Catholic Church was moti-
vated mainly by Marxism-Leninism, but also by the
fact that it was a Western Church with strong ties
to Italy, a former colonial power and enemy during
World War II.  In 1967, the Albanian government
announced that Albania had become the first atheist
state and from that point on all religious practices
have been outlawed.[52]

The Albanians follow closely the developments
between the Catholic Church and the Communist governments of Eastern Europe.  With the advent of Papal
Ostpolitik, the Albanian authorities opened up a
bitter and sharp attack upon their fellow Communists
in Eastern Europe and the Soviet Union.  Moscow is
accused of cultivating the Vatican as an ally in its
"counter-revolutionary activity."[53]  Edward Gierek
is accused of outdoing the "Gomulka clique in
[granting] concessions to the Catholic Church."[54]
Kadar and his "revisionist clique" are charged with
attempting "to glorify the image of the Church and
the Vatican."[55]  Almost no one though, pays attention
to Albania, which undoubtedly is the proper response
to its hostility and withdrawal from European
affairs.  The fact that China, as already mentioned,
has broken its alliance with Tirana might force the
Albanian government to adopt a more reasonable
attitude.

NOTES

1.  Simon, "Catholic Church," p. 217.
2.  Beeson, Discretion, p. 172.

3. Simon, "Catholic Church," p. 217.
4. Ibid.; Beeson, Discretion, p. 176.
5. Beeson, Discretion, p. 172.
6. Ibid., p. 174.
7. Simon, "Catholic Church," p. 217.
8. Herter Korrespondence 3 (March 1973): 114-115.
9. East German News Agency, May 3, 1972.
10. Ibid., August 24, 1972.
11. Ibid.
12. Ibid., January 12, 1973; New York Times, January 12, 1973.
13. Herter Korrespondence 3 (March 1973): 114.
14. New York Times, July 24, 1973.
15. East German News Agency, October 11, 1973.
16. "Voice of the GDR," November 9, 1974.
17. Ibid., June 9, 10, 1975; The Tablet (London), June 28, 1975.
18. The Times (London), June 16, 1975.
19. Polish Press Agency, October 24, 1975.
20. East German News Agency, August 2, 1977.
21. Ibid., September 29, 1977.
22. Beeson, Discretion, p. 309.
23. Keston News Service, Issue No. 45, November 17, 1977, pp. 1-2.
24. Beeson, Discretion, p. 309.
25. Ibid., p. 304.
26. Simon, "Catholic Church," pp. 197, 201.
27. Radio Free Europe Research, Rumanian Situation Report/3 (January 24, 1975), p. 15.
28. The Tablet (London), December 2, 1967.
29. Radio Free Europe Research, Rumanian Situation Report/3 (January 24, 1975, p. 15; New York Times, January 25, 1968.
30. Radio Free Europe Research, Rumanian Situation Report/3 (January 24, 1975), p. 16; Romanian Press Agency, November 11, 1971.
31. Radio Free Europe Research, Rumanian Situation Report/3 (January 24, 1975), p. 16.
32. Ibid.
33. New York Times, May 27, 1973.
34. Radio Free Europe Research, Rumanian Situation Report/3 (January 24, 1975), p. 15; Jewish Chronicle, May 31, 1974.
35. Radio Free Europe Research, Rumanian Situation Report/3 (January 24, 1975), p. 16.
36. Ibid., pp. 14-15; The Tablet, February 1, 1975.
37. Radio Vatican, October 22, 8, 1976.
38. Romanian Press Agency, March 31, 1977.
39. Keston News Service, Issue No. 52

179

(May 25, 1978), p. 5.

40. Radio Vatican, May 20, 1978.

41. Beeson, Discretion, p. 288.

42. Ibid., p. 289.

43. Ibid., p. 293.

44. Ibid.

45. Ibid., p. 297.

46. Radio Free Europe Research, Bulgarian
Situation Report/19 (July 11, 1975), pp. 5-6;
Bulgarian Telegraph Agency, June 26, 1975.

47. Radio Vatican, November 4, 1976; Bulgarian
Telegraph Agency, November 11, 1976.

48. Bulgarian Telegraph Agency, November 9,
1976.

49. Ibid., October 3, 1977.

50. Beeson, Discretion, p. 281.

51. Ibid., pp. 584-85.

52. Ibid., p. 281; Peter Prifti, "Albania--
Towards an Atheist Society," in Bociurkiw and Strong,
Religion and Atheism, pp. 388, 393-98.

53. Radio Tirana, January 27, 1971. Also see
Albanian Telegraph Agency, August 29, September 6,
December 29, 1971; Albanian Telegraph Agency,
March 16, 1978.

54. Radio Tirana, February 10, 1971. Also see
Albanian Telegraph Agency, February 18, 1971; Radio
Tirana, February 25, 1972, February 10, 1971; Al-
banian Telegraph Agency, February 7, 1974; Radio
Tirana, November 22, 1974, March 6, 1975, November 2,
1977, January 9, 10, 1978.

55. Radio Tirana, March 9, 1972, February 27,
1972.

# 9. Conclusions

So far as there is a definable policy of détente in the politico-religious sphere, it is directed by the Communist governments of Eastern Europe at the Vatican rather than at the local Catholic hierarchies. The Communist hope is that the latter can be influenced by and held to agreements made with the Papacy. The desire of the Papacy, of course, is to establish a modus vivendi with the Communist regimes and to improve the position of Catholics in Eastern Europe and the USSR. From the Catholic side, the policy of détente, then, can be judged in accordance with two criteria: Whether or not it achieves improvement of relations between the Vatican and the various Communist governments and alleviates the conditions of local Catholic Churches in each Communist country.

In the USSR the policy has to be deemed a failure on both counts. Vatican officials, to be sure, have been welcomed in Moscow and exhorted and praised for supporting specific foreign policies of the Soviet government. But the reality is that the Papacy, the Catholic Church, and religion in general continue to be viciously attacked in Soviet internal propaganda. Discrimination and persecution of Catholics have indeed been on the increase since the early 1970s, particularly in Lithuania and the Ukraine. These two Catholic communities are, with the exception of Albania where every vestige of religious practice is brutally suppressed, those which suffer the most from Communist rule in the whole of Europe. The Lithuanians are the one complete Latin Catholic nation, which, since the last war, has formed part of the USSR. It is for this reason that they can hope for nothing like the relative freedom of their Polish Catholic neighbors, which the internationally recognized independence of

the Polish Republic has made it possible to secure.
Whether the Holy See could have done more than obtain
the Soviet government's consent to the appointment
of one or two bishops to keep alive a vestige of
ecclesiastical organization is open to question.  But
in this case there is no opportunity for a reciprocal
exchange, as in Poland, Hungary, or Yugoslavia, where
the restoration of certain religious facilities is
the price of controlling the discontent of large
populations.  For Soviet citizens themselves, as the
Lithuanians are, it is the only kind of pressure from
the Western industrial powers, suggested later in
this chapter, which might obtain any safeguard of
their basic human rights.

The same consideration applies to the Uniate Catholics of the Ukraine which has been annexed to
the Soviet Union.  They certainly have deserved more
consistent and effective help from the Holy See, let
alone the United States and other friendly governments than they have received, regardless of Cardinal
Slipyi's determined agitation--after his liberation
at Pope John's intervention--for an Ukrainian Patriarchate.  But in their case there is an additional
complication which was unknown in their earlier history of alternate repression and tolerance by the
tsars.  It is that their forced conformity to the
Russian Orthodox Church, which it had been for centuries their characteristic tradition to resist because of their loyalty to Rome, is now found to be,
not only not condemned but apparently condoned by
the Holy See, because of its novel ecumenical preoccupation with the possible reunion of the Russian
and Catholic Churches.  To most observers who realize
the extent to which the Moscow Patriarchate is in
effect an organ of the Soviet State, such a possibility seems a will o' the wisp, and, even if exter-
nally attainable, of doubtful spiritual merit.  But,
whether as excuse or justification for inaction, this
attitude of the Vatican can only appear to the
Uniate Catholics as a betrayal.

In Poland, the government has taken meaningful
steps to improve the situation of the Catholic
Church.  In 1971 it returned land, churches, and
property to the Church which had been in the Oder-
Neisse regions.  The Polish Catholic press and educational facilities have considerable influence,
although they are hampered.  On the other hand, the
regime is uncompromising on such important issues as
the Church's social and welfare functions and it is
only with difficulty that new churches can be built.
The Catholic leaders are under no illusions as to

what the Communists would like to do to Catholics in
Poland, but realize that the government is prevented
from taking offensive measures by the Church's per-
vasive influence with the people.  The regime in
Poland has now established fairly close relations
with the Holy See and would no doubt like to obtain
some leverage against Cardinal Wyszynski and the
other indigenous bishops.  But there is at present
no evidence of tension between Rome and the Polish
episcopate.

     In Hungary the situation has certainly been
transformed from the one of internal warfare between
an oppressive Communist government, using the party
apparatus for aggressive interference at every level,
and the bulk of the Catholic and Protestant people,
to a regime of mutual cooperation between believers
and unbeievers in political, social, and economic
life for "the building up of the homeland," sponsored
equally by the government and the Church leaders.
This state of affairs, symbolized for instance by the
participation of Cardinal Lekai the Primate in the
1977 Congress of the Patriotic National Front, is
unique in Eastern Europe.  Whether or not this com-
promises the Church in its freedom to defend faith
and morals is a matter of opinion.  It has disappointed some young Catholics whose "basic groups"
were stifled by the bishops, but it has undoubtedly
brought an appreciable easing of restrictions on religious instruction and the prospects of Catholics
in the universities and professions, and on popular
religious events--50,000 people were reported at a
pilgrimage last year and 30,000 attended the first
masses of newly ordained priests.  This transformation had begun under the Kadar regime during the
economic easement of the late 1960s, but was only
made possible by the decision of the Pope to sacrifice Cardinal Mindszenty and enforce his retirement
from the see of Esztergom.  Intense bitterness was
caused to many Catholics, more outside than in Hungary, by this abandonment of the brave, old champion
of the Faith, but it is undeniable that it was in-
dispensable to the main aim of the Holy See, which
was to secure government agreement to the restoration
of the Hungarian hierarchy.  This objective, starting
with the partial agreement of 1964, was fully attained in 1977 when bishops installed in every diocese made their joint ad limina visit to the Pope,
followed, in June, by his receiving Mr. Kadar in a
long private audience.  The Communist Party leader
said that he believed that this encounter "would
lead to further efforts to stabilize Church-State

relations."

In Czechoslovakia restriction and intolerance characterize the position of the Catholic Church. Though repression has not been as bad as it was between 1948 and 1968, few of the improvements affecting the clergy made during the Dubček regime have survived. The Vatican has not succeeded in filling the majority of the vacant sees but has accepted three politically compromised "peace priests" as bishops. Whether the installation of the archbishop of Prague will lead to any such solution as has been reached in Hungary remains to be seen; but the character of the Communist Party leader, Mr. Husak, and his subservience to Soviet direction are against it.

Yugoslavia has been the success story to date. The Vatican has diplomatic relations with Belgrade and the local Catholic Church in Croatia and Slovenia has made many gains, although its educational and social functions are still curtailed.

In East Germany, the Church is suffering from growing secularization and official atheism, but enjoys relative freedom compared to the other East European Communist states except for Poland and Yugoslavia. This situation is the result of the GDR's unique position between Eastern and Western Europe and the fact that the East German authorities have decided they need not make religion a major issue. Vatican-East German relations are evolving, with the East Germans waiting for the Holy See to name East German bishops for the new dioceses which formerly had been part of West German dioceses and administered by West German bishops.

In Romania, the Romanian Orthodox Church remains the religion of the bulk of the people and, in return for the complete political acquiescence of the Orthodox Patriarch and clergy, there is little interference by the Communist government in the life of that Church. It is different for the religious minorities who, despite the freedom accorded in the constitution to belief and worship, have suffered considerable molestation. There has been outright persecution of some small Protestant communities and their ministers. But it is mainly the consequences of Romanian annexation (or recovery) of territory from Hungary after the Second World War which has been the occasion of religious repression on nationalistic grounds. The Hungarian population of Transylvania was either Latin Catholic or Calvinist in the case of the Magyars, or Uniate Catholic in the case of the people of Romanian origin. For the former who did not migrate to Hungary, a tolerable

184

condition has been assured, but the Uniate bishops, priests, and people have suffered from the same policy of enforced conformity with the national Orthodox Church as had been inflicted on the Uniates of the former Polish Ukraine and of sub-Carpathian Ruthenia. And the Holy See has failed to secure any appreciable aleviation of their lot.

In Albania the Church has been brutally suppressed. The Vatican is attacked as "reactionary" and the other Communist states as "revisionist." The Church in Bulgaria is small, but the Bulgarian government has shown interest in improving its relations with the Vatican.

Apart from the specific purposes of the Ostpolitik of the Holy See in different countries, whether to reduce, if possible, the hostile pressure upon the Catholic clergy and people in some countries or to reinforce in others (as in Poland) the already strong position of the Church and in every case to secure the presence of bishops, there are two major considerations which have evidently impelled the Pope to pursue a policy of rapprochement with the Soviets and their Eastern European dependents. One is the reality of power. Whatever the errors of Marxism, and the Papacy never has and never can unsay its condemnation of atheism, materialism, and the overriding of the dignity of human personality, however strong, on the other hand, is the tendency nowadays to look for whatever is constructive in socialist institutions, it is undeniable that socialism is making remarkable progress not only in Western Europe but throughout what is called the Third World and in the United Nations. Behind this movement stands the expanding military strength of the Soviet Union, already superior to that of its political adversaries. The universal Church has never, since the fading of the Roman Empire, identified itself with a particular political system; and, though the difficulties of securing respect for its essential freedom to fulfill its mission under a government which denies the existence of God are greater even than they were under the pretensions of eighteenth century monarchs, it is inevitable that many millions of Christians in fact live under such governments. It can be argued, therefore, that to be on speaking terms with the Communist rulers of those socialist states is the duty of the head of the Catholic Church. There is little doubt that it is for that reason that Paul VI was determined during his pontificate to establish a firm bridge between the Catholic Church and socialism. It is, of

185

course, a policy full of pitfalls and misunderstand-
ings, and one which is difficult to pursue without
outraging the sentiments of Catholics who have
suffered most from antireligious repression and
others throughout the world who are devoted to the
fight against Communism and Soviet power.

The other overriding consideration which favors
Papal rapprochement with the Soviet bloc as well as
friendship with the United States and other democratic powers, is the devotion of international peace
which is part and parcel of the Papal tradition. The
danger of thermonuclear war hangs over the world.
It is for fear of this that the Soviet Union, while
rivalling and even outbidding the United States in
its strategic nuclear weapons, has committed itself
to the more subtle "policy of peaceful coexistence"
to advance the world revolution to which it is dedicated. It is also to avert it that the Western an-
tagonists of the Soviets seek the mutual limitation
of armaments while arming themselves sufficiently,
as many hope, to deter an attack. The Pope and his
advisors have had little taste, and, maybe, little
competence for these strategic arguments. It was
simply for peace that he worked, and prayed, and
exhorted; and, since peace, cooperation in Europe,
and the resolution of tension were proclaimed as
the purpose of the Helsinki Conference, we found the
Pope praising it in uncritical terms which seemed
naïve to those diplomatic observers who were well-
aware of the Soviet strategy which brought it about.
He was at the same time quite firm in insisting--for
example, in his recent conversation with the leaders
of the Hungarian and Polish Communist Parties and
governments--upon the obligation to secure the safeguard of human rights for which the Final Act, to
which the Holy See is a party, provides. Support
for peace, which their Communist interlocutors interpret after their fashion, is consequently a con-
genial topic for such Papal visitors as Mgr. Casaroli
or Cardinal Koenig or Father Arrupe in Communist
capitals.

There is little difficulty in assessing the
practical consequences in Eastern Europe of the
attempts of Papal diplomats to repair the hierarchi-
cal structure of the Church and improve conditions
for the spiritual life of the faithful through contacts with the Communist governments. We have seen
how far these governments on their side have or have
not found it useful in controlling their populations
to give any satisfaction to these attempts. What is
far more difficult is to foretell the future of

186

these Catholic-Communist relations, particularly
with the death of Paul VI on August 6, 1978.
One school of thought, steeped in the habits of
the free society and the legacy of Christian civilization, is instinctively optimistic. Believing in
the creed of human progress, it is convinced that a
regime which denies natural rights and liberties to
its people and presents to the world an attitude of
absolute political and military defiance will, as
the result of increased economic intercourse with the
democratic peoples and their amicable posture, be
inevitably converted in due course of time from its
naughty ways. It is this school of thought, so prominent in the English-speaking countries and in
Western Europe which from the moment the so-called
"détente" movement was initiated in the early 1960s,
with a view to reduce the military configuration between the Soviet bloc and the Western Alliance in
Europe and to seek a limitation of strategic nuclear
weapons, conceived that a lasting peace was the
terminus ad quem of détente for the Communist Party
of the Soviet Union and their subordinates, as it is
for the United States and other civilized peoples.
Despite the accumulation of evidence to the contrary,
from the military subjugation of Czechoslovakia to
the drastic consequences of the Communist conquests
in Vietnam and Cambodia, the Communist despotism
established in Portuguese Africa and the Soviet-Cuban
military intervention in Angola and Ethiopia, despite
the wholesale disregard by both the Soviets and their
satellites of obligations to which they subscribed in
the Final Act of the Helsinki Conference for the respect of basic human rights, something of this same
optimism is to be found among certain Western religious leaders, beginning with the late Pope Paul VI
himself. Rome, it is true, thinks in centuries;
and it is very possible that the Soviet revolutionary
empire will eventually wear itself out, as the other
great empires of human history have done. But it is
to go in the face of reason to pretend that minor
concessions made to the Church in Hungary or Czechoslovakia or Romania or the exchange of public courtesies between Russian Orthodox prelates and Roman
Catholic visitors to the USSR portend a repudiation
of atheism which is inherent in the constitutions
of the Soviet bloc of states, just as it is simply a
matter of wishful thinking to see in the wordy out-
pouring of the "peaceful coexistence" propaganda the
beginning of any fundamental change in the world
strategy of Communist Russia. It is possible, of
course, that relations between the state and churches

187

in Hungary may develop into something like the modus vivendi which exists for specific reasons in Yugoslavia; it is probable that the existing truce will continue in Poland.  It is also possible, though not probable, that the remarkable concession to foreign pressure represented by the permission given in ten years for 150,000 Jews to migrate from the Soviet Union to Israel might be followed by permission to other groups to emigrate:  only rare individual permits, however, seem likely.  One thing is clear from the experience of recent years.  The internal pressure from a minority of dissidents for the respect of human rights has a certain nuisance value in the East European satellites of the Soviet Union.  But there is not the remotest prospect of verbal protests on the infringement of personal, civil, or religious rights by the President of the United States, or any other Western spokesman, or the Vatican having the slightest effect upon the Soviet government, unless they could be reinforced with the denial of the one great tangible advantage which détente is bringing to it, namely the increasing supply of sophisticated technical processes and machinery from the West. Here indeed is one possibility of modifying the inhuman rigidity of Communist rule; the vested interests of Western industrialists in the lucrative contracts of the Communist bloc are, however, now too strong for this to be a practicable proposition for politicians.

It is more prudent therefore to view such concessions as have been made to the Catholic Church in Eastern Europe, as well as the courting of ecclesiastical goodwill for the current peace campaign of Soviet propaganda, as the tactics of expediency, a phase which may or may not last.  The value of the former is certainly that, because of the popular welcome which they have received (e.g. the restoration of the Hungarian hierarchy and Cardinal Tomasek's installation at Prague) they will be difficult to undo.  But on the major question of Soviet policy, the only safe judgment must be based upon the purpose of détente as consistently expounded by President Brezhnev and the ruling Communist Party of the Soviet Union.  Though this has been defined as applying to inter-state relations between socialist and capitalist countries, there is no reason to suppose that it does not encompass important elements such as the churches, within capitalist states.  Further, the principle of courting the participation of religious, anti-militarist, pacifist, and liberal bodies in the West in favor of Soviet policies has been a recurrent

feature of Communist propaganda from the days of the
"Ban the Bomb Campaign" and the attempted "Common
Front against War and Fascism" in the late 1930s.
Since the early 1960s, the process has become much
more intensive through the increasing involvement of
the churches in Europe and the Americas in the anti-
colonial "liberation campaign" and the Marxist pene-
tration of large sections of the Catholic clergy
which has resulted from the novel preoccupation of
the post-Counciliar Church with secular causes.  The
great advantage of this development to the advancement of the Soviet-Communist strategy throughout the
world, including particularly Western Europe, the
United States--where the "leftward lurch" is most
marked among the Catholic bureaucracy--Latin America,
and Southern Africa is so great that it is well
worth a mild flirtation with the Papacy, some concessions which are of local political value to the
satellite governments, and encouragement to ecumenical courtesies between Papal representatives and the
tightly controlled Russian Orthodox Church.

None of this involves the slightest deviation
of the Soviets from their pursuit of détente governed
by the well-defined purpose of "peaceful coexistence,"
which was laid down by the CPSU as the "main aim of
Soviet foreign policy" at its congress in 1961 and
has been an essential part of the party's program
ever since.  The purpose is to promote the achievement of the Communist order within the Soviet Union
and the victory of socialism throughout the world.
The aim is to advance this cause without provoking
the capitalists to war and particularly the thermonuclear war which Khrushchev believed--though it is
doubtful whether his successors do--would probably
be fatal to the prospects of the World Revolution.
Hence peaceful intercourse and the peaceful settlement of disputes between the socialist and capitalist
states were to be encouraged, but without affecting
the "class struggle" (which Marxism-Leninism teaches
to be an inexorable law of life) and "peaceful coexistence will create more favorable conditions both
for the advancement of the workers' cause within the
capitalist states and the liberation of the dependent peoples."  The proposals for military and nuclear
détente first made by President Johnson and the
NATO Council, taken up, after long delays by the
Soviet leadership, were adopted to this general purpose; and, through Mr. Brezhnev's persistence, the
Helsinki Conference on Security and Cooperation in
Europe was eventually convened as an attempt to in-
ternationalize the Soviet "policy of peaceful

coexistence." Within months, the Soviets launched
a major military operation, with its Cuban surro-
gates for the Communist conquest of Angola. This
was a severe shock to Western opinion and Dr. Kissinger, in particular, threatened, it will be remembered,
that such a military aggression carried out far from
its own frontiers by the Soviet Union endangered for
the United States the whole prospect of the policy
of détente. To which President Brezhnev replied at
the next Congress of the CPSU that it was "as clear
as can be that détente and peaceful coexistence apply
solely to inter-state relations" and that it was
"obtuse" for a capitalist spokesman to imagine that
it affected a people's struggle for "liberation" and
the Soviet Communists' support for it.

This then is the kind of "détente" into which
any consideration or speculation on the prospects
of the Catholic Church, and in general of any better
respect of religious rights and liberties, in Eastern
Europe and in the Communist-ruled countries of other
continents depend. The policy itself has, of course,
no relation to religion. It is an extremely adroit
and logical method of achieving victory without war.
It has already had considerable success in its primary aim which is to weaken the coherence of the
Atlantic Alliance, the main core of capitalist re-
sistence to the Soviet strategy; and there is no
doubt that the cooperation of Catholic as well as
the World Council of Churches in the anti-militarist
and Russophile movements, which have gained strength
among the left wing parties of Western Europe, is
giving considerable help to the Soviet aim of the
neutralization of the continent and the loosening of
the American-European defensive coalition. It may
well be that, as viewed from Moscow, it is this,
rather than local accommodations in Eastern Europe,
that is the central importance of the temporary
rapprochement with the Papacy.

# Bibliography

DOCUMENTS

Acta Apstolicae Sedis.  Citta del Vaticano, 1923-
     1978.
Annuario Pontifico, Official Yearbook.  Citta del
     Vaticano, 1945-1978.
Chronicle of the Catholic Church in Lithuania, 1972-
     1978; 31 issues to date.  English translation
     of early issues available from the Lithuanian
     Roman Catholic Priests' League of America,
     Maspeth, New York.  Recent issues in Russian
     and Lithuanian are available at Keston College
     (Centre for the Study of Religion and Commu-
     nism), London.
Sobranie documentov samizdata, 1971-1978.  Munich,
     Radio Liberty, 1972-1978.
Summary of World Broadcasts (SWB), Part 1: The USSR,
     and Part 2: Eastern Europe.  Caversham Park,
     Reading, England.  British Broadcasting Corpora-
     tion, 1945-1978.  (All Radio, Television, and
     News Agency reports have been taken from the
     SWB.)
Slipyi, Joseph Cardinal,  Letter to Paul VI,
     April 14, 1977. (Personal collection, photo-
     copy.)

ARCHIVES

Roosevelt, Franklin D., Papers, Franklin D. Roose-
     velt Library, Hyde Park, New York.  Documents
     cited here are from the President's Secretary's
     File (PSF).

BOOKS

Akademiia nauk Belorusskoi SSR, Institut filosofii i
     prava, Prichiny sushchestvovaniia i puti preo-
     doleniia religioznykh perezhitkov. Minsk, 1965.
Akademiia nauk SSSR--Institut nauchnogo atheizma;
     Akademiia obshchestvennykh nauk pri Tsk KPSS--
     Institut nauchnogo atheizma, Stroitelstvo
     kommunizma i preodolenie religioznykh
     perezhitkov. Moscow, 1966.
Alexeev, Wassilij. The Foreign Policy of the Moscow
     Patriarchate, 1939-1953. New York, 1955.
Anderson, Paul B. People, Church, and State in Mod-
     ern Russia. New York, 1944.
Andras, Emmerich and Morel, Julius. Bilanz des
     Ungarischen Katholizismus. Munich, 1969.
Andreev, M.V. Katolitsizm i problemy sovremennogo
     rabochego i natsional'no-osvoboditel'nogo
     dvizheniia. Moscow, 1968.
Armstrong, John A. Ukrainian Nationalism. New York,
     1963.
Babosov, E.M. Nauchno-teknicheskaiavi modernizatsiia
     katolitsizma. Minsk, 1971.
Bach, Markus. God and the Soviets. New York, 1958.
Barron, J.B. and H.M. Waddams, eds. Communism and
     the Churches: A Documentary. London, 1950.
Beeson, Trevor. Discretion and Valour. London, 1974.
Bello, Nino L. The Vatican Empire. New York, 1968.
Berdyaev, Nicholas. The Origin of Russian Communism.
     Ann Arbor, Mich., 1966.
Billington, James. The Icon and the Axe: An Inter-
     pretive History of Russian Culture. New York,
     1966.
Bishop, Donald. The Roosevelt-Litvinov Agreement:
     The American View. Syracuse, N.Y., 1965.
Bissonnette, Georges. Moscow Was My Parish. New
     York, 1956.
Blanshard, Paul. Communism, Democracy, and Catholic
     Power. Boston, 1951.
Blet, Pierre et alii., eds. Actes et documents du
     Saint Siège à la seconde guerre mondiale.
     9 vols. Citta del Vaticano, 1967-1976.
Blit, Lucian. The Eastern Pretender. London, 1965.
Bober, M.M. Karl Marx's Interpretation of History.
     New York, 1965.
Bociurkiw, Bohdan R. and John W. Strong, eds. Reli-
     gion and Atheism in the USSR and Eastern Eur-
     ope. Toronto, 1975.
Bol'shaia sovetskaia entsiklopediia, 1st Edition,
     65 volumes with supplementary volume on "Soiuz
     Sovetskikh Sotsialisticheskikh Respublik USSR."

Moscow, 1926-47; 2nd Edition, 51 volumes, 1950-
1958.
Bourdeaux, Michael, ed. Religious Minorities in the
Soviet Union (1960-1970). London, 1970.
_____. Land of Crosses. London, 1978.
Bromke, Adam. Poland's Politics: Idealism vs.
Realism. Cambridge, Mass., 1967.
Bronowski, J. The Ascent of Man. London, 1973.
Browne, Michael, ed. Ferment in the Ukraine. London,
1971.
Brzezinski, Zbigniew K. The Soviet Bloc: Unity and
Conflict. Cambridge, Mass., revised edition,
1967.
Burks, R.V. The Dynamics of Communism in Eastern
Europe. Princeton, N.J., 1961.
Busek, Vratislav and Nicholas Spulber, eds. Czecho-
slovakia. New York, 1957.
Ceranić, Ivan. "Religious Communities in Yugoslavia,"
in Zlatko Frid, Religions in Yugoslavia.
Zagreb, 1971.
Cianfarra, Camille. The Vatican and the Kremlin.
New York, 1950.
Ciszek, Walter S. with Daniel L. Flaherty. With God
in Russia. New York, 1964.
Conquest, Robert. Religion in the U.S.S.R. New
York and Washington, 1966.
Cousins, Norman. The Improbable Triumvirate. New
York, 1972.
Czerski, M. and A. Walicki, eds. Dialog episkopatow
Polski i Niemiec. London, 1966.
Daim, Wilfried. The Vatican and Eastern Europe.
Trans. Alexander Gode. New York, 1970.
Diiannia Soboru Hreko-Katolyts'koi Tserkvy, 8-10
bereznia 1946, u L'vovi. Lvov, 1946.
Dunn, Dennis J. The Catholic Church and the Soviet
Government, 1939-1949. Boulder, Colo., 1977.
_____. Religion and Modernization in the Soviet
Union. Boulder, Colo., 1977.
Dushnyck, Walter. Martyrdom in Ukraine: Russia
Denies Religious Freedom. New York, n.d.
Dziewanowski, Marian K. The Communist Party of
Poland. An Outline History. Cambridge, Mass.,
2nd Edition, 1976.
Dziuba, Ivan. Internationalism or Russification?
London, 1970.
Engels, Friedrich. Anti-Dühring. New York, New
World Paperbacks, New Printing, 1966.
Feuer, Lewis, ed. Marx and Engels: Basic Writings
on Politics and Philosophy. Gardon City, N.Y.,
1959.
Fireside, Harvey. Icon & Swastika: The Russian

Orthodox Church Under Nazi and Soviet Control.
Cambridge, Mass., 1971.
First Victims of Communism: White Book on Religious
Persecution in the Ukraine. Rome, 1953.
Fischer-Galati, Stephen, ed. Man, State, and Society
in East European History. New York, 1970.
Fletcher, William C. Religion and Soviet Foreign
Policy 1945-1970. London, 1973.
_____. A Study in Survival: The Church in
Russia, 1927-1943. New York, 1965.
_____ and Max Haywood, eds. Religion and the
Soviet State: A Dilemna of Power. New York,
1969.
Floridi, Ulisse A. Mosca e il Vaticano. Milan, 1976.
_____. Dr. Hromadka and the Christian Peace
Conference. Failure of an Experiment in East
West Dialogue. Boston, 1970.
Frid, Zlatko, ed. Religions in Yugoslavia. Zagreb,
1971.
Foreign Relations of the United States, 1939-1949.
Washington, D.C., 1956-74.
Free Europe Committee. The Red and the Black. New
York, 1953.
Galter, Albert. The Red Book of the Persecuted
Church. Westminster, Md., 1957.
Garkavenko, F., ed. O religii i tserkvi. Sbornik
dokumentov. Moscow, 1965.
Geanakopolos, Deno J. Byzantine East and Latin West:
Two Worlds of Christendom in Middle Ages and
Renaissance. New York, 1966.
Gill, Joseph. The Council of Florence. Cambridge,
Mass., 1959.
Graham, Robert A. Vatican Diplomacy. Princeton,
N.J., 1959.
Griffith, William, ed. Communism in Europe. 2 Vols.
Cambridge, Mass., 1964, 1966.
Grunwald, Constantine de. The Churches and the
Soviet Union. New York, 1962.
Gsovski, Vladimir. Church and State Behind the Iron
Curtain. New York, 1955.
Halecki, Oscar. From Florence to Brest (1439-1596).
New York, 1958.
Hebblethwaite, Peter. The Runaway Church. London,
1975.
Heyer, Friedrich. Die orthodoxe Kirche in der
Ukraine von 1917 bis 1945. Cologne, 1953.
(Hungarian Government). Documents on the Mindszenty
Case. Budapest, 1949.
_____. The Trial of József Mindszenty. Buda-
pest, 1949.
Huntington, Samuel P. and Clement H. Moore, eds.

Authoritarian Politics in Modern Society. New
York. 1970.
Hutten, Kurt. Iron Curtain Christians. Trans. Walter
C. Tillmanns. Minneapolis, Minn., 1967.
Iablokov, I.N. Krizis religii v sotsialisticheskom
obshchestve. Moscow, 1974.
Institite for the Study of the USSR. Genocide in the
USSR. New York, 1958.
_____. Religion in the USSR. Munich, 1960.
Itogi vsesoiuznoi perepisi naseleniia 1970 goda.
Vol. 4: Natsionalnyi sostav naseleniia SSR.
Moscow, 1973.
Johnson, A. Ross. The Transformation of Communist
Ideology: The Yugoslav Case, 1945-1953.
Cambridge, Mass., 1972.
Johnson, Chalmers, ed. Change in Communist Systems.
Stanford, 1970.
Just, Bela. Un process prefabrique, l'affaire
Mindszenty. Paris, 1949.
Khrushchev, Nikita. The Crimes of the Stalin Era:
Special Report to the 20th Congress of the
C.P.S.U. The New Leader, 1962.
Koch, Hans-Gerhard. Staat und Kirche in der DDR.
Stuttgart, 1975.
Kolarz, Walter. Religion in the Soviet Union. New
York, 1962.
Kouroiedov, Vladimir (also see Kuroedov, Vladimir).
L'Eglise et la religion en U.R.S.S. Moscow,
1977.
Koval'skii, N.A. Katolitsizm i mirovoe sotial'noe
razvitie. Moscow, 1974.
_____. Religioznye organizatsii i problemy
Evropeiskoi bezopasnosti i sotrudnichestva.
Moscow, 1977.
Kubijovyc, Volodymyr. Ukraine: A Concise Encyclo-
pedia. 2 Vols. Toronto, 1971.
Kuroedov, Vladimir. Religiia i zakon. Moscow, 1970.
_____ and A.S. Pankratov, eds. Zakonodal'stvo
o religioznykh kultakh: Sbornik materialov i
dokumentov. Moscow, 1971.
Laszlo, Leslie. "Church and State in Hungary, 1919-
1945." Ph.D. Dissertation, Columbia University,
1973.
Leclerc, Hervé. Marxism and the Church of Rome.
London, 1974.
Lencyk, Wasyl. The Eastern Catholic Church and Czar
Nicholas I. Rome-New York, 1966.
Lenin, V.I. Religion. New York, 1933.
_____. Sochineniia. 35 Vols. Moscow, 4th
Edition, 1941-50.
_____. V.I. Lenin ob ateizme religii i tserkvi.

Moscow, 1969.

Leveque, M. Persecution en Pologne. Paris, 1954.

Lichtheim, George. Marxism: An Historical and Critical Study. New York, 1964.

Lithuanian American Community. The Violations of Human Rights in Soviet Occupied Lithuania. A Report for 1971. Delran, N.J., 1972.

Lowry, Charles W. Communism and Christianity. New York, 1962.

Luchterhandt, Otto. Der Sowjetstaat und die Russisch-Orthodoxe Kirche. Cologne, 1976.

Lytvyn, K.Z. and Pshenychnyi, A.I., eds., Zakonodavstvo pre relihiini Kulty. Kiev, 1973.

MacEoin, Gary. The Communist War on Religion. New York, 1951.

Mackiewicz, Józef. Watykan w cieniu Czerwonej Gwiazdy. London, 1975.

McLellan, David. Karl Marx: His Life and Thought. New York, 1973.

Mailleuz, Paul, S.J. Exarch Leonid Fedorov: Bridge-builder Between Rome and Moscow. New York, 1964.

Manhattan, Avro. The Vatican in World Politics. New York, 1949.

Markham, R.H. Communists Crush Churches in Eastern Europe. Boston, 1950.

Markiewicz, Stanislaw. Kościół rzymskokatolicki a państwa socjalistyczne. Warsaw, 1974.

_____. Państwo i Kościół w okresie dwudziesto-lecia Polsi Ludowej. Warsaw, 1965.

Markus, Vasyl. Nyshchennia Hreko-Katolyts'koi Tserkvy v Mukachivs'skii Ieparkhii v 1945-1950. Paris, 1962.

Marshall, Richard H., Jr, et alii, eds. Aspects of Religion in the Soviet Union, 1917-1967. Chicago, 1971.

Marx, Karl. Das Kapital. Edited by Friedrich Engels and condensed by Serge L. Levitsky. Vol. 1. Chicago, Gateway Edition, 1961.

_____ and Friedrich Engels. Harold J. Laski on the Communist Manifesto. New York, Vintage Books, 1967.

McCullagh, Capt. Francis. The Bolshevik Persecution of Christianity. London, 1924.

Mchedlov, M.P. Evoliutsiia sovremennogo katolitsizm. Moscow, 1967.

_____. Katolitsizm. Moscow, 1970.

_____. Sovremennia bor'ba idei i religiia. Moscow, 1977.

Medvedev, Roy A. Let History Judge: The Origins and Consequences of Stalinism. New York, 1972.

Mikhnevich, D.E. Ocherki iz istorii katolicheskoi

reaktsii. Moscow, 1953.

Mindszenty, Cardinal Jozsef. Four Years' Struggle of the Church in Hungary. London, 1949.

_____. Memoirs. London, 1974.

Moroz, Valentyn. Boomerang: The Works of Valentyn Moroz. Baltimore, 1974.

Morozov, M.A. and Lisavtsev, E.I. Aktualnye zadachi atheisticheskogo vospitaniia. Moscow, 1970.

Mourin, Maxime. Le Vatican et l'URSS. Paris, 1963.

Nemec, Ludwig. Church and State in Czechoslovakia. New York, 1955.

Persits, M.M. Otdelenie tserkvi ot gosudarsvta i shkoly ot tserkvi v SSSR (1917-1919 gg.). Moscow, 1958.

Piasecki, Boleslaw. Zagadnienia istotne. Warsaw, 1945.

_____. Patriotysm polski. Warsaw, 1958.

Plantonov, R. Vospitanie ateisticheskoi ubezhdenosti. Propaganda nauchnogo ateizma v sisteme ideologicheskoi deiatelnosti partiinykh organizatsii Belorussii 1959-1972 gody. Minsk, 1973.

Powell, David E. Antireligious Propaganda in the Soviet Union. Cambridge, Mass., 1975.

Pruden, Salme. Pan-Slavism and Russian Communism. New York, 1976.

Raffalt, Reinhard. Wohin steuert der Vatikan? Munich, 1973.

Reddaway, Peter, ed. Uncensored Russia. London, 1972.

Rhodes, Anthony. The Vatican in the Age of the Dictators 1922-1945. London, 1973.

Roter, Zdenko. Katoliška cerkev in država v Jugoslaviji 1945-1973. Ljubljani, 1976.

Rudnyts'ka, Milena. Nevydymi stygmaty. Rome-Munich-Philadelphia, 1971.

Savasis, Jonas. The War Against God in Lithuania. New York, 1966.

Schuster, G.W. Religion Behind the Iron Curtain. New York, 1954.

Seton-Watson, Hugh. The East European Revolution. New York, 3rd Edition, 1954.

Shakhnovich, M.I. Lenin i problemy ateizma. Leningrad, 1961.

Sheinman, M.M. Ot Piia IX do Ionna XXIII. Moscow, 1966.

Shuster, George N. In Silence I Speak. New York, 1956.

Simon, Gerhard. Church, State and Opposition in the U.S.S.R. Berkeley and Los Angeles, 1974.

Slipyĭ, Josyf. Tvory. Rome, 1968-69.

Smith, Hedrick. The Russians. New York, 1976.

Solzhenitsyn, Alexander. Gulag Archipelago. New
York, 1973-74.
Stehle, Hansjacob. Die Ostpolitik des Vatikans.
Munich, 1975.
_____. The Independent Satellite: Society and
Politics in Poland Since 1945. New York, 1965.
Struve, Nikita. Les Chretiens en URSS. Paris, 1963.
Szczesniak, Boleslaw. The Russian Revolution and
Religion. Notre Dame, 1959.
Taborsky, Edward. Communism in Czechoslovakia 1948-
1960. Princeton, N.J., 1961.
Theodorowitsch, Nadeshda. Religion and Atheismus in
der UdSSR: Dokumente und Berichte. Munich,
1970.
Timasheff, N.S. The Great Retreat. New York, 1946.
_____. Religion in Soviet Russia 1917-1942.
New York, 1942.
Tobias, Robert. Communist-Christian Encounter in
East Europe. Indianapolis, Ind., 1956.
Tökes, Rudolf, ed. Dissent in the USSR: Politics,
Ideology and People. Baltimore, 1975.
Treadgold, Donald W. The West in Russia and China.
Vol. 1: Russia, 1472-1917. Cambridge, England,
1973.
Tucker, Robert C., ed. The Marx-Engels Reader. New
York, 1972.
Ulam, Adam B. The Bolsheviks. New York, 1965.
_____. Expansion & Coexistence: The History of
Soviet Foreign Policy 1917-1973. New York, 1974.
_____. Stalin: The Man and His Era. New
York, 1973.
_____. Titoism and the Cominform. Cambridge,
Mass., 1952.
Vardys, V. Stanley, ed. Lithuania Under the Soviets:
Portrait of a Nation. New York, 1965.
Vasilii, Diakon, OSBM. Leonid Fedorov, Zhizn' i
deiatel'nost.' Rome, 1966.
Velikovich, L.N. Iezuity vchera i segodnia. Moscow,
1972.
Von Rauch, Georg. The Baltic States. Berkeley and
Los Angeles, 1974.
Weingartner, Erich, ed. Church Within Socialism:
Based on the Work of Giovanni Barberini. Rome,
1976.
Wetter, Gustav A. Dialectical Materialism: A Histor-
ical and Systematic Survey of Philosophy in the
Soviet Union. Trans. Peter Heath. New York,
1958.
Winter, Eduard. Russland und das Papsttum. 3 Vols.
Berlin, 1960.
Zaninovich, George. The Development of Socialist

Yugoslavia. Baltimore, Md., 1968.

Zatko, James J. Descent into Darkness. Notre Dame, 1965.

Zizola, Giancario. L'Utopia di Papa Giovanni. Assisi, 1973.

Zubek, T. The Church of Silence in Slovakia. Whiting, Ind., 1956.

## ARTICLES

_____, "Communism's Struggle with Religion in Lithuania," Lituanus 9 (March 1963): 1-17.

_____, "Die Ostpolitik des Vatikans aus Weiner Sicht," Menschenvecht 4 (January 27, 1975): 13-14.

_____, "Marxisme et Chretiens," Bulletin du secrétariat de la conférence épiscopale francaise, no. 11 (juin 1975), pp. 1-12.

_____, "Poland in the Vatican's Eastern Policy," Contemporary Poland (Polish Interpress Agency) vol. 7, no. 10 (October 1973): 20-23.

_____, "Vatikan pered vyzovom ateizma," Kommunist (Lithuania), no. 9 (1974), pp. 78-87.

Adler, Erwin, "Lenin's Views on Religion," Studies on the Soviet Union 10 (1970): 61-69.

Alexander, Stella, "Archbishop Stepinac Reconsidered," Religion in Communist Lands 6 (Summer 1968): 76-88.

_____, "Church-State Relations in Yugoslavia Since 1967," Religion in Communist Lands 4 (Spring 1976): 18-27.

Antic, Zdenko, "Tension Between State and Catholic Church in Yugoslavia Continues," Radio Free Europe Research (July 1, 1975), pp. 1-9.

_____, "Attacks Continue Against Catholic Church in Yugoslavia," Radio Free Europe Research (February 13, 1975), pp. 1-6.

_____, "More Strain Between State and Catholic Church in Yugoslavia?" Radio Free Europe Research (April 1, 1975), pp. 1-4.

Bajsić, Vjekoslav, "The Standpoint of Christians Towards a Dialogue with Marxists," in Frid, Religions, pp. 146-53.

Barberini, Giovanni, "Introduction," in Erich Weingartner, ed. Church Within Socialism. Rome, 1976.

Bartoli, Edguardo, "The Road to Power: The Italian Communist Party and the Church," Survey 21 (Autumn 1975): 90-106.

Bennigsen, Alexandre, "Modernization and Conservatism in Soviet Islam," in Dennis J. Dunn, ed.,

Religion and Modernization in the Soviet
Union, pp. 239-279.
Blane, Andrew, "Protestant Sectarians and Modern-
ization in the Soviet Union," in Dennis J.
Dunn, ed. Religion and Modernization in the
Soviet Union, pp. 382-407.
Bociurkiw, Bohdan R., "The Catacomb Church:
Ukrainian Greek Catholics in the USSR," Re-
ligion in Communist Lands 5 (Spring 1977):
4-12.

_____, "The Catholic Church and the Soviet
State in the 1970s," (Unpublished manuscript).

_____, "Church-State Relations in the USSR,"
in William C. Fletcher and Max Haywood, eds.,
Religion and the Soviet State: A Dilemna
of Power. New York, 1969, pp. 71-104.

_____, "Lenin and Religion," in Leonard
Schapiro and Peter Redaway, eds. Lenin:
The Man, The Theorist, The Leader. A
Reappraisal. New York, 1967, pp. 107-34.

_____, "Religion in Eastern Europe,"
Religion in Communist Lands 1 (July-October
1973): 9-14.

_____, "Religious Dissent and the Soviet
State," in Bohdan R. Bociurkiw and John W.
Strong, eds. Religion and Atheism in the
USSR and Eastern Europe. Toronto, 1975,
pp. 58-90.

_____, "Religious Dissent in the USSR:
Lithuanian Catholics," in James Scanlan and
Richard DeGeorge, eds. Marxism and Religion.
Dordrecht, 1976, pp. 147-75.

_____, "The Religious Situation in the
Soviet Ukraine," The Ukrainian Quarterly,
forthcoming.

_____, "Religion and Atheism in Soviet So-
ciety," in Richard H. Marshall, Jr. et alii,
eds. Aspects of Religion in the Soviet Union
1917-1967. Chicago, 1971, pp. 45-60.

_____, "Religion and Nationalism in the Soviet
Ukraine," in G.W. Simmonds, ed. Nationalism in
the USSR and Eastern Europe in the Era of
Brezhnev and Kosygin. Detroit: University of
Detroit Press, 1977, pp. 181-93.

_____, "Soviet Religious Policy," Problems of
Communism (May-June 1973): 37-51.

_____, "The Uniate Church in the Soviet Ukraine:
A Case Study in Soviet Church Policy," Canadian
Slavonic Papers 7 (1965): 89-113.
Bromke, Adam, "From 'Falanga' to Pax," Survey,
no. 39 (December 1961), pp. 29-40.

_____, "A New Juncture in Poland," <u>Problems of Communism</u> (September-October 1976), pp. 1-17.

_____, "Poland Under Gierek: A New Political Style," <u>Problems of Communism</u> (September-October 1972), pp, 1-19.

Casaroli, Archbishop Agostino, "Interview with Otto Schulmeister," <u>Die Presse</u> (Vienna), December 21, 1974.

_____, "La Santa Sede e l'Europa," <u>Civiltà Cattolica</u> (February 19, 1972), pp. 367-81.

Cousins, Norman, "The Improbable Triumvirate: Khrushchev, Kennedy, and Pope John," <u>The Saturday Review</u>, no. 54 (October 1971), pp. 24-35.

Cviic, Christopher, "Martyrs & Ostpolitik," <u>The Tablet</u> (London), February 15, 1975.

_____, "Tito Tightens Up," <u>The Tablet</u> (London), January 26, 1974.

"Declaration by the Priests of the Catholic Church in Lithuania," (August 1969), addressed to the Chairman of the Lithuanian Council of Ministers and the Catholic Church Leaders in Lithuania by forty priests of the Vilnius Archdiocese, published in <u>Lituanus</u>, 19 (Fall 1973): 46-53.

Deminski, Ludwik, "The Catholics and Politics in Poland," <u>Canadian Slavonic Papers</u> 15 (1973): 176-83.

Denitch, Bogdan, "Religion and Social Change in Yugoslavia," in Bociurkiw and Strong, <u>Religion and Atheism</u>, pp. 368-87.

Devlin, Kevin, "The Challenge of Eurocommunism," <u>Problems of Communism</u> (January-February 1977), pp. 1-20.

Dinka, Frank, "Sources of Conflict Between Church and State in Poland," <u>Review of Politics</u> 28 (July 1966), pp. 322-49.

Dolan, Edward, "Post-War Poland and the Church," <u>American Slavic and East European Review</u> (1955), pp. 84-92.

Draper, Theodore, "Appeasement & Detente," <u>Commentary</u> (February 1976), pp. 27-38.

Drašković, Cedomir, "Orthodoxy and Ecumenism," in Frid, <u>Religions</u>, pp. 120-31.

Dunn, Dennis J., "The Catholic Church and the Soviet Government in the Baltic States, 1940-41," in V. Stanley Vardys and R.J. Misiunas, eds. <u>The Baltic States in Peace and War, 1917-1945</u>, forthcoming.

_____, "The Catholic Church and the Soviet Government in Soviet Occupied East Europe, 1939-1940," in James Scanlan and Richard DeGeorge,

eds. <u>Marxism and Religion</u>. Dordrecht, 1976,
pp. 107-18.

_____, "The Disappearance of the Ukrainian
Uniate Church:  How and Why?" <u>Ukrains'kyi
Istoryk</u> (Munich-New York, 1972), pp. 57-65.

_____, "The Kremlin and the Vatican:  <u>Ostpoli-
tik</u>," <u>Religion in Communist Lands</u> (London)  4
(Winter 1976): 16-19.

_____, "Papal-Communist Détente: Motivation,"
<u>Survey</u>, no. 99 (Spring 1976), pp. 140-54.

_____, "The Papal-Communist Détente, 1963-73:
Its Evolution and Causes," in Bernard Eissenstat,
ed. <u>The Soviet Union:  The Seventies and Be-
yond</u>. Lexington, Mass., 1975, pp. 121-40.

_____, "Pre-World War II Relations Between
Stalin and the Catholic Church," <u>Journal of
Church and State</u>, no. 15 (Spring 1973), pp.193-204.

_____, "Religious Renaissance in the U.S.S.R.,"
<u>Journal of Church and State</u> 19 (Winter 1977):
21-30.

_____, "Stalinism and the Catholic Church Dur-
ing the Era of WWII," <u>The Catholic Historical
Review</u> 59 (October 1973): 404-28.

Dziewanowski, Marian K.,  "Communist Poland and the
Catholic Church," <u>Problems of Communism</u> (September-October 1954), pp. 1-2.

Feiffer, George,  "No Protest:  The Case of the Passive Minority," in Tökes, <u>Dissent</u>, pp. 418-38.

Hebblethwaite, Peter,  "The Vatican Power Game,"
<u>The Observer</u> (London), December 22, 1974.

Hotz, Robert,  "I cattolici ucraini e il Vaticano,"
<u>Russia Cristiana</u> (Milan), no. 123 (May-June 1972),
pp. 3-11.

Iastrebov, I.,  "Pacem in terris:  Katolicheskaia
tserkov' o mire i voine," <u>Nauka i religiia</u>, no. 1
(1970), pp. 49-50.

Kertesz, Stephen,  "Church and State in Hungary,"
<u>Review of Politics</u> 11 (April 1949): 208-19.

Kichanova, I.M.,  "Problema cheloveka," <u>Voprosy
nauchnogo atheizma</u>, 6 (Moscow, 1968): 268-69.

Kolakowski, Leszek <u>et alii</u>,  "The Polish Resistance,"
<u>The New York Review of Books</u> (January 20, 1977),
p. 61.

Korotynski, Henry,  "Church and State in Poland,"
<u>New Times</u>, no. 36 (September 7, 1966), pp. 14-16.

Kravchenko, I.I.,  "Katolicheskaia traktovka sotsial'-
nykh otnosheniiv razvitykh kapitalisticheskikh
stranakh," <u>Voprosy nauchnogo atheizma</u>, no. 6
(Moscow, 1966), pp. 270-306.

Lacko, Michael, S.J.,  "The Re-Establishment of the
Greek Catholic Church in Czechoslovakia," <u>Slovak</u>

Studies 11 (Cleveland, Ohio-Rome, Italy, 1971 reprint): 159-89.

Lamonin, Christian, "Les rapports juridiques entre Saint-Sèige et les Etats communists," Revue général de droit international public (Paris) no. 3 (1972), pp. 689-767.

Laqueur, Walter, "'Eurocommunism' and Its Friends," Commentary (August 1976): 25-30.

Larrabee, F. Stephen, "Initial Soviet Reaction to the Security Conference," Radio Liberty Research (August 18, 1975), pp. 1-7.

Laszlo, Leslie, "Towards Normalisation of Church-State Relations in Hungary," in Bociurkiw and Strong, Religion and Atheism, pp. 292-313.

Lavretski, I.V., "Nekotorye voprosy politiki Vatikana v Afrike," Voprosy istorii religii i ateizma 7 (Moscow, 1958): 105-29.

Lazić, Ivan, "The Legal and Actual Status of Religious Communities in Yugoslavia," in Frid, Religions, pp. 43-79.

Leclerc, Hervé, "L' 'Ostpolitik' du Vatican: Le point de vue de Rome," Est & Ouest (16-31 decembre 1971), pp. 506-9.

Levitin (Krasnov), A.E., "The Situation of the Russian Orthodox Church," in Gerhard Simon, Church, State and Opposition, pp. 188-201.

_____, "Open Letter to Archbishop Casaroli," Religion in Communist Dominated Lands 16 (1977): 174-77.

Luchterhandt, Otto, "Wie verhalten sich die Rechtsordnungen der sozialstischen KSZE-Statten zu dem in der Schlussakte der Konferenz von Helsinki verankerten Menschenrecht der Religionsfreiheit," Die Religionsfreiheit in Osteuropa nach Helsinki. Küsnacht-Zürich, 1977, pp. 11-17.

Mailleux, Paul S.J., "The Roman Catholic," in Marshall, Aspects of Religion, pp. 359-78.

Markus, Vasyl, "Religion and Nationality: The Uniates of the Ukraine," in Bociurkiw and Strong, Religion and Atheism, pp. 101-22.

_____, "Vatikan'ka 'Skidnia politika' i sprava Ukts," Svoboda, November 29, 30, 1972.

Maximov, Vladimir, "Wir leben am Vorabend," Deutsche Zeitung, June 24, 1974.

Mirski, J., "Wrazenia z ZSSR 1970-1973," Kultura (Paris), no. 11/314 (1973).

Nemec, Ludvik. "The Communist Ecclesiology During the Church-State Relationship in Czechoslovakia," Proceedings of the American Philosophical Society 112 (August 1968): 245-76.

Novak, Theodore, "L' 'Ostpolitik' du Vatican et

l'eglise catholique Ukrainienne," L'Est Europeen,
no. 124 (janvier 1973), pp. 12-25; no. 125
(fevrier-mars 1973), pp. 21-26.

Nowak, Jan, "New Thaw in Church-State Relations in
Poland," East Europe (February 1969), p. 11.

Nunka, V.U., "Natsonal'no-osvoboditel'noe dvizhenie
i religiia," Novoe v zhizni nauke tekhnike
(Moscow, 1972).

Pekar, Rev. Athanasius, OSBM, "Restoration of the
Greek Catholic Church in Czechoslovakia," The
Ukrainian Quarterly 29 (Autumn 1973): 282-96.

Pipes, Richard, "Liberal Communism in Western Europe?" Orbis 20 (Fall 1976): 595-600.

Podhoretz, Norman, "Making the World Safe for
Communism," Commentary (April 1976), pp. 31-41.

Popov, S., "Sotsial-reformizm i religiia," Politiche-
skoi samoobrazovanie, no. 11 (1970), pp. 89-96.

Reshetar, J.S., "Ukrainian Nationalism and the Orthodox Church," The American Slavic and East European Review, no. 1 (1951), pp. 38-49.

Revel, Jean-Francois, "The Myths of Eurocommunism,"
Foreign Affairs 56 (January 1978): 295-305.

Rosales, Juan, "Revolution, Socialism, Theology,"
World Marxist Review (Toronto), no. 6 (June 1975),
pp. 80-90.

Roter, Zdenko, "The Sense of the Dialogue Between
Marxists and Christians," in Frid, Religions,
pp. 154-62.

Rothenberg, Joshua, "The Legal Status of Religion in
the Soviet Union," in Marshall, Aspects of
Religion, pp. 61-102.

Sadovskii, N.A., "Novye momenty v sotsial'noi doctrine katolicheskoi tserkvi," Voprosy filosofii,
no. 1 (1971), pp. 87-96.

Sagi-Bunić, Tomislav, "Catholic Church and Ecumenism," in Frid, Religions, pp. 107-19.

Sani, Giacomo, "The PCI on the Threshold," Problems
of Communism (November-December 1976), pp. 27-51.

Sheinman, M.M., "Problemy sovremennogo katolitsizma,"
Nauka i religiia, no. 10 (1970), pp. 82-84.

Simon, Gerhard, "The Catholic Church and the Commu-
nist State in the Soviet Union and Eastern
Europe," in Bociurkiw and Strong, Religion and
Atheism, pp. 109-221.

Staron, Stanislaw, "State-Church Relations in Poland," World Politics 21 (July 1969): 575-601.

Stehle, Hansjakob, "Vatican Policy Towards Eastern
Europe," Survey, no. 66 (January 1968), pp.108-116.

Strashun, B., "Socialist Democracy Triumphs," International Affairs, no. 1 (Moscow, 1977), pp.16-25.

Stremooukhoff, Dmitri, "Moscow the Third Rome:

Sources of the Doctrine," Speculum 28 (January 1953): 84-101.

Syzdek, Eleonora, "Gosudarstvo i Katlicheskaia tserkov' v narodnoi Pol'she," Politicheskoe samoobrazovanie, no. 4 (1966), pp. 138-44.

Theodorovich, N., "The Political Role of the Moscow Patriarchate," Studies on the Soviet Union 4 (1965): 241-47.

Tiersky, Ronald, "French Communism in 1976," Problems of Communism (Jan.-Feb. 1976), pp. 20-47.

Toma, Peter A. and Milan J. Reban, "Church-State Schism in Czechoslovakia," in Bociurkiw and Strong, Religion and Atheism, pp. 273-91.

Toufar, Vaclav, "Religiia i nauka," Nauka i religiia no. 5 (1975), pp. 84-85.

Triska, Jan F., "Messages From Czechoslovakia," Problems of Communism (November-December 1975): 26-42.

Tyszka, Zygmunt, "Polityka Wschodnia Watykanu," Zycie i myśl 21 (May 1971): 12-25.

U.S. Foreign Broadcast Information Service. Daily Reports, Foreign Radio Broadcasts. Washington, D.C., 1947-78.

Urban, George, "A Discussion with Robert F. Byrnes," Survey, no. 93 (Autumn 1974), pp. 41-66.

Valkenier, Elizabeth, "The Catholic Church in Communist Poland, 1945-1955," Review of Politics 18 (July 1956): 305-26.

Vardys, V. Stanley, "Catholicism in Lithuania," in Marshall, Aspects, pp. 379-403.

_____, "Geography and Nationalities in the USSR: A Commentary," Slavic Review 31 (September 1972): 546-70.

_____. "Modernization and Baltic Nationalism," Problems of Communism (Sept-Oct. 1975), pp.32-48.

_____, "Modernization and Latin Rite Catholics," in Dennis J. Dunn, ed., Religion and Modernization, pp. 348-81.

Velikovich, Lazar., "Catholicism and the Time," New Times, no. 48 (November 1972), pp. 18-20.

_____, "Contrary to the Understanding," New Times, no. 32 (August 1976), pp. 21-23.

_____, "Voina i mir viotsenke sobora," Voprosy nauchnogo ateizma 6 (Moscow, 1968), pp. 307-25.

Vetö, Miklos, "The Catholic Church," Survey, no. 40 (January 1962), pp. 133-39.

_____, "Kremlin and Vatican," Survey, no. 48 (July 1963), pp. 163-72.

Walf, Knut, "The Vatican's Eastern Policy," Aussen Politik (April 1973), pp. 416-26.

Wrzeszcz, Maciej, "Ważny krok na drodze do

normalizacji," Życie i myśl (Warsaw) 24 (1974):
1-7.

Wynot, Edward, Jr., "The Catholic Church and the
Polish State, 1935-1939," Journal of Church and
State 15 (1973): 22-40.

NEWSPAPERS AND PERIODICALS

Agitator (Moscow).
America (New York).
Ateismo e dialogo (Rome).
Begegnung (East Berlin).
Bratskii Vestnik (Moscow).
Bulletin of the Secretariat for Promotion of Christ-
    ian Unity (Rome).
Catacombes (Paris).
Catholic Herald (London).
The Christian Science Monitor, Midwestern and Inter-
    national editions.
Civiltà Cattolica (Rome).
Current Digest of the Soviet Press (Columbus, Ohio).
Christianity Today (Washington, D.C.).
Church and State (Silver Spring, Md.).
East Europe (New York).
Eastern Churches Review (New York).
The East European Quarterly (Boulder, Colo.).
L'Est Europeen (Paris).
L'Humanité (Paris).
Izvestiia (Moscow).
Katolické Noviny (Prague).
Kommunist (Moscow).
Komsomolskaia pravda (Moscow).
Kontinent (Paris).
Keston News Service (London).
Laboro (Rome).
Liudyna i svit (Kiev).
Le Monde (Paris).
The Month (London).
Nauka i religiia (Moscow).
Nauka i zhizn (Moscow).
New Times (Moscow).
New York Times (New York).
The Observer (London).
l'Osservatore Romano (Rome).
Politicheskoe samoobrazovanie (Moscow).
Pravda (Moscow).
Pravda Ukrainy (Kiev).
Pravda Vostoka (Alma Ata).
Pravoslavnyi visnyk (Kiev).
Problems of Communism (Washington, D.C.).
Religion in Communist Dominated Lands (New York).

Religion in Communist Lands (London).
Rude pravo (Prague).
Russia Cristiana (Milan).
Slowo Powszechne (Warsaw); Kierunki (Warsaw).
Sovetskaia Litva (Lithuania).
Sovetskaia Rossiia (Moscow).
Tablet (London).
The Times (London).
Trybuna Ludu (Warsaw).
Tygodnik Powszechny (Cracow).
Ukrains'kyi Visnyk (Baltimore).
Ukrainian Quarterly (New York).
Unita (Rome).
Voprosy nauchnogo atheizma (Moscow).
Zhurnal Moskovskoi Patriarkhii (Moscow).
Zycie Warszwy (Warsaw).

# Index

Dubček, Alexander, 151-52, 158, 161-62, 165, 184
Dulbinskis, Bishop Kazimirs, 59
East Berlin Conference of Communist Parties, 6, 51
East Germany(GDR), ix, 2, 15-16, 17, 39, 42, 108, 170-73, 184
Eastern Europe, ix-x, 1-3, 5, 11, 14-17, 23, 25-33, 35-36, 38, 40, 42-45, 58, 62, 75, 83-84, 88, 91, 94, 114, 117, 150, 157, 164, 178, 181, 183-88, 190
Eisenhower, General Dwight, 150
Engels, Frederick, 6-9
Eppstein, John, x
Estonia, 15, 52-53
Etchegaray, Archbishop Roger, 71
Ethiopia, 187
European Conference on Security and Cooperation, ix, 1, 6, 32, 40, 43, 67, 70-72, 112, 117-119, 143-144, 162, 165-66, 175, 177, 186-87, 189
Fedorov, Exarch Leonid, 5, 13
Feranec, Bishop Jozef, 164-165
First World War, 11, 14, 35
Ford, President Gerald, 163
Four Powers Agreement on Berlin, ix
France, 6, 14, 16, 32-33, 34, 36, 43
Franco, General, 67
French Communist Party (RPCF), 6, 14-15, 32
Fuchs, Otto Harmut, 74, 172
Gabris, Bishop Julius, 164-65
Gasperi, Alcide de, 16
German Catholic in the USSR, 13, 41-42, 52, 60-61, 76
Germany, Weimar, 13-14; Germany, Nazi, 14, 34-35,

Germany (cont.), 57, 59, 89, 100, 108, 128, 151-52; Germany, West (FRG), viii-ix, 16, 23, 24, 43, 63, 95, 109-11, 171, 173
Gherghel, Monsignor Petru, 176
Gierek, Edward, 42, 100, 109, 111, 115, 119-20, 178
Goidych, Bishop Pavlo, 158
Golden Horde, 3
Gomulka, Wladyslaw, 100, 104-105, 107, 109-10, 119, 178
Gottwald, Klement, 150-52
Grabner, Bishop Rudolf, 175
Great Britain, 34
Grechko, Marshal, 162
Gremillon, Mgr. Joseph, 172
Gromyko, Andrei, 29, 44, 64, 67, 70-71
Grosz, Archbishop Jozsef, 133
Hamer, Archbishop Jerome, 74-75
Heenan, Cardinal, 63
Helsinki Conference, see European Conference on Security and Cooperation
d'Herbigny, Bishop Michael, 14
Hitler, Adolph, 58
Hlond, Cardinal, 103
Holy See, see Vatican
Hopko, Bishop Vasyl, 158
Hruza, Karel, 161-62, 165-66
Human Rights Committee (Sakharov), 62
Hungarian Catholics in the USSR, 52-53, 60
Hungarian Revolution (1956), 17, 23, 34,